A new paradigm of reality?

Gonzalo Rodríguez-Fraile

A new paradigm of reality?

Foundation for Consciousness Development

© Gonzalo Rodríguez-Fraile Díaz, 2015
© Foundation for Consciousness Development, 2015
Calle María de Molina 1, 28006 Madrid
(Spain)

First Edition: November 2015
Legal deposit: M-34178-2015
ISBN: 978-84-608-2830-3
Cover design: 267estudiográfico
Photograph author: Codis, Inc.
Typeset by BibliotecaOnline SL
Printed in Spain by Manuel Heras Alcalde (Imprenta Comercial)

Table of contents

Part I: The New Paradigm of Reality

Author's foreword

Some fifteen years ago, I started out on a journey that ended up changing how I perceive the meaning of life. When I was about 40 years old, one day I decided to sit down and ask myself: Why wasn't I happy all the time, despite having everything I needed? Apparently everything around me was fine (I had great kids, a successful career, was well-off financially, in good health, etc.); but all too often I felt anxious, stressed out, worried and had minor health problems due to my state of mind.

Just like everyone else, there had been ups and downs in my life, but more ups than downs and I hadn't had to deal with many of the dramatic situations that other people close to me had faced. Even so, something wasn't right inside me, despite my extensive academic and religious background.

So I said to myself: What good is external success unless it lets me always feel happy and at peace? I realized that nothing I could learn from the prevailing culture would solve that problem and decided to embark on a journey of external research and, at the same time, introspection, to which I have devoted several thousands of hours. This journey has become a core purpose of my life ever since.

As I was more of a mind-oriented person, and my education had been rational, I decided to start by investigating the available knowledge. I began studying both the wisdom expressed by all kinds of thinkers throughout history (in the East and West), and the conclusions of new research in some of its facets (physics, cosmology, psychology, philosophy, epigenetics, theology, etc.).

I spent the first part of my several year-long journey just gathering data, and as I steadily started understanding reality in a new light, I became convinced that I needed to begin living in line with that new information I had acquired, and that was my focus over the following years. When I saw the extent to which both this new understanding and my training had affected and transformed me, I thought it could do the same for other people, which is why in recent years I have devoted much of my life to passing on that information. The next objective was to summarize it to let others take it in faster.

Yet while doing so, I first realized that my mind was interpreting reality the wrong way. The culture in which I had been brought up had not yet understood the workings of the Universe, as modern physics explains it nowadays, and that precisely was what was stopping me from comfortably putting my spiritual teachings into practice. For example, I'd been taught to "turn the other cheek" if attacked, and also to "strive for inner peace and rely on whatever else comes about", but my mind didn't think one could put such teachings into practice in the real world. In the first case, I thought I'd be killed if I didn't fight back when attacked; and, in the second, that nothing would happen unless I focused on working hard to solve the problems and situations that arose "out there".

My mind was an obstacle that still believed —despite my religious faith— in a "materialist" view of reality, triggered by my knowledge of classical physics, in which essentially you think of reality as a set of objects suspended in space and separate from one other, without being connected.

Through my research of new knowledge about science and philosophy and its relationship with Mankind's great spiritual teachings, I realized that things were not as I had thought until then, and that Man was not what I had believed either.

I discovered that the Universe is not fragmented, but instead is a unitary system that combines all parts and in which everything is interconnected. What's more, that Universe has its own intelligence and intention, and that intention is creative evolution. The human being is not a body and a mind that also has a soul, but fundamentally a soul with a temporary body and mind to let it experiment and evolve in the material world.

These two discoveries changed my whole understanding. Shortly after I also drew the conclusion (thanks to new scientific and old mystical knowledge, without confusing the different levels to which they apply) that the Universe is multidimensional and that the higher-vibration dimensions (the subtler dimensions that are not perceived through the senses or their extensions) have a total influence and enormous causative power over the denser dimensions (the third dimension that can be perceived through the senses).

In this book I endeavor to explain that everything that happens is perfect and necessary in order for souls to evolve; otherwise it would not happen, because the intelligence of the Universe that causes the manifestation is very efficient and does not make mistakes or waste energy. This idea will become clearer throughout the book.

If all this were so, it became apparent that a change in one's inner polarity was required: the emphasis had to be placed "inside" oneself, not "outside". That is, if reality is perfect and necessary and I have come into the world with the sole purpose of growing, I have to work inside myself to "lose my own agenda" and be able to flow with the manifestation (reality) instead of working "outside" to change it so that it suits my particular tastes.

When I realized the existence and the significance of the levels of consciousness (see chapter 3, Part I), for the first time my mind had before it a clear and sure "map" that really helped me to know where to steer my efforts. It also helped me to finally and correctly identify the root cause of human difficulties.

This new knowledge also shed light on how available human potential increases as one moves to higher levels and that happiness correlates with those levels.

At the same time, I understood how one's ego works, and that spiritual growth consists in a gradual loss of ego, which results in a change of inner psychic experience rather than control of external behaviour. Once internal change has taken place, external issues change alone and effortlessly.

Therefore I reached the conclusion that this new view of reality was triggered by the convergence of many disciplines of knowledge that could no longer be studied separately, one specialty at a time, but had to be integrated to better understand the unified, and no longer fragmented, reality. Physics, astronomy, epigenetics, integral philosophy, transpersonal psychology and other disciplines seem to be converging in a New Paradigm of reality.

This New Paradigm fits perfectly with what mystics have been arguing throughout the history of Mankind. This understanding led me to a second degree of certainty. When I studied both the teachings and processes of mystics in the East and West alike, I was surprised to find that their testimonies were essentially the same, despite the cultural differences under which they were expressed.

I also realized that the spiritual masters of the past, as a whole, had talked about almost everything, even though not all of them talked about everything. For instance, Jesus spoke in depth about Love, but not about the structure of the cosmological reality. So I found it very useful to find out about many of the masters' teachings, so as to cover all aspects of reality.

All these understandings changed my mind and my heart and I got ready to try practicing this new information in everyday life.

I ran into certain difficulties to start with, of course. Yet slowly I came to better understand what internal changes had to be made. Tradition has it that the teacher always appears when the disciple is "ready" and right then I got my hands on the information I needed, and found the right teachers.

Throughout the process, I realized that I had to accept and take responsibility for my own growth. In other words, come to terms with it. I also began to understand how to use the tool of thought and how to "let go" of attachments and constraints to generate greater inner peace, which is the gateway to the higher powers of consciousness.

Yet above all, and for the first time ever, I realized that there are Universal Laws and how they work. This let me try to flow with them, because one cannot avoid complying with them and not knowing about them does not free us from experiencing their results. I realized that my ignorance of those laws had not brought the expected results in my life or that of others.

I trust that anyone looking for information and understanding so as to evolve their consciousness faster and more efficiently (which, in a nutshell, is the purpose of our existence in this world of form) will find this book useful.

A fitting end to this foreword is the reproduction of the letter that Einstein is attributed to have written to his daughter at the end of his life. "Attributed" because the veracity of its origin has not been confirmed, but even if it were not his, it deserves to be.

> "When I proposed the theory of relativity, very few understood me, and what I will reveal to you, for you to pass onto Mankind, will also clash with the incomprehension and prejudice in the world. Even so, I ask you to keep it for as long as necessary, years, decades, until society has advanced enough to accept what I explain below.
>
> There is an extremely powerful force for which so far science has not found a formal explanation. It is a force that includes and governs all the others, and is even behind any phenomenon operating in the Universe and has not yet been identified by us. This universal force is LOVE.
>
> When scientists were looking for a unified theory of the Universe, they forgot the most invisible and powerful of forces.
>
> Love is Light because it illuminates the one who gives it and the one who receives it. Love is gravity, because it makes people feel attracted to each other.
>
> Love is potency, because it multiplies the best we have, and keeps humanity from extinguishing itself in blind selfishness. Love reveals and

unveils. For love one lives and one dies. Love is God, and God is Love.

This force explains everything and gives great meaning to life in capitals. This is the variable that we have ignored for too long, maybe because we are afraid to love hence it is the only power in the Universe that man has not learned to control at will.

To give visibility to love, I made a simple replacement in my most famous equation. If instead of $E = mc2$ we accept that the energy to heal the world can be obtained through love multiplied by the speed of light squared, we come to the conclusion that love is the most powerful force there is, because it has no limits. We must give love to everyone with whom we relate.

After the failure of humanity in the use and control of the other forces of the Universe that have turned against us, it is urgent that we nurture ourselves with another kind of energy. If we want our species to survive, if we are to find meaning in life, if we want to save the world and every sentient being that inhabits it, love is the only and the last answer.

Perhaps we are not yet ready to make a love-bomb, a device powerful enough to destroy all hate, selfishness and greed plaguing the planet. However, each individual carries within them a small but powerful generator of love whose energy is waiting to be released.

When we learn to give and receive this universal energy, Lieserl dear, we'll prove that love conquers all, transcends everything and can do everything, because love is the quintessence of life.

I deeply regret not having been able to express to you what is in the depths of my heart, which has quietly beaten for you all my life. Maybe it's too late to apologize, but as time is relative, I need to say I love you and thanks to you I've come to the last answer.

Your father: Albert Einstein."

Introduction: a change of context

This book is about spirituality in the age of globalization, secularization and reductionist materialism, and outlines the ideal of living in line with Man's spiritual nature. So it is not a book about religion, philosophy or theology, or about science, even though it does touch on philosophical, theological, religious and scientific issues. The fact is that spirituality is like a sword, inasmuch as it passes through all five human dimensions: religious, political, social, moral, and family. Yet it does not require a definitional connection because it does not fully identify with any of them.

This book has been written for anyone, whether they have religious beliefs or not, and regardless of the religious community to which they belong. It mentions great religious leaders, such as Jesus and Buddha, but only in their spiritual dimension, for their contribution to spirituality, not for their religious contribution.

It is worth mentioning here that when the term science or scientific is used, I am referring to science in the broad sense of the term and not only empirical-analytical science, because some of the realities being investigated cannot be subject to experimentation as of now. This will become clearer in chapter 8 of this work that deals with the problem of verification.

Broadly speaking, there is a common moral for all Mankind (murder is not "spiritual" in China, Honolulu or London), so too there is a common spirituality for the West and East that transcends all barriers when one opens up to transcendence. This book aims to unite, not divide, helping Mankind to raise its level of consciousness, allowing us to live a higher quality existence in accordance with our spiritual dimension.

Though it is not religious, this book speaks about God, the beauty of evolutionary creation and the gratitude that Man must feel at being part of the Universe. It presents a God who is transcendent and immanent, personal and impersonal at the same time, and whose presence in the Universe is real. The intention is not to create a new dogmatism but rather to offer a glimpse of what some of the new knowledge is pointing to. In this regard, this book may be rather eclectic, because it broaches issues that cannot be explained in depth in one single book.

The first part of this book outlines what some of the leading thinkers on science and philosophy have to say about reality and how this new vision of the world seems to be converging with what the Perennial Wisdom of Mankind has stated throughout history.

The book also aims, in the second part, to explain what can happen to us when we are exposed to this new knowledge and how all of us can change inside ourselves in the light of this information.

The book can be read in any order. It all depends on which part of the brain you want to use first: people with an analytical mind (predominant use of the left hemisphere) might first read Part I and if they feel in tune with it, continue with Part II. More intuitively-minded people might prefer starting with Part II and if they feel in tune with it, go onto Part I to understand it even better or to find tools with which to explain it to others who are looking for the same information.

In short, everything has to be verified both on the inside and the outside, because that is how integral wisdom is built. Internal verification is unlimited, but external verification is not, and instead progresses through levels of knowledge and is limited by the technology available at any given time —the realities being researched are imperceptible by our senses, which is why high energy devices are needed–, by the mental paradigm from which the research is designed and by the researched realities. Science and logic can be confirmed, defined and are objective. Spirituality, on the other hand, is subjective and experiential (although it can also be confirmed). Spiritual truth cannot be proven via linear logic, but its results can be verified. Consciousness research deals with linear and non-linear domains and serves as a bridge between them. Everything in life can be described from two different approaches: linear versus non-linear, i.e., science versus spirit.

The **(linear) domains of ordinary consciousness** have to do with form, logical sequence and perception, which separates, divides and establishes categories. This kind of perception and its language allow relatively accurate predictions to be made. When events fall outside predictable boundaries, data is often ignored as background noise or chaos. The weakness underlying this domain is that it projects the mental mechanisms of cognition on an objective Universe that exists independently of its observer; it is the world of effects and interaction of forces. This domain fails to recognize the crucial substrate of subjectivity, which is the basis of all experience and observation. Its supposed objectivity rests on subjectivity. The mere fact of stating that objectivity exists is a subjective statement in itself; it is the domain of everything that is conceptual, mental and sensory (physics, philosophy, mathematics, theology, etc.).

In contrast to the tangible and visible world, there is the infinite and all-encompassing domain that is referred to as **nonlinear.** Science has recently begun to address it by studying consciousness, chaos theory and nonlinear dynamics. Our whole life in its essence is nonlinear, non-measurable and non-definable; it is purely subjective. The nonlinear domain is the ability to experience, without which knowledge would be worthless. Until now, science had ignored it as a minor issue and had relegated it to the study of philosophy, theology and mysticism. However, the world of power and of creation or emergence lies in nonlinear domains that can lead to form through exercise of the will which, in turn, has the ability to activate possibilities and options. Non-linearity is the spirit world, which has no duality; it is the world of mystical experience and all creative inspiration, which is not conditioned by learned concepts.

Linearity lies within non-linearity. They are not two different realms, but one realm seen from two different perspectives. One can talk about holistic versus specific, duality versus non duality, visible versus invisible, definition versus meaning, force versus power, lasting versus eternal, local versus non local, quality versus essence, knowing "about" versus Being, material versus spiritual, illusion versus reality; about that "or" that versus that "and" that, divided versus united and finite versus infinite. In a nutshell, Caesar versus God.

All information has to be interpreted by the receiver in a given context. That is how we internalize and subsequently experience. The new vision of the world, or New Paradigm, broadens the context in our minds, giving us a far deeper understanding of ancient philosophy, allowing us to redefine our purpose of life and, above all, change intention, which is the driving force behind any evolutionary progress. Thus, understanding comes not just from examining data, but from doing so in a given context. When the context changes, the intellectual explanations of the previous context no longer fit.

Reality is always interpreted. All mental concepts are provisional by nature. Being aware of that limitation is a necessary quality for wisdom. Wisdom has a component of humility and another of flexibility; it sees all knowledge as provisional and subject to change, not only in meaning but also in value. **Wisdom** could be defined with a mathematical formula: Wisdom = Knowledge + Love or, to put it another way, knowledge "in" Love.

A paradigm is a generalized context or point of view. It can also mean "general field". A paradigm, therefore, predetermines the range of possible experiences or discoveries and is a factor about which ordinary consciousness is not aware.

A paradigm is like the "glasses" that we use to "see" the world. This book intends to help us change the glass in our glasses to let us see what would happen when we do so.

Due to recent discoveries, today we can stay within logic and rationality and at the same time understand spiritual realities, supported by plenty of evidence. The New Paradigm has expanded the existing context to include scientific and spiritual realities at the same time, rather than one or the other. An expanded paradigm always facilitates conflict resolution.

As discussed later on, everything that exists is a "holon" (a whole/part) and a paradigm is too. As such, it is subject to the properties of holons. One of them is to transcend and include; not transcend and dissociate, because this would lead to pathology. So, any new paradigm must transcend and include the previous one and not just deny it.

Most human beings are "subscribed" to a certain paradigm and assume that our perception/experience represents reality. Opening up to a new way of thinking and understanding life brings bad news and good news: the bad news is that it can be frightening, as it involves moving away from the safety of what is "known"; the good news is that when this new paradigm of reality is understood and verified, it is amazing how fast it can transform people's lives.

New science sees an intelligent design in the whole Universe. Quantum physics has revolutionized knowledge of reality. All scientists are now aware of the quantum "enigmas" but not everyone agrees on how to interpret them. This book offers an interpretation that might explain them, and one that is based on the idea of "science within consciousness". As you read the book, it will become evident that this interpretation most closely resembles the vision of reality that both the Perennial Wisdom of Mankind and the teachings of the great spiritual masters have offered us throughout history.

Jung used to say that Freud and many other thinkers of his time had failed to free themselves of the scientific materialism of their time, and so tried to clarify any complex spiritual creation in line with a mechanistic picture of the Universe.

Recently, a lot more can be said, and from a perspective that is far more novel than the one that existing culture has offered to date. However, readers must be warned that what they are about to read may well seem more science-fiction than science. At least that is what it seemed to me, as the author, when my mind began to open up to some of these ideas. Yet these ideas brought peace to my mind even before I could check them out.

A new paradigm should integrate using the three modes of acquiring knowledge available for the soul: transcendent knowledge, rational knowledge and science. This integration must also acknowledge the hierarchical order of these three "eyes" —the higher one cannot be reduced in the lower one— and their realms of application to avoid category errors.

Perhaps the best way to make the most of this book is for the reader's mind to neither accept nor reject the ideas outlined in it, but instead for the mind to open a "hypothetical" window that says: "If everything it says were true, how would it change my life and my attitude towards things?" Then all that would remain would be an easier task: verifying to what extent these ideas are true.

For simplicity's sake, some numerical scales will be used. Readers should know that when dealing with issues such as energy, energy waves and different vibrational frequencies, any artificial numerical division and subdivisions become far more subtle. Experts can divide levels of consciousness into four, forty or four hundred levels, depending on how accurate they want to be in describing their differences.

On the other hand, always bear in mind that a map is not the same as the land; by that I mean that knowing a concept is not the same as experiencing it.

This book cannot explain all the issues covered in detail. Instead, it aims to shed some light on important issues, so as to try to summarize many of the disciplines of current knowledge. Much work remains to be done in compiling such a summary, and a second book might be required to further explore how to better integrate some of the ideas that are presented here.

The following brief summary of the chapters in Part I of this book will let readers focus their attention on whatever interests them most:

Chapter 1 discusses the scientific basis of the New Paradigm:

Section 1.1 runs through the evolution of physics, starting with classical (mechanistic) physics and ending with a cosmological concept open to spirituality, and the current string theory. It explains how many scientists nowadays conceive a multidimensional Universe, where each dimension represents a different vibrational frequency and probably also represents a different world that our senses cannot perceive.

Section 1.2 focuses a little more on the current scientific view of reality and explains that everything that exists is made up of "in-formed" energy. It talks about the primacy of consciousness in the manifestation of the world of form and describes the possibility of making science within consciousness. It also describes a Universe with intelligence and purpose.

Section 1.3 analyses one of the recent lines of scientific research that seeks to determine if the Universe is holographic, with all the implications that would bring.

Section 1.4 discusses the observer's effect in quantum physics and the fact that material reality cannot be separated from the consciousness that observes and causes it.

Section 1.5 explains the concept of downward causality and shows how the 3D world is a world of effects, not cause and effect. This section explains that the cause of everything that is manifested lies in the invisible dimensions that have a higher vibrational frequency and, therefore, may contain more information. This idea leads to another very powerful one: everything that happens is perfect and necessary, or else it would not happen. It also shows that everything that happens is aligned with the universal purpose.

Chapter 2 deals with the new holistic vision of the human being.

Section 2.1 offers a new vision of the human being as an evolving spiritual being. It argues that the human being is a spiritual being that is experiencing growth in the physical worlds, not a physical being having a spiritual experience. It also talks about the four bodies or filters that the soul uses to interact with reality, and examines the three archives that contain information in humans and the differences between them.

Chapter 3 discusses the levels of consciousness, which is where everything said so far converges and is one of the key points to consider in personal growth.

Section 3.1 introduces a novel concept that is highly important to scientific research: levels of consciousness. The level of consciousness is an energetic attractor field that determines our view of life and our behaviour. Some descriptive scales of these levels are presented, some of its features are analyzed and some of the tools available to ascend through these levels are discussed. It shows how knowing about these levels of consciousness can help to understand individual and social problems, and how it can help distinguish primary causes from secondary causes.

Section 3.2 analyses the direct correlation between the level of consciousness and inner experience of happiness.

Section 3.3 provides a detailed description of the levels of consciousness located above rational levels and discusses how a view of reality changes when perceived from those levels. It takes a quantum leap between linear and nonlinear, between reason and Love.

Section 3.4 describes how human behaviour is manifested through different levels of consciousness, and does so by choosing two topics of interest to almost everyone: Professional work and sex. Readers will see how human behaviour in these two matters varies depending on the level of consciousness that has been reached.

Section 3.5 studies the different lines of development and shows that the level of consciousness is the average score of all of them. Readers will see that these lines are relatively independent, but also that they all develop "holarchically".

Chapter 4 takes a look at the "holarchic" progression of one of the lines of development, the cognitive line. Readers will see how it advances both in the individual and in society, and how it passes through the archaic, magic, mythic, rational and vision-logic levels and, finally, the four subsequent mystical levels.

Chapter 5 addresses the three broad forms of manifestation of consciousness in the animal and human kingdoms. It describes simple consciousness (animal kingdom), and two large possibilities of manifestation of consciousness in the human kingdom: self-consciousness and cosmic or mystical consciousness.

Chapter 6 studies integral philosophy and also the "holonic" nature of reality, and shows how the four quadrants of any manifestation can bring an end to the reductionist view of reality. It also explains whether or not you need a certain psychological development before attempting spiritual development.

Chapter 7 analyses the difference between spirituality and religion from this new paradigm and the different function of each one of them. It describes the difference between an activity that "translates" reality and one that "transforms" it. It also shows that both new science and mystical consciousness offer us an opportunity to achieve greater convergence between the different existing religious beliefs in today's world.

Finally, **chapter 8** discusses verification, the three different "eyes" that people have for investigating reality and how to prevent more categorical mistakes in knowledge research.

Chapter 1. A new vision of the Cosmos and the person

1.1 The evolution of physics

As it has developed, physics has gone through five stages since its inception. This chapter runs through them and shows how the vision of reality changed in each of them.

Classical reality

First to emerge was what we call now the classical view of reality or classical physics, whose pioneers were fundamentally Copernicus, Galileo and Newton, among others.

These scientists were the first to discover that events in the Universe could be explained and predicted mathematically. Newton was the first to use mathematical equations to express the movements of bodies in space. Thus began classical physics, which is characterized by a deterministic view of reality.

Yet what did people know about the environment where all movement happened? What is space? Is it an independent physical reality or an abstract reality created by the human mind to understand the Universe? When Newton addressed the problem of space and time, he conceived both as absolute and immutable entities that turned the Universe into a rather rigid, mechanistic and fragmented entity.

For over 200 years, this view of the Universe became dogma in science.

Relativity

Newton's vision and his equations worked well, and mathematics fitted our ordinary experience, derived from the perception of our senses.

Even today, those same equations are used to send rockets to the moon, for example. So they still remain valid within their scope of application. Newton also included gravity in his equations.

It was not until 1860 that the Scottish scientist James Clerk Maxwell extended the framework of classical physics to also consider electric and magnetic forces. It seemed that by including the mathematical equations that describe these forces, theoretical physics would soon be completed.

However, the British physicist Kelvin realized that there were two matters that did not fit the model: one had to do with the properties of light in motion, and the other with radiation of some objects when heated.

The next decade, everything changed. The issues that Kelvin raised were studied and were found not to be mere minor details that had to be resolved in order to complete the classical view of the Universe.

A revolution occurred between 1905 and 1915, when Einstein postulated the **special and general theories of relativity.** He discovered flaws in Newton's concepts of space and time, and concluded that they were not absolute and independent, but instead interdependent entities. He also ended up destroying classical physics by rewriting the laws of gravitational physics.

This scientist discovered that through its flexibility and its curvature, space itself takes part in cosmic evolution. Einstein argued that what matters is space-time and that the relationship between them is flexible and dynamic.

His famous equation E=mc2 means that energy and matter are interchangeable because one becomes the other and vice versa. If an adult person turned their mass into energy, they could supply a medium-sized town with electricity for a couple of days.

Einstein also discovered that there is no global time. The passage of time depends on speed and the observer's position. Imagine two simultaneous stellar explosions and an observer positioned equidistant from both: he will see the two events simultaneously. Yet if the observer is closer to one of the stars than to the other, he will see one explosion "before" the other, even if they happen at the same time. So, what is "past" for one observer, may be "future" for another, and what has already happened for one has not yet done so for the other, even if the event itself has already occurred and it is finally observed by both. Somehow, for the observer, the future is determined.

As space is curved, time also curves with it. The greater the mass of an object, the slower time passes on its surface. Time passes faster on Earth, than time on the surface of a star, for example.

Even so, since the difference between classical physics and the theory of relativity only occurred under extreme circumstances (high speeds and high gravity), Newtonian physics continued being used for everyday experiences. Yet utility and reality are two different things and, as will be seen below, the characteristics of time and space that most people keep playing with in their minds, have been rejected as fragments of the Newtonian perspective that is no longer correct.

Quantum physics

The second anomaly that Kelvin pointed out in his criticism of classical physics (radiation) has led us to

the quantum revolution, because quantum physics transformed human knowledge as never before.

One of the principles of classical physics argued
that if the position and velocity of bodies in space are
known, Newton's equations (combined with Maxwell's) can
be used to predict the velocity and position of these bodies at any other time in the past or future. Classical physics
certainly states that the past and future are entangled with
the present. This idea is also maintained in Einstein's theory
of relativity.

However, quantum physics has shown that even if
we measure the current state of objects as accurately as
possible, we can only expect to measure the "probability"
of how those things might be at any point of time in the future. Quantum physics is a physics of probabilities.

Just as classical physics –according to human sensory perception– postulates that reality is one way "or" another, quantum physics explains that things are sometimes
presented one way "and" sometimes another.

Something can only be defined when an observation "forces" it to take a specific form among all the quantum possibilities. This result cannot be predicted, and only
the odds of it happening can be predicted. As very strange
as this may seem, it is not so strange in the light of quantum
physics. The fact is that people are not used to thinking of
reality as something ambiguous.

Another amazing discovery of quantum physics implies that something that occurs somewhere has instant effects on reality elsewhere, however far away it is. Einstein
struggled with this observation, to which he once referred
as "spooky action at a distance".

Yet experiments made in this field since 1980 have shown it to be true. It is what is known as "entanglement", which is when the behaviour of one or more particles depend on the behaviour of others; i.e., they interact regardless of the distance between them and they do so simultaneously.

When one thinks of space, it is generally thought that spatial separation means physical independence, yet the Aspect experiment demonstrated the instant influence between particles, which seems not to depend on signals. The experiment by Alain Aspect and his collaborators directly shows that when two quantum objects are correlated, if we measure one (thus collapsing its wave function), the other's wave function is instantly collapsed as well even at a macroscopic distance, even when there is no signal in space-time to mediate their connection. Einstein, however, proved that all connections and interactions in the material world must be mediated by signals traveling through space (the locality principle) and thus must be limited by the speed of light. Where, then, exists the instantaneous connection between correlated quantum objects that is responsible for their signal-less action at a distance? The succinct answer is: in the transcendent domain of reality.

Hence it must be deduced that this relationship is due to the fact that they constitute a single entity; their separation is an illusion. Therefore the different things that are seen and felt are different manifestations of the same reality.

According to the classical view, the only way to have an effect on what was happening elsewhere in space was to physically go there. Yet we now know that quantum connections transcend space and time.

Cosmological reality

One of the everyday experiences that remained unexplained in the three evolutions of physics already mentioned was the "arrow of time", or "time's arrow", as the physicist Arthur Eddington called it.

It is normally taken for granted that there is a direction in time: the past exists, as does the present and the future, and the impression is that time always flows in this direction. For example, a glass can be broken, but not put back together again, and people get older, but not younger. These asymmetries govern everybody's lives.

Yet where does this asymmetry stem from? It is nowhere to be found in the known laws and equations of physics, thus contradicting everyday experience of time. Solving this puzzle entails looking at what happened at the beginning of the Universe.

The mathematician Roger Penrose tried to do so by showing how special conditions in the Big Bang attributed directionality to the arrow of time. His equations explained part of the puzzle, but not all of it. It was from 1970 onwards that the Big Bang theory –which dates back far earlier– was postulated as the dominant theory in modern cosmology.

However, this theory still failed to answer certain questions. For instance: why is space shaped the way that it is? Why is the temperature of radiation what it is? And, above all, why was there was so much order in the beginning that it produced directionality in time?

The answers were sought in the light of a new theory in cosmology: inflation. **The theory of cosmic inflation** is being underpinned by the evidence found by the international team of scientists working with the microwave telescope BICEP2 at the Amundsen base in the South Pole. This theory (despite the current ongoing discussion about the interstellar dust problem) explains that the Universe expanded very rapidly and uniformly, in an infinitesimal space of time after the Big Bang. Issues as surprising as the fact that the Universe has a constant temperature and density everywhere, could not be explained unless all of space had been in contact previously, as demonstrated by the theory of cosmic inflation.

This theory, combined with other discoveries about cosmic radiation, is prompting many physicists to investigate the possibility that there is not a Universe but a **Multiverse** (infinite number of universes), and right now, plenty of scientists and thinkers argue that there is a Multiverse (e.g., Greene, Susskind, Guth, Stephen Hawking, Weinberg, Tegmark, Kaku and many others). Another group of scientists think that the question of the Multiverse is more philosophical than scientific, but this matter will be addressed in more detail in the last chapter of the first part of this book, which tackles the problem of verification.

As time and space are entangled in the origin of the Universe, understanding them in depth entails formulating equations that can cope with the extreme conditions of high density, energy and temperature that existed at the beginning of the Universe.

Unified Reality

For many years, physicists thought that one of the obstacles they had to overcome in order to develop a unified theory, was the conflict between the theory of relativity and quantum physics. Although both deal with different areas (the former deals with galaxies and the latter with sub-atomic matter), both theories remain universally applicable. Any attempt to use the equations together does not work.

The first theory to make headway with this combination is called the **"super-string theory"**.

This begins by proposing a new answer to an old question: What are the smallest, individual components of matter? For many decades these components were thought to be particles, such as electrons or quarks. These particles combine in different ways to produce protons, neutrons and the variety of atoms and molecules that make up the material Universe.

Yet according to the super-string theory, these particles are not points but are made up of tiny filaments of string-shaped vibrating energy, millions of times smaller than the nucleus of an atom. Just as a violin string can vibrate with different patterns that produce different sounds, these filaments produce different properties in the particles through their possible vibrations. A "string" vibrating according to a certain pattern, can produce the mass and electric charge of an electron.

To get an idea of the size of these "strings", imagine a drop of water, which contains one quadrillion atoms of oxygen and hydrogen. If a hydrogen atom were increased ten billion times, it would measure one meter. But its size would have to be increased much more, to the size of the known Universe, to see the strings inside it, which would be like a ten-meter tree in relation to the size of the entire Universe.

Scientists believe that space and time cease to exist as we know them when these scales (the Planck scale) are reached. To understand what happens there, researchers are changing the ideas of space and time for the idea of the existence of new dimensions and, at these scales, they have found conditions similar to those that existed just before the Big Bang.

According to this theory, the "vibrating string" would be the equivalent of what was previously thought to be an electron. All species of particles come together in the super-strings theory because each originates from a different "vibrational pattern", executed by the same underlying entity.

The super-string theory is the first capable of integrating quantum physics with the theory of relativity.

Yet for the super-string theory equations to work, we have to accept another great revolution in human perception. Instead of three space dimensions and one time dimension, the super-string theory involves considering at least nine or more spatial dimensions and one time dimension. In a revised version of this theory called "M-theory", unification requires at least ten spatial dimensions. As these other dimensions cannot be observed, the super-string theory implies that only a small part of reality in the Universe is accessible to human perception.

Brian Greene concludes:

"The idea of more spatial dimensions allows us to glimpse something much more dramatic: the existence of other worlds in the Universe, not in ordinary space but in those other dimensions about which we have not been aware until now."

The super-strings theory can offer the world the first, non-subjective rational evidence of the "non-visible" dimensions and forces us to accept the fact that until now we have only been aware (at least through ordinary consciousness) of a tiny part of the whole universal reality.

To a certain extent, this view matches what mystics have always said about reality throughout the history of Mankind.

1.2 How does current science regard the Cosmos?

The idea that consciousness affects matter is the main, and apparently irreconcilable difference between how classical physics sees the world and the new vision of modern physics. This interpretation of Wigner, von Neumann and many others is still widely debated. Yet as will be seen later (when speaking of the observer and the three eyes of knowledge), it may actually be the correct view.

Classical physics and the other sciences of the old paradigm stem from the laws of motion and gravity developed by Isaac Newton in his *"Principia"*. Newton's laws describe a Universe in which all objects move in three-dimensional space of geometry and time, according to certain fixed laws of motion. Matter was considered inviolable and independent or autonomous with its own fixed boundaries. It was thought that some sort of physical force had to be applied to objects to have any kind of influence on them. This way of explaining reality, which held that things exist independently of each other, is the basis of classical philosophy, in which most of the world's population still believes. We believe that life simply happens around us, whatever we do or think.

This mechanistic and organized view of the Universe as a collection of isolated objects whose behaviour seems predictable, has been replaced by modern physics. It has been shown that the smallest components of the Universe, which make up the great objective world we see, do not behave at all according to the rules of classical physics.

For instance, atoms are not like miniature solar systems, but something far more complex: small clouds of probability. Each subatomic particle is not a solid and stable element, but instead exists as a potentiality of any of its future states. This is known to physicists as "superposition" or sum of all the probabilities inside it; just like a person looking at himself in a hall of mirrors.

A "quantum particle" can manifest itself both as a particle, i.e., as something solid and stable and as a "wave", i.e., a broad region of space-time. Subatomic reality does not resemble the solid and reliable state described by classical science, but is rather a fleeting possibility of seemingly endless options. According to new science, matter cannot be divided into units that exist independently, nor can it be described in full.

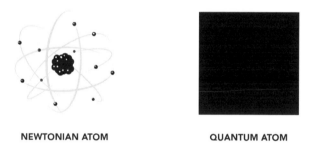

NEWTONIAN ATOM **QUANTUM ATOM**

Figure 1

The basic conclusion of quantum field theorists is that the raw material of the Universe is immaterial, and its essential substance is insubstantial. All present-day technology is based on that fact: computers, radios, television sets and plenty of other devices are possible because scientists no longer believe that the atom, the basic unit of matter, is a solid entity. The difference between an atom of lead and one of silver does not lie in the material level (because the particles are the same), but in the arrangement and number of energy and information impulses that make them up.

Human beings have to consider what it means to live in an "illusion" because, according to new science, that is the physical Universe. The atom, which serves as the basis for all matter, lacks any physical qualities, and instead consists of energy patterns that emerge from the invisible fields. And those fields mainly exist in a virtual state, which means that they are not present in the physical Universe. Some physicists would say that is a different ontology to the ordinary world's.

Things do not make sense in isolation, but rather in a network of dynamic interrelationships. Quantum physics' pioneers also discovered the surprising ability of quantum particles to influence each other despite not exchanging forces at a finite speed. Matter is organically bound, such that each object is a different representation of the same thing.

At subatomic level, changes are produced by dynamic changes of energy. The small bundles of vibrational energy constantly exchange energy through "virtual particles" that form a huge layer of underlying energy in the Universe.

Furthermore, subatomic matter is involved in a constant exchange of information causing continuous refinements and subtle alterations. The Universe is not a room full of separate, static objects suspended in space, but a single body of interconnected energy fields in a permanent state of probability of becoming something, in a constant state of transformation.

The only factor that seems to turn this cloud of probability into something solid and measurable is the participation of an "observer". Some people might regard this interpretation as over idealistic, but every day there is more evidence, as will be seen later on, that material objects (such as a ball) and mental objects (such as the thought of a ball) are both objects in consciousness. In an experiment, there is also a subject (the experimenter).

The living consciousness or field of consciousness provides the observer's influence and, to a certain extent, turns "the possibility of something" into "something real". This suggests that the most important ingredient in the creation of the Universe is the consciousness that observes it. Several of the leading figures of quantum physics say that the Universe is democratic and participatory, a joint effort between observers and the observed. Reality is not fixed but fluid and changing and, therefore, exposed to other influences.

Understanding those influences involves knowing that most of the matter and the energy of the Universe exist in dimensions that cannot be explored externally from our dimension. It is said that 85% of the matter in the Universe, also known as "dark matter", has never been observed. Yet even stranger is the fact that this universal "matter" or "energy" is crucial in the formation of planets and galaxies. Nothing of observable reality would exist without it; it is a force capable of bringing everything together to form structures and, without it, the matter that can be observed would not exist. As surprising as it might sound, in the Universe there is nine times more of a "substance" that is invisible than that which can be observed.

Not only are we not the centre of the Universe, but we're not even made of the same substance that forms much of it.

It has been found that "dark matter" is not made of neutrinos, because they travel very fast, thus preventing large-scale structures from forming.

So what is this exotic particle that forms dark matter? Is it a particle? Scientists call it **WIMP** or **"weakly interacting massive particle"** and right now they are trying to find WIMPS in the particle accelerator in Geneva.

A growing number of scientists say that this dark matter is not a new element, but rather, a new place: new dimensions that would have an effect on ours. This is not so strange if you think that, inside an atom, you'll find a vast territory that is far more complex than the observable Universe.

In this context, one could say that mind and consciousness are not an epiphenomenon of the brain, but rather that consciousness is seen, today, as the fundamental reality, the setting where all manifestation occurs.

To a certain extent, when scientists tried to explain how nature works according to this new data, eventually they came face to face with nothing less than the Universe described by the mystics; the fact is that the new models of consciousness portray it as an entity capable of transcending physical limits of all kinds. Intention seems to be something like a tuning fork, whose tuned vibration causes other forks in the Universe to echo at the same frequency.

Even before quantum physics was developed, Albert Einstein said:

> *"A human being experiences himself, his thoughts and feelings as something separated from the rest, a kind of optical delusion of his consciousness."*

The existence of this field of consciousness, referred to as *"A-Field"* by physicists and as *"Akashic Field"* by mystics, implies that all matter in the Universe is connected on the subatomic level through a constant dance of quantum energy exchange.

Other kinds of tests have shown that, at the most basic level, each of us is also a bundle of pulsating energy constantly interacting with this vast energy field called the Universe. Scientific experiments suggest that consciousness is a substance outside the confines of our body; a highly ordered energy with the ability to change physical matter. The power of mind over matter seems to cross time and space.

Scientists have found that directed thought plays some sort of role in creating reality. Guiding one's thoughts intentionally seems to produce an energy powerful enough to change physical reality. Each thought is tangible energy with the power to transform. A thought is a real entity, just as a table is, but subtler, in other words, it has a greater vibrational frequency. Thoughts have weight and substance at a subtle level and can influence other things.

To summarize, new scientific theories have the following basic premises:

- We live in a Universe that has its own intelligence: logos, self-regulation and creativity.

- Consciousness precedes the brain, created life and then created the brain itself.

- Consciousness is primary in the world; matter is secondary.

- Evolution is conscious and therefore creative. It does not work randomly.

- What science finds at the origin of Creation is a field of pure consciousness.

- Pure consciousness is the source of all qualities that are manifested in the Universe.

These new discoveries made by today's scientists and thinkers undermine the ideas that previous generations were brought up with, such as:

- The Newtonian view of the primacy of a physical-mechanical Universe.

- The belief that genetics controls biology.

- The idea that evolution is driven or led by a struggle for survival of the "fittest".

- The belief that evolution is the result of random genetic mutations.

What follows is another summary of the differences between the old paradigm and the new vision of reality:

Old Paradigm

- We're disconnected from our primary source and everything that exists, does so outside us in space-time.

- The world is made up of visible matter and invisible energy.

- Reality is whatever can be perceived via the senses or their extensions.

- Mind and matter are separate substances and different from each other.

- The physical body is a machine that has somehow learned to think.

- Humans are distinct entities with bodily limits.

- Our needs are separate from the needs of other living organisms.

- The outside world is real because it exists in space-time. The inner world is not real because it exists in our imagination.

- We exist in a "local" Universe, i.e., we have space-time location and exist irrespective of the act of observation.

- The thinking mind is located in the brain and nervous system.

- Time is an absolute phenomenon and also exists regardless of the observer.

- Things happen in a linear sequence of cause and effect.

- How we interpret our own experience in time has no effect on our biology.

- We exist in an objective Universe.

- Observation is an automatic phenomenon. Our senses objectively interpret a reality that is also objective.

- Our inner and outer world depend on our relationships, our environment and external circumstances.

New Paradigm
- We are fully connected to our source and all other living beings.

- The world is made up of fields of energy and information that manifest themselves through the infinite diversity of the Universe.

- That field of intelligence is the mind when it is experienced subjectively. When experienced objectively, that field becomes external objects.

- "Solid" objects are not solid at all, nor are they separated from each other in space-time.

- Mind and matter are essentially the same. Both are different expressions of the field of consciousness that produces every manifestation.

- Consciousness creates the mind and body so that the mind can express itself.

- At the most fundamental level of nature, no boundaries are defined between our body and everything else in the Universe. The body and mind are pulsating and changing patterns of that field of consciousness in space-time that re-create themselves constantly.

- Our needs are interdependent with the needs of all living beings in the Universe.

- Both the internal and the external world are projected from a single source. Both are patterns of movement of energy within the infinite field of consciousness.

- We live in a non-local Universe. Nothing can be confined to a single point in space-time.

- One's location in space-time depends on the observer's perception.

- The mind is not located in the brain but is part of a vast field of intelligence that extends beyond the Cosmos.

- We live in a timeless Universe. Time is a relative phenomenon and physicists no longer talk about time but about a space-time continuum. Everything happens simultaneously and everything is correlated with everything else.

- The unified field of consciousness determines that we live in a subjective Universe. The outside world does not exist without an observer; it is a response to the act of observation.

- We live in a participatory Universe. Our internal and external worlds arise interdependently according to the vibratory level of our soul.

Quantum physics stresses that the invisible energy realm, collectively referred to as "the field", is the primary governing force of the material realm. "The field" is defined as "invisible moving forces that influence the physical realm". This is the same definition as used for the concept of "spirit". Therefore new physics can be said to provide a modern version of what was known in ancient spirituality: in a Universe formed by in-formed energy, everything is entangled and everything is one.

Quantum physics and epigenetics provide amazing insight into the mystery of the mind-body-spirit connection. While classical physics and genetic theory dismiss the power of our mind, new science accepts that consciousness endows us with powerful creative abilities to shape our lives and the world in which we live.

According to science's new discoveries, all living organisms continuously emit light radiation that forms a field of coherence and communication. The visible part of the body simply is, or can be observed, wherever the wave activity is densest. Invisible quantum waves extend from each of us and penetrate all other organisms. Similarly, each of us receives the energy waves from other beings, that become entangled with our own.

The prospect of a "living" Universe invites us to change our thoughts from indifference, fear and cynicism to curiosity, love and wonder. Seeing ourselves as part of a continuous creation awakens in us a feeling of connection, belonging and compassion towards all life. From then on, it starts to make sense that each of us could have a direct experience of communion with and affection for the welfare of others.

As can be seen, Mankind is experiencing a paradigm shift driven by the growing number of observations that do not fit into the commonly accepted theories and would not do so even if these theories were extended.

For example, a vacuum is now known to be a cosmic medium carrying the waves of photons (light) and density-pressure waves, and that it is this vacuum which endows particles with "mass". This medium is not an abstract theoretical entity, or even a vacuum, but something with a full physical reality. The quantum vacuum is the "holographic information mechanism that records the historical experience of matter".

Why is this field referred to as the Akashic Field? In Sanskrit culture, Akasha is an all-encompassing medium that also underlies everything and becomes everything. It is real, but so subtle that it cannot be perceived until it becomes the many things that populate the manifested world. Physical senses do not register Akasha, but it can be reached with spiritual practice and training.

The Akashic vision of a cyclic Universe —of a "metaverse" that creates universe after universe— is essentially the vision that modern cosmology now offers. In new physics, the real vacuum is equivalent to Akasha. It is the original field from whence emerged particles and atoms, stars and planets, human bodies and animals and, in general, all reality that can be seen and touched. It is a dynamic environment, full of constantly fluctuating energy. The vacuum is Akasha and Prana at once, all in one the matrix of all the "matter" and all the "strength" of the Universe. In Sanskrit literature, Prana is like the air we breathe, the cosmic energy that gives everyone strength. The Akashic field becomes matter when Prana, cosmic energy, acts upon it. When the action ceases, matter disappears and returns to the Akashic field.

Energy + Information

One of the most important and revolutionary scientific discoveries is the idea that lying at the innermost root of reality, not only is there energy but also a very subtle but equally important factor: **active and effective information.** This information represents all things in the Universe: atoms and galaxies, bodies and minds. This discovery transforms current Western culture's fragmentary conception of the world into a holistic and comprehensive vision of the world. Nor is this information a human artifact but, as wise men used to say, and scientists are now rediscovering, it is present in the Universe, independently of human beings' will and action.

Thanks to the information that the Akashic field preserves and conveys, the Universe is extraordinarily coherent. Nothing is "local", limited to where and when it is happening, but instead everything is global and interconnected.The memory of all things extends to all places and all times.

Information is rather like an almost instant, non-evanescent and non-energetic subtle connection between objects and realities in different places in space and at different times. Such connections are referred to as "non-local" in natural science, and "transpersonal" in consciousness research.

Throughout life, almost all the atoms in our bodies change. These atoms were elsewhere before, but as long as the information structure is maintained, "I am still me". This quantum vacuum, the subtle energy and information that underlies all "matter" in the Universe, did not originate with the Big Bang that produced our known Universe, and will not disappear when the particles created by the blast return to the source.

The multidimensional Universe and the vibratory frequency

What does the new scientific paradigm say about the ultimate nature of reality? The answer to this question is relatively easy for today's scientists: the most fundamental element of reality is the quantum vacuum, the energy and the informed whole that underlies, generates and interacts with the Universe and other Universes that might exist in the past and in the future. This response stems from an old idea: The Universe we observe and live in is a product of the sea of energy that was here before there was anything else at all. Chinese and Hindu cosmologies have always maintained that the objects and beings that exist in the world are a concretization or distillation of the basic energy of the Cosmos, descended from the original source. The physical world is a reflection of the energy vibrations of the subtler worlds –higher vibrational frequency– which, in turn, reflect the more subtle fields of energy that exist in a multidimensional reality.

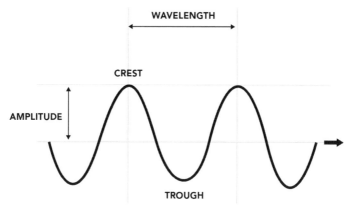

Figure 2

Any element that exists in the Universe is made of energy plus information. Energy is measured by its vibrational frequency (Hz or repetition of cycles per second): the higher it is, the more information it can contain. Learning or understanding is raising one's vibrational frequency.

Everything that exists in the Universe is energy plus information. Just as the only way to measure any object is by its weight, density or size, the only way to measure energy is by the vibrational frequency. There are low vibrational frequency energies and other very high vibrational frequency energies, and a principle says: "the higher the vibration, the more information it can contain".

If we want to boost our ability to store information about the truth, we have to raise our vibrational frequency. If we could invent a machine that, once connected to our body, would increase our vibration, then all information would be included in it and the natural process of evolutionary increase of understanding could be avoided. Yet as there is no such machine, vibration can only grow by raising the level of consciousness, which is its cause. A higher level of consciousness will always be accompanied by a higher vibration as an inseparable effect.

So, a multidimensional Universe is starting to emerge. Each dimension has a different vibrational frequency, which is what characterizes it. In this model, one could imagine the multidimensional Universe gradually increasing its frequency, from dimension to dimension, until it reaches the last one, which is the Absolute. Here the vibrational frequency is infinitely fast, so time is zero and can contain all the information of the Universe. The Absolute includes everything, even the lowest frequencies of manifestation.

As the dimensions below the Absolute reduce their vibrational frequency, supposedly there is some information missing in them and there is some sense of time passing. Therefore, until the complete unification that characterizes the last dimension is achieved, it could be logical to suppose that there are individualized consciousnesses in all these dimensions. This implies the likelihood that there could be non-physical beings experiencing in them. Different cultures have called these beings in different ways: Angels, Ascended Masters, etc. We are not concerned here with what to call them, because that is not going to change who they are, and it does not matter to them. All that matters is that, seen from this vision of the Universe, their existence is deemed more than likely and there are understood to be different hierarchies of non-physical beings moving up the different dimensions until they merge with the Absolute. In fact, and according to this model, that is the "future" of the experiences of human souls when they have finished acquiring information (or learning) in the human realm.

The Creation and all subsequent existence is a progression downwards and outwards from the primary source, in a process that is first downward and then upward. The path of ascent from "the many" to "the one" is the path of wisdom, which consists in seeing that behind all forms and diversity of phenomena lies "the one". The path of descent is the path of compassion because all forms of life spring from the one and, therefore, should be treated with the same respect. Compassion shows that emptiness is form and wisdom helps one understand that form is emptiness. The upward or transcendental current of wisdom (eros) must be harmonized by the downward or immanent current of compassion (agape). The combination of eros with agape is what underlies all true wisdom.

The new scientific vision of reality corresponds to the Perennial Wisdom of Mankind. According to ancient Hindu thought, in the Akashic field, all attributes of the manifest world arise in a state that lies beyond attributes: the "state of Brahman". Although undifferentiated, Brahman is dynamic and creative. Its ultimate "Being" causes the temporary manifestation of the world of matter. The cycles of the "*Samsāra*", from the Being to the manifestation and from the manifestation to the Being, are the "lila" of Brahman and its never-ending pastime of playing at creating and dissolving. In this philosophy, the absolute reality is the reality of Brahman. The manifest world enjoys a derivative, secondary reality, which is why it is mistaken for the illusion called "maya". The absolute reality is Brahman which, together with the reality derived from the manifested world, forms a co-created all, in constant co-creation: this is the Advaitavada, the non-duality of the Universe.

As in ancient philosophies, what new physics describes as the unified emptiness —the reality of all fields and forces of the physical world— is, in fact, the most fundamental and real element in the Universe. What is deemed to be matter is only a semi-stable set of energies that flow from this emptiness. Ultimately, matter is a disturbance of the quasi-infinite energy and information field that is the connected field.

New ideas are also being developed from the viewpoint of epigenetics. Dr. Bruce Lipton, a cell biologist at Stanford University, argues in his highly interesting book "*The Biology of Belief*" that the life of a cell is governed by the physical and energetic environment –including the system of beliefs– and not by genes; these are merely molecular drawings used to build cells, tissues and organs.

It is the environment that acts as the "contractor" that reads and interprets these energy drawings. It is the perception of the environment of the individual cell, not its genes, that triggers the mechanism of life.

According to Lipton, and many other researchers today, the character of our existence is determined not by our genes but by our response to environmental signals that drive life.

This new insight into the nature of life caused a big stir at its time because for more than two decades, medical students had been taught the central "dogma" of biology: the belief that life is controlled by genes.

If one believes that people are more than just fragile biochemical machines controlled by genes, this gives way to the understanding that they are powerful creators of their own lives and the world in which they live.

The body and mind and, therefore, life, are not controlled by the hormones and neurotransmitters produced by the genes, but by beliefs: energy signals are many times more effective and infinitely faster than chemical signals.

According to Lipton, all organisms, including humans, communicate with one another and interpret their environment by evaluating energy fields.

The new vision of the Universe's mechanics shows that the physical body can be affected by the immaterial mind. Thoughts, which are the mind's energy, directly influence the brain's control over the body's physiology. The "energy" of thoughts can activate or inhibit protein production in cells through constructive or destructive interference. That is the reason why, whenever you take the first step to change your life, the first thing to consider carefully is on what you are spending your mental energy. You must consider the results of the energy invested in thoughts as much as you consider what you eat to strengthen your physical body.

1.3 Is the Universe holographic?

A hologram is a two dimensional entity that projects a three-dimensional image when bathed in the light of a laser beam.

At the start of the 1990s, the Dutch Nobel prizewinner Gerard Hooft and Leonard Susskind (co-inventor of the superstring theory) suggested that the Universe could operate as a hologram. These two scientists put forward the incredible idea that the 3D Universe we perceive could be nothing more than an illusory holographic projection originating from a distant 2D plane. Just like in *Star Wars*, where certain characters appeared as holograms in videocalls.

Just as Plato, back in ancient times, conceived the idea that our common perception only offered a shadow of reality, the holographic theory offers a twist on this idea. The "shadow" that exists in a 2D surface would be reality and what appears to be a richer, 3D reality, would be like an evanescent projection of those shadows. It is a well-grounded, albeit unprecedented idea (not so for mystics who have always said that the world of 3D shapes is "illusion" or "Maya").

The maximum entropy of a region of space matches its surface area and not the volume inside it. What we experience in the "volume" of the Universe would be determined by the information encoded on the surface, as in the holographic projection. It is as if all the events in a room can be known by what happens on the walls. The laws of physics act as the Universe's laser, illuminating the processes taking place in a thin, distant two-dimensional surface, which generates the illusory holograms of everyday life.

Holography could be regarded as something that articulates a form of duality in which people, based on their sensations (not on physical reality), can choose a more familiar description of reality, in which the fundamental physical laws operate here in the "volume". We could also accept a less familiar description in which fundamental physics originates in some two-dimensional boundary of the Universe.

In 1997, the physicist Juan Maldacena made a great discovery: he discovered a hypothetical Universe in which the abstract meanings of holography could be made more concrete and precise using new mathematical equations. Maldacena showed that the physics observable by someone located in the "volume" could be completely described in terms of existing physics at that two-dimensional edge of the Universe.

This brings to mind another film, Matrix, where the world that seems real, is actually virtual, a computerized projection. So what if the reality that we know is generated by a supercomputer? Would reality be a dream of the soul just as night dreams are an illusion of the mind?

Greene says that all mathematical calculations made to date support this theory.

Meanwhile Michael Talbot, in his book *"The Holographic Universe"* offers more arguments to delve further into this theory. One of them is based on the holographic functioning of the human brain demonstrated in experiments by the reputed scientist Karl Pribram, whose conclusions dovetail with those of David Bohm. This holographic interpretation would, for the first time, explain phenomena such as telepathy, precognition, the mystical feeling of Oneness with the Universe and even psychokinesis.

Indeed, the increasingly larger group of scientists who have come to embrace the **holographic model** immediately saw that it helped explain virtually all known paranormal and mystical experiences.

In 1980, Dr. Kenneth Ring, a psychologist at the University of Connecticut and President of the International Association for Near Death Studies, also suggested that the holographic model could explain such experiences. Dr. Ring argues that both these experiences and death itself are merely a change in a person's consciousness from one level of the reality hologram to another.

In 1985, Dr. Stanislaf Grof, Chief of Psychiatric Research at the Maryland Psychiatric Research Center and Professor of Psychiatry at Johns Hopkins University School of Medicine, published a book in which he concluded that the existing models of brain neurophysiology were inadequate and that only the holographic model could explain such things as archetypal experiences, encounters with the collective unconscious, and other unusual phenomena experienced in altered states of consciousness.

At the annual meeting of the Association for the Study of Dreams, which in 1987 was held in Washington

DC, the physicist Fred Allan Wolf gave a talk in which he assured that the holographic model explains lucid dreams. Wolf believes such dreams are actually trips to parallel realities and the holographic model will allow us to eventually develop a "consciousness physics" with which to start an in-depth exploration of the levels of existence of these other dimensions.

In his book entitled *"Synchronicity: The Bridge Between Matter and Mind"*, Dr. F. David Peat, a physicist at Queens University in Canada, said that synchronicity –a coincidence that is so unusual and so significant, psychologically speaking, that it does not seem to just be by chance– can be explained with the holographic model. In his opinion, such coincidences show that thought processes are connected with the physical world far more closely than has been suspected before.

The holographic model is still hotly debated and many scientists have not accepted it yet. However, many important thinkers do support it and believe it may be the most accurate picture of reality that we have to date.

This holographic model has also received great backing from quite a few experiments. In the field of neurophysiology, for example, numerous studies have shown several Pribram predictions about the holographic nature of memory and perception. Similarly, a famous experiment conducted in 1982 by a research team led by physicist Alain Aspect at the Institute of Theoretical and Applied Optics of Paris showed that the network of subatomic particles that make up the physical Universe, the very fabric of reality per se, has what appears to be an undeniable holographic property.

The holographic theory has yet to be proven as a whole but it is mentioned here to let readers whet their minds and get ready for what lies ahead, as far as understanding reality goes.

Despite seeming an unheard of idea, this physical model has equivalents in the world of mystics, who have always said that the world of forms is "illusion" or "Maya".

If reality were holographic, somehow science would have ended up discovering a mystical Universe, with the enormous consequences that this would have for human beings and how they conceive the Universe and how they act in it.

1.4 The "observer" effect in quantum physics

Scientists had to tackle the problem of measuring a solitary event or object, and the "observer effect", in other words, how does observation per se change (or "collapse") possibility in reality? If the electron is a probability wave, what or who makes it collapse into a "ball" of matter?

The collapse event not only manifests the electron as a particle, but also collapses space and time with it.

Yet, what is this "quantum enigma" all about? What follows is one possible explanation:

An atom is approximately one ten-billionth of a meter. What happens in those magnitudes is very strange, and science is governed by new rules to describe it; indeed, in the study of the very small, the boundaries between science and philosophy are becoming blurred.

Perhaps the most famous quantum physics experiment is the double slit experiment. In it, scientists fired electrons through two slits in front of a screen. On doing so, they observed that this did not produce two hit or impact lines on the screen as happened when firing marbles but many, as would occur when pushing water through the same two openings. How was that possible? Why did an electron behave like a wave and not a particle?

The researchers then saw something amazing: if they observed the electron while it passed through the slits, it behaved like a particle, but if they did not observe it, it behaved like a wave, a possibility wave. So the electron behaved like a wave or a particle, depending on whether or not it was observed. They then realized that measurement itself changed the nature of what was observed and called this discovery the "quantum enigma".

When observing, light has to be concentrated on the subatomic particles and that changes their location and the way they move. Yet why does light not only change the direction of the particles, but also their nature? This was the big mystery.

In a more advanced version of the same experiment, the scientists observed how the electrons behaved "after" passing through the slits but "before" hitting the screen. They found that they behaved again as particles from the moment they left the barrel. It was as if they went back in time before passing through the slits and decided to go through one or the other and not through both, which is what they would have done if they were waves.

Which experiment is chosen determines the previous state of the electron. One way or another, the observer exerts an influence on the electron travelling "back" in time.

There is a Universe just as mysterious as science-fiction. Quantum physics suggests that reality is just a figment of our imagination, an "illusion" and, maybe, a hologram?

Upon further investigation, they came across another unexpected discovery: nature refuses to reveal its mystery due to its immense complexity or subtlety. There is a fundamental uncertainty in everything one wants to measure, yet it is not a measurement problem, but rather, nature itself does not know what the result will be; it is a matter of probability. Scientists call it the "uncertainty principle", and it is one of the most profound concepts to have emerged from the microscopic Universe. In a nutshell: nothing can be known with absolute certainty. It is impossible to find out for certain where a particle is from its wave properties. Even stranger still, if you try to trap a particle, it always has enough energy to get out of the trap before its speed and position are determined.

Edward Lorenz demonstrated in his weather forecasting studies that a very slight alteration of the initial parameters had a great impact on forecasts. This observation led to the study of chaos theory (small changes, big effects). The most famous example is the "butterfly effect", according to which a butterfly flapping its wings in one place, can cause tiny disturbances in the air that influence the whole planet's climate. When one tries to predict the effect of everything that can move in the world, the conclusion drawn is that it is unpredictable. The long-term behaviour of the material world cannot be predicted even if it is determined.

The behaviour of subatomic particles is chaotic, cannot be determined, and this is also due to the influence of observation. The entire present state of the Universe cannot be ascertained. Godel's "incompleteness theorems" show that natural reality cannot be apprehended in its entirety; that is to say, logical systems cannot prove all the statements that they contain. The uncertainty principle, chaos systems and Godel's theorems all serve to show us that the Universe hides the ultimate truth from us. Everything can be determined (Laplace), but that does not mean it is determinable. Humans are not forbidden from seeing the signs, but are not allowed to see the final evidence.

The uncertainty principle says that nature does not allow its constituents to remain enclosed. Uncertainty extends beyond the particles' location and applies to everything, including the energy that gives rise to the phenomenon called "tunneling".

Although they are not the only ones, the four most widespread ways of interpreting the quantum enigma problem are as follows:

1. The Copenhagen interpretation

This basically states that the electron wave function collapse occurs randomly. Einstein rejected this interpretation in his famous phrase "God does not play dice" and does not tie in well with the vision of reality of Perennial Philosophy or any present day religion, either in the East or the West. However, there are many scientists who defend it.

2. The parallel universe theory

This is the stance of some physicists such as Wheeler and Everett. This theory holds that all possibilities of the wave function end up happening. Since all of them cannot occur in the same space-time, i.e., in the same Universe, they occur in parallel universes that emerge just as branches emerge from the trees. No Universe appears to know about the other.

3. Hidden variables theories

According to this interpretation, the wave function collapse occurs due to the influence of variables that remain unknown but could be known in the future. Researchers who champion this approach believe that the collapse is not random; instead, there is an instantaneous causality not separated by time or space, but due to unknown variables. Bohm is one of this interpretation's advocates and Bell's theorem also fits with it well. The "implicit" order gives rise to the "explicit order" or outward manifestation, according to Bohm.

4. Science within consciousness

According to this interpretation, it is Consciousness that collapses the electron wave function. There is a "superior" intelligence that directs the manifestation. This perspective is very similar to the previous one and merely asserts that the hidden variable is Consciousness. It is currently being investigated by scientists such as Wigner, Sarfatti, Walker, Muses, Goswami, Hawkins, Wolf, Radin and others, and is the interpretation taken in this book.

According to this vision, the "collapse" is the result of a choice made by a non-local (outside space-time) consciousness.This interpretation would dovetail much better with the vision of reality outlined in the texts of the Perennial Wisdom and the Gospel, both in the East and the West.

1.5 Downward causality

We face the fact that the manifested Universe is not a Universe of "causes" and "effects", as had been thought previously, but only a Universe of "effects", and the last cause always lies in the subtler world, in the unmanifested universe. In other words, in the higher-vibration dimensions.

This is a key finding of the new vision that, as will be seen later on, will have a major bearing on human beings' understanding.

Many scientists now argue that the 3D world is a world of effects, and not of cause and effect as previously believed, and as most of the population still believes.

There are no causes in the observable world, but rather it is a world of effects.

Reference will be made to several of the scientists who are debating this idea, among them David R. Hawkins and his book *"Power vs. Force: The Hidden Determinations of Human Behaviour"*.

Within the observable world, causality has conventionally been presumed to work in the following manner:

Figure 3

This is called a deterministic linear sequence. The implicit presumption is that A causes B, which in turn causes C. But his research indicates that causality operates in a completely different manner:

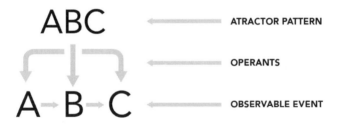

Figure 4

From this diagram we see that cause (ABC), which is unobservable, results in the sequence A→B→C, which is an observable phenomenon in the measurable three-dimensional world. The typical problems the world tries to deal with exist on the observable level of A→B→C; yet our work is to find the inherent attractor pattern, the ABC out of which the A→B→C arises.

In this simple diagram, the operants transcend both the observable and the non-observable; we might picture them as a rainbow bridging the deterministic (subtle) and non-deterministic (physical) realms.

This description of how the Universe works is in accord with the theories of physicist David Bohm, who has described a holographic Universe with an **invisible implicate** (enfolded) **order** and a **manifest explicate** (unfolded) **order.** It is important to note that this scientific insight corresponds with the view of reality experienced through history by certain enlightened sages who have evolved beyond ordinary consciousness to a state of pure awareness.

Thus, the visible world is created from the invisible world. It is also influenced by the future, not only by the past. Our minds find it very hard to grasp the future's causative influence on the present. We are used to the idea that the past influences the present and know, for instance, that if you drink several bottles of wine today, tomorrow you'll have a hangover; but would struggle to understand how the future can influence the present, because the idea clashes with the senses and everyday experience.

Consciousness can transform the understanding of causality. As perception itself evolves with each level of consciousness, it becomes clear that what is usually known from the human perspective in the Universe as the causes field is, in fact, the effects field.

Here's how Goswami explains this idea in his book *Quantum Activism*:

> *"In materialist science, there is only one source of causation: material interactions. This is*

called upward causation since cause rises upward from the base level of the elementary particles to atoms, to molecules, and to bulkier matter that includes the living cells and the brain."

This is fine, except that, according to quantum physics, objects are waves of possibility and all that material interactions do is change possibility into possibility but never into the actuality that we experience. Like the paradox of dualism, this, too, is a paradox.

As we have seen in "double slit" kinds of experiments, observation influences the experiment, and particles behave differently on whether they are observed (they become corpuscle-shaped) or not (they behave like waves).

To change possibility into reality, a new source of causality, or **downward causality,** *is needed. When we realize that consciousness is the ground of all being and material objects are possibilities of consciousness, then we also recognize the nature of downward causation: it consists of choosing one of the facets of the multifaceted object of the possibility wave that then becomes manifest as actuality. Since consciousness is choosing from its own possibilities, not something separate, there is no dualism.*

"Why can't I use my freedom of choice to make my own reality and make good stuff happen all the time?", you might ask. The answer is crucial. The state of consciousness from which we choose is a subtler, non-ordinary state of one interconnected consciousness in which we are

all one, a "higher" quantum consciousness. That is why causation should be referred to as "downward" and as stemming from the Absolute.

Hence, to use the physicist Henry Stapp's words, "nonlocal downward causation must take place from "outside" space and time, yet it can bring about an effect, the actuality, in space and time."

According to this theory, an observable reality does not cause an effect that is also observable, but instead a change in the purpose (or in the behaviour) acts as an energy field in which the possibilities of obtaining one or another effect increase, as postulated by the Universal Law of Correspondence. So if our level of consciousness is not very advanced yet, when we are not expressing everything in our lives, Consciousness will be doing it for us.

Despite what has been explained so far, for each person reality is "their observable reality", and that is so because their soul still has a fate to follow, or in other words, some karma to "burn". In the absence of fate or karma, intentions manifest themselves effortlessly because they have no opposing force. Inner work is like opening a bank account, but an account from which we cannot withdraw money whenever we want to. What money we can take out depends on a subtle energy field that awaits a trigger to release this energy back to us.

This new notion of downward causality was what prompted the physicist Fred Alan Wolf to coin his famous phrase: "We create our own reality". This is also the idea put forward, for instance, in the best-seller, The Secret. Yet in this case, would-be-creators were unaware of something important: as human beings we create our own reality, yes, but we don't do that in an ordinary state, but in a "non-ordinary state of consciousness". This quantum consciousness, the author of downward causality, is non-local and unitive.

There is one final question: how can we know what consciousness intends so we can align our intention with it? The answer is **creative evolution.** Consciousness intends to evolve us toward greater good for everyone through creative evolution, evolution that seeks greater information and depth.

This shows that there is a parallelism between these new scientific ideas and the evocative statements often made in highly spiritual debates: God is both transcendent and immanent to the world.

Before the advent of quantum physics, spiritual Masters tried to convey the idea that the relationship between God and the world is not dualistic. When people complained that these remarks were too vague, they said that "God is ineffable", i.e., cannot be explained with concepts or words; making it difficult for people to understand spiritual wisdom.

In the light of new science, the difference between God's consciousness and ordinary self-consciousness is clear: in the latter, connections and communications use signals, whereas in God's consciousness, communication occurs without signals. Interactions can never imitate non-locality. This is the final evidence of the existence of "God" at least when conceived as a higher Consciousness, a non-local interconnectedness of all beings, with complete causative power.

So it seems that humans have long been mistaken with their notion of "causality", because it has always been thought, from the paradigm of Newtonian classical physics, that the world was governed by "causes and effects". Yet the New Paradigm demonstrates that this is only a world of effects, and that the cause of everything that happens here lies in these higher vibration and information dimensions. At the start, the author himself thought: "What on earth are they talking about? That's impossible".

Downward causality could mean that everything that happens is "perfect and necessary" because the collapsing field of Consciousness has far more information than humans and a higher vibrational frequency. When the Gospel says that "even every hair on your head has been counted", it is telling the truth, because everything is done from above, by the Absolute and through Consciousness.

Everything that happens to everyone is "perfect and necessary", from the point of view of their souls' evolution. Coming to terms with this takes the stress, anguish and other negative emotions out of life, because whatever happens is what the Universal Intelligence desires. This conclusion does not imply there is no need for action or inner freedom, as is explained in the second part of this book.

This idea is based not only on science, but also on an internal verification, namely intuition and rationality. This is borne out by the fact that, when taken literally, there is a peace and acceptance that spread to others, removing fear. This is a key finding of the new vision that, as will be seen later on, will have a major bearing on our understanding.

To take this one step further, one might say that everything that happens "out there" is what people cause within themselves. If you want things "out there" to go better, it is far more useful to work "inside" than "outside". Why? Exactly how the "Laws of the Universe" work will be explained later on, and here a brief note suffices: the Universe is governed by a set of "Laws", but not the known physical laws, such as the law of gravity; the Universal Laws govern how the whole Universe works at all times, such that nothing can happen outside the Laws, because if anything did, the Universe would become disorganized. When the Laws are described in further detail later on, it will become easier to understand the core idea that is being explained now: downward causality. Thanks to this, the traditional clash between evolution and creation disappears, and is replaced by an "ongoing creation" or "emergence", that combines the concepts of evolution and creation.

Thus, among the various possible interpretations of the "collapse" problem, the most likely one is that it is the unitary Consciousness which collapses reality between all possibilities. This collapse follows the Laws of the Universe, which have a pedagogic purpose. The hypothesis put forward here, backed by the quoted literature, is as follows: this "collapse" would be the result of a choice made by a non-local Consciousness.

On the one hand there is a statistical determinism that argues the predictive power of a science of the non-living, objects and events that are distributed in a probability curve. Yet there is also the freedom of choice of individual acts of biological beings when they operate from non-local Consciousness (outside space-time). In the common consciousness, which is known as the ego or personal self, the memories learned from previous responses to stimuli push behaviour in one direction, making it more or less predictable and conditional. Humans' challenge is to go beyond the ego to a greater, non-local Consciousness that lets them access creativity and transformation.

To enter a world of real solutions is to solve the conflict between materiality and spirituality; the external and the internal. This, indeed, is the power of the new science: its ability to integrate apparent opposites. Hence, when consciousness is non-local, it is inclusive. When inclusion is practiced in settling conflicts, one is closer to non-local Consciousness.

In the light of new science, one could say that the conscious collapse with true freedom of choice is:

- discontinuous.

- non-local.

- hierarchically entangled or inter-connected.

Everybody and what they choose forms part of the same co-creation, because something is hierarchically inter-connected when causality fluctuates back and forth indefinitely, ad infinitum.

We practice discontinuity in creativity, non-locality in developing social consciousness and hierarchical entanglement in intimate relationships.

Chapter 2. The human being in the New Paradigm

2.1 We are an evolving soul

The definition of a human being according to the old paradigm could be as follows: a human being is an animal (with a physical body), which also has a rational brain (with a neocortex that other animals do not have) and a soul (you only believe the latter if you are spiritual/religious). Therefore the human being is seen as a rational animal capable of transcendence; in short, as a physical being having a spiritual experience, instead of a spiritual being having a learning experience in the physical world. According to this definition, the mind is an epiphenomenon of the brain; in essence, it is the brain (inanimate matter) that causes the mind, or put another way, that makes the mind exist.

Yet the current emerging vision regards man as a spiritual being. The more "real" and more significant reality of the human being lies in the soul, which has eternal existence. The soul has an evolutionary and temporary experience in a physical body and in an individual personality in order to gain insight aligned with the truth and purpose of the universal evolutionary plan. The soul can be regarded as an individualized packet of energy with information.

The four bodies

Both Mankind's Perennial Wisdom (e.g., Upanishads, Zohar, etc.) and new science believe that human beings have a physical body and other subtle bodies. The human soul has four bodies or filters for interacting with the world of matter. These filters determine our experience and the level of consciousness determines how and in what percentage we use them. The four bodies are:

A **physical body** that can be seen and touched. It is in this body that sensations are experienced.

A **vital body** related to individual life processes. It is in this body where the emotions that are then regulated by the midbrain, are experienced.

A **mental body** with different individualized forms of mental activity. This is where sequential mental reasoning is experienced and it is also called the "lower mind".

A **supramental body** that contains the learned aspects of the movements of the mind. This is the root of intuition. It is also called "higher mind", "supramental body" or "ethereal brain".

The picture below shows these bodies as well as the fifth body, which is included in perennial philosophy and is known as the **body of Grace** or Joy that is used for connecting with divinity. Science has not reached this fifth body yet.

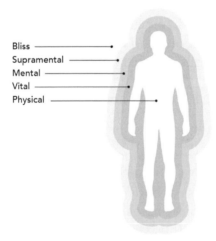

Figure 5. The five bodies of consciousness. Taken from Goswami, "Physics of the Soul"

Due to the science within Consciousness, it can be argued that there are other bodies besides the physical one, without resorting to dualism. These bodies do not need to interact with each other or with the physical body. Instead, it is Consciousness that controls their interactions and maintains their parallelism. The following is an excerpt from *"Physics of the Soul"* by Dr. Amit Goswami (PhD, a quantum theoretical physicist):

> *"The biologist Rupert Sheldrake reaches the same conclusion by noting that genes do not have the programs for morphogenesis or form-making. In Sheldrake's terminology, morphogenesis (development of the forms or organs that carry out biological functions) in living organisms is guided by nonlocal extra-physical morphogenetic fields. What is experienced as "feels" is operationally the morphogenetic fields; these are equivalent descriptions of the vital body."*

Morphogenetic fields (morpho = shape or form) are patterns or structures that confer order to everything that exists, be they crystals, molecules or animals.

Similarly, the biologist Robert Sperry, the philosopher John Searle, the mathematician Roger Penrose and the artificial-intelligence researcher Ranan Banerji all have pointed out that the brain which can be looked upon as a computer cannot process meaning that we so covet. Our lives centre around meanings, but where does meaning come from? Computers process symbols, but the meaning of the symbols has to come from outside. The mind gives meaning to the symbols that the brain generates. You may ask why can't there be some other symbols for meaning, call them symbols meaning. But then we would need further symbols for the meaning of the meaning, ad infinitum (Sperry, 1983; Searle 1992, Penrose, 1989; Banjeri 1994).

The feels behind the vital functions of a living organism come from the **vital body of consciousness.** Consciousness maps the vital functions in the form of the various functional organs in the physical body of the organism using its vital body.

Since only consciousness can inject meaning in the physical world, it makes sense to hypothesize that consciousness "writes" the meaningful mental programs in the brain. When we write software for our personal computer, we employ a mental idea of what we want in the programming. Similarly, consciousness must use the mental body to create mental "software" (the representations of the meanings that mind processes) in the brain.

To summarize, the behaviour of nonliving is law-like, but the behaviour of living and thinking matter is program-like. Thus, logic dictates that we have both a vital and a mental body of consciousness. Consciousness uses the physical hardware to make software representations of the vital and the mental. What argument can we give for the essential existence of the supramental?

Goswami broaches the question from the concept of **creativity:**

> "What is creativity? Only a little thought is needed to see that creativity has to do with the discovery or invention of something new of value. But what is new? The new in creativity refers to either new meaning or new contexts for studying new meaning. When we create new meaning using old, already-known contexts, we call it invention or, more formally, situational creativity. For example, from the known

theory of electromagnetic waves, Marconi invented the radio. The radio gave new meaning to a particular portion of the electromagnetic spectrum, but the context for the invention was already present.

In contrast, the creativity of Clerk Maxwell, who discovered the theory of electromagnetic waves, is fundamental creativity, because it involves the discovery of a new context of subsequent thinking or inventions.

This creativity in some people can put them ahead of their time. Take the case of Nikola Tesla, the precursor of alternating current. He was ahead of his time in many fields of knowledge, and what he had to say about the subject covered in this book was:

"If you want to find the secrets of the Universe, think in terms of energy, frequency and vibration."

Goswami continues:

"Thus, the fact that we have two types of creativity, situational and fundamental, invention and discovery, necessitates the hypothesis for a supramental intellect body which processes the context of mental meaning.

A little thought will show something else. The mental body not only gives meaning to the physical objects of our experience, we also use it to give meaning to the vital body feelings. So similarly, the supramental is used not only to give contexts of mental meaning, but also to provide context for the movement of the vital as well as of the physical. In other words, the supramental intellect is the very same as what I previously called the theme body the body of archetypal themes that shapes the movement of the physical, the mental and the vital."

The same thing is to be seen in ancient wisdom's tenets. As explained earlier, then humans were thought to have five bodies, the physical body being the densest of them (annamaya); the next would be the vital body (pranamaya); the following one was even subtler than the previous ones, the mental body of movement of mind and thought, or (manomaya). Finally, if we stick to the four bodies that science admits do exist, was the body of supramental intelligence (vijnanamaya).

So it seems clear that scientific points of views and that of ancient wisdom are very similar. Yet Perennial Wisdom adds a fifth body to the equation: (anandamaya), body of Grace and joy, made of spiritual joy, ecstasy and happiness.

Information in the human being: the consciousness archive

Like everything else in the Universe, the human being is essentially made up of energy and information. By now it will be clear that we are dense energy or "matter". The next questions could be where information is in human beings and how it works. It is argued that humans have different information archives for the different bodies. For simplicity's sake, let's say that the human being has three information archives and each one vibrates at different frequencies, as do the bodies to which the archive is attached. These archives are:

• **Genetic archive:** associated with the physical body and "hardware" needed to support the other bodies; it is corruptible, can be damaged or destroyed and dissolves with physical death. For example, if you drink five bottles of alcohol every day, you may end up with cirrhosis and cause other kinds of damage to your genetic archive.

• **Mental archive:** includes character, personality and conditioning, i.e., the software. It is also corruptible: e.g., if you let too many negative thoughts nest for too long in your mind, they will have an influence, through downward causality –from the subtlest to the densest– on the brain's physiology and probably trigger a depression or any other symptom, thereby damaging the mental information archive. This archive also dissolves upon physical death.

• **Consciousness archive:** records the understanding obtained from each evolutionary experience, but only the understanding that correlates with the Universe's evolutionary purpose. It does not record false understanding and cannot be corrupted in any way. This archive does not disappear or dissolve upon physical death; it is linked to the soul and the entire evolutionary process involves "filling" this archive with information about truth. After physical death, it continues its evolutionary experience. This may include other physical experiences.

Any understandings that are recorded in the consciousness archive first occur in the other less subtle bodies where the soul's evolution is anchored in each of its experiences in the physical worlds,. As mentioned earlier, many cosmologists believe that we live in a "Multiverse", and this has prompted some thinkers to assert that a soul might well have developmental experiences in many different mental and physical worlds.

Therefore the body and mind are not the ultimate human reality. They must be deeply valued, but only as a tool and to meet the needs of one's true Self: the evolving soul.

According to the latest findings of scientific and transpersonal psychology research, the very essence of Mankind can be said to consist of a **"higher consciousness"**. As soon as human beings travel through any internal development, they can feel the existence of this reality and, finally, experience it directly and clearly.

The Self exists as a higher vibrational level than the other three bodies –physical, emotional-vital, and mental– and needs a tool to express its will through these three lower-vibration levels.

Life as a learning process: the higher consciousness and the Self

In her book *"Free Your True Self - The Power of Free Will"*, Annie Marquier describes the human being as follows.

According to Marquier, human beings are a soul that has an instrument. This is what we know as the **human form,** consisting of a physical-etheric body, an emotional system and a mental system. This instrument can be referred to as **personality** or **ego,** and it is what lets the soul express itself in the world.

The aim of the process of evolution, the goal of existence on this planet is not to achieve a level of perfection that already exists (at the level of the divine essence inside us), but to build an instrument –the personality or ego– that is fully flexible and receptive to the energy and will of the soul, so that its perfection can be expressed directly and specifically in this world. When that goal is finally reached, the three bodies –physical, emotional and mental– will be a direct expression of perfection, beauty, intelligence and power. In fact, they will be an expression of all the "divine" qualities of the Self.

Meanwhile, the instrument is still being built, as it has not yet reached the goal of what is generally referred to as the process of "evolution".

To better understand how we function and the source of our difficulties, there is an Eastern analogy that shows how our consciousness is structured. In it, a human being is compared to a combination of factors, including a carriage pulled by a horse, a coachman who controls the horse, and the master or owner sitting in the carriage behind the coachman.

This combination of elements moves along a road. The carriage represents the physical body; the horse is the emotional body; the coachman is the mental body; and the master is the Self or soul. The road symbolizes the soul's great journey so that it can experience the world of matter and gain mastery over it through a well coordinated personality.

To travel along the road effectively, you need a carriage that is in good shape: a healthy physical body, including a brain and nervous system that is in the best working conditions.

You also need a good horse. The stronger the horse, the faster you'll travel along the path and the more opportunities you'll have to discover and experience. This means it is good to have a powerful emotional system. Even so, a strong horse has to be controlled, otherwise it could get carried away and start galloping out of control or inappropriately. When this happens, you usually end up in a ditch with a severely damaged carriage (the physical body). This is what happens when we let our lives be controlled only by our emotions. Yet the horse is needed to move the carriage effectively. Our physical body's condition depends largely on the number of times it has been carried away and ended up in the ditch and therefore with a damaged carriage, or the number of times that the coachman (our mind) has failed to control the horse. We know the condition of our physical body depends largely on our emotional state.

In principle, the coachman ought to be able to keep the horse under control intelligently, and use all its strength wisely. The role of the horse (the emotions) is to provide the energy needed to make the material world work. The role of the coachman (the mental body) is to control this energy wisely.

Yet the coachman does not know the way. In this sense, it has to listen to the instructions of the Being/I (the master sitting in the carriage) and follow them. To make the journey worthwhile, the master, who is the only one with an accurate perception of reality at all times, must direct the whole combination of elements.

Similarly, in order for the mental part of a human being to fulfill its entire purpose, first it has to develop its ability to be in direct and conscious contact with the soul, so as to clearly understand its instructions. Secondly, it has to develop a deep understanding of its emotional nature in order to channel its energy wisely. It should also know how to ensure the route is efficient and intelligent. When you manage to work in this ideal, balanced way, you have a personality —a physical, emotional and mental combination of elements— that is completely subordinate to the Master. The Being/Self/soul can then fully express all its qualities in the physical world.

To understand our current situation, we have to take a closer, more accurate look at how the coachman works. Actually it is a two-faced character. In fact, according to spiritual teachings, which have verified through countless practical observations, the **mental body** is regarded to consist of two parts.

The first, or **lower mind,** belongs to the personality. For now, it is closely linked to emotional mechanisms. This part of the mind has no knowledge and works like a machine, based on automations from past experiences. Yet it is very active in the collective consciousness; overactive in fact, in the sense that it does not let the higher mind act, leaves no room for intuition and hinders enlightenment.

The second, which is called the **higher mind,** which is in direct contact with the Being/Self. It is, in fact, the link between the soul and personality. Through its relationship with the Being/Self, it has access to knowledge. When the higher mind is active, and the lower mind is quiet and receptive, personality is guided by the power of the Being/Self and shows the best of itself in the world. So, life is very satisfactory.

The carriage analogy is useful because it lets us grasp the mind's importance in ensuring that the human system works properly. The quality of our life depends on which part of the mind is exercising control. If the higher mind is in charge, then we are in contact with the Being/Self, and the consequences are radically different. It is worth remembering that both the physical body and the emotional body have their own laws of functioning and the mind's role is precisely to learn to control these mechanisms effectively and following the will of the Being/Self.

Any experience of inner transformation should aspire to put the higher mind, not the lower mind, in control of the personality. The process involves the consciousness ceasing to identify with the lower mind and instead do so with the soul through the higher mind. So the inner transformation occurs when our consciousness harmonizes with the Being/Self instead of with the ego.

On the other hand, if consciousness identifies with our ego through the lower mind, we end up with an inadequate perception of reality, live in ignorance, and depend on automatisms from the past. Our life experience becomes difficult and limiting both for ourselves and for others.

On the contrary, when our consciousness manages to identify with the Being/Self through the higher mind, your understanding is correct and accurate at any time, we have a joyful experience of the world and an enormous sense of mastery and freedom. Our very behaviour and quality of our life experience depend directly with which of the two aspects our consciousness identifies.

The task of changing our consciousness' point of identification is, therefore, essential for this transformation process. To understand our present difficulties, in our attempt to live in a permanent state of peace and harmony, we must understand both the **process of identification with the ego** –which the consciousness has to undergo for the ego to be built– and the opposite process, namely **de-identification,** to which we must submit to regain our freedom. The natural order of things is that consciousness has to first identify with the ego to build it. During this construction period, in the absence of knowledge of the Being, the ego develops an operating mechanism, the lower mind.

Nowadays, many people do not need to reinforce their personality because it is already well built. Burning within these people's consciousness is a desire to break free from the shackles of their lower mechanism. Right now, the fact that we identify with our ego mechanism is not only not appropriate, but instead has become a source of suffering and limitation. What was useful at a certain point of our evolution has become an obstacle. It is a question of perfecting an imperfect ego and then releasing it. You can only let go of a perfected ego.

Depending on each person's level of development, one can find many human beings who still identify with the ego, while a few others have managed to identify with the Being/Self in varying degrees. In this context, what come into play are two different dynamics that depend on whether the consciousness identifies with the ego or the Being/Self.

While it is true that we must aspire to cease feeling attached to this world, this should not be taken in the sense of trying to escape from this relationship, but rather in the sense of trying to gain mastery over it.

Identifying with one's personality is not a mistake. It remained necessary for thousands of years, to permit the construction of a physical, emotional and mental instrument and so allow God to appear in this world, and for spirit and matter to come together.

When that instrument is sufficiently well built, it is time for the consciousness to let go and become less attached to matter; i.e., for separation and identity at the ego level, so as to put the instrument under the control of the Being/Self. So "negating" the ego is not bad, one just has to adopt the right perspective.

Many people today are willing to change their operational approach to the soul, but the old mechanisms remain active in our consciousness, so we keep on experiencing both approaches depending on the circumstances. Then we come to a crossroads where we have to make a decision: either we let our consciousness keep on identifying with the ego and open ourselves up to possible harmful consequences, or we shift our consciousness's identification to the reality of the soul through conscious internal work to reconnect with our true nature, with the deeper meaning of this life and the joy and freedom of being.

What do we have to do so that, over time, our personality can be considered fully built and receptive to the will of the soul?

Some general recommendations in this regard:

Become familiar with the mechanisms of the instrument (ego), its components, how they work at this point in time; become fully aware of these unconscious mechanisms (i.e., knowledge of oneself in terms of both the conscious and unconscious mechanisms of our personality); recognize the fact that one is NOT the instrument, but is responsible for building it, and through this knowledge, start to stop identifying with the instrument (the ego).

Weigh up the needs and improvements lacking in the current structure, so that the instrument can manifest the qualities of the Being/Self, such as healing, the ability to rid oneself of past complexes etc.).

Recognize the need to develop the higher elements so as to activate the full potential of the instrument: development of the higher mind, intelligence, the heart and all the qualities of the Being/Self; strengthen direct contact with the Being/Self, and increasingly identify consciousness with the soul.

The successive experiences of the soul

To explain this idea, we will follow the argument put forward by Annie Marquier in her aforementioned book.

For a long time, Mankind has been working to build and progressively align the ego through a specific process, which takes place mainly through a series of "trips" to the world of matter, a series of successive "lives". Through these trips to the three worlds, we can keep on refining our instrument to express the will of the Being/Self.

Upon completing each trip, we gain wisdom and mastery and acquire valuable and some not so valuable luggage –obsessions, negative memories, failures, suffering, etc.– as well as aspects that we have not yet mastered and need to be worked upon.

The fact that we have the opportunity to make several trips in the world of matter, rather than just one, is something that has become more widely accepted in our collective consciousness in recent decades. These trips are made to build and refine our instrument and its alignment with the soul, and even though more and more people are embracing this idea, it needs to be clarified because there is still plenty of confusion about this issue.

In simple terms: it is not the ego that is "reincarnated". On the contrary, with each "reincarnation" the old personality dissolves and the Self turns into another that is completely different from all the previously experienced personalities, in order to perfect its instrument. It is true that past life experiences will play a relevant role in building the new level of personality; we are immortal in terms of the Being/Self/soul, but mortal in terms of personality and, to the extent that we remain identified with our personality, we will actually die.

So in this context, "reincarnation" may be regarded as the process of building our instrument for manifesting the Being/Self in the three worlds, and not as an illusion of permanence for the ego. That is why it is better referred to as "successive experiences", rather than reincarnation, to avoid confusion such as the belief in the possibility of the whole of a person being reincarnated, or the likelihood of being reincarnated as something less evolved, such as a cat, because the consciousness archive always evolves towards a greater convergence with the Absolute.

Instead, what really happens is that after each "death", we return to the universal consciousness, where the material that needs to be worked in subsequent experiences is selected.

Based on our observations, this principle seems very useful for seeing things from the perspective of a string of "individual" lives. Indeed, each unit (soul) is responsible for working on its own transformation. This approach makes it easier for us to identify with the soul, because it is based on the sum of the experiences gained by the different personalities. Rejecting the prospect of a series of individual "lives" automatically removes the possibility of doing any internal work focused specifically at what needs to be done at the level of the unconscious.

All we have to do is simply avoid considering these life courses "personally" at the ego level; these different lives do not belong to our current personality but to our soul, as part of the material that it has to work with. The fact is that, as far as the soul goes, we are not separate from one another, nor can we really say that these lives are ours. Yet on the other hand, it is "my" soul. Once again, it's the paradox that something is not individual "or" collective but individual "and" collective. Both approaches finally converge in what seems a paradox, as is always the case when trying to describe reality at the soul's level, rather than at the level of the ordinary mind, with its obvious limitations. It is almost impossible to describe the reality of the Self/Being/ soul through personality-related concepts. However, once we have assimilated the paradox, what remains is the fundamental reality that the **soul is building an instrument through successive experiences in the world of matter**. These lives are "not us": they are simply experiences of the Being/Self. On the other hand, humans have a responsibility to do something with such experiences.

As everyone knows, at the end of any life, the physical body dies, and its substance or matter breaks down completely. That, according to materialistic science, is when we disappear forever. And, indeed, the fact is that the physical body has done so.

However, the consciousness that inhabited that body has not ceased to exist. In fact, after leaving the physical body, the soul's consciousness continues having experiences on the emotional plane –also called the astral plane– and on the mental plane. Therefore "we" continue to exist, for a time, in the astral world, with all the thoughts and emotions that we had throughout the physical life that we have just left. The body of its personality is then only made up of emotional and mental matter.

Then it's time to leave the emotional world, after having done what was needed at that level. Now we are "dead" in the emotional world, we move away from our emotional body, which then bonds with the universal astral matter, and the physical body merges with universal physical matter after its physical death.

Furthermore, the Self/Being/soul only exists in the mental field. The process is the same as for the previous levels: after some time having experiences at this level, we depart from our mental body, which in turn merges with universal mental matter and at last we are at the soul's level.

Our personality, which the Self used as a means of experience, has now dissolved altogether. The ego has died and will not reappear as it was before. So what remains after our journey through this life that just ended? Where, and at what level, is there some form of continuity?

The explanation is that when our consciousness leaves the physical/etheric body, all the information about this body's experiences in the life that has just ended is recorded in a unit of consciousness known as a **permanent atom** or **consciousness archive.** So when our consciousness departs from our astral and mental bodies, it takes away permanent atoms that contain the essence of our experience at the emotional and mental levels. When our personality completely disintegrates and the consciousness inside us has returned fully to the Self, what are left are these permanent atoms in which the Being can access all the information about the experiences acquired during this life in the three worlds. This is added to the experiences gained during previous lives.

That is when the Self "takes stock", so to speak, both of what it possesses and what it has failed to master; of the ability or inability of its instrument to express its will in the three worlds. On this basis, it also decides what "lessons" have yet to be learned, selects an appropriate date and establishes the conditions for recreating a new instrument in a context suited to further learning. So it is not the form or shape —be it physical, emotional or mental—, nor is it our last lived personality that is "reincarnated", as it no longer exists. The Self is simply another instrument, in the light of past experiences, another "personality" to undergo a new set of experiences. Yet it is not entirely independent of other previous personalities, because it is based on what has been learned to date, in all the aspects of consciousness that have already been developed, in all the lessons that have been learned or remain to be learned.

Therefore the physical birth of a being comes with a relatively well-defined mental, emotional and physical potential, through the integration of all the past experiences that we have yet to encounter in this life. This potential encompasses all conscious understandings, the positive wealth of knowledge acquired in terms of physical, emotional and mental proficiency, and the Being can use all this proficiency directly to express its will on the earthly plane.

This is the part of the ego that is flexible, intelligent, creative, free and serene, and that makes it an effective tool.

Moreover, since the evolution process has not been completed, this being also carries the "fragments" of the ego that are still relatively undeveloped or have become solidified or blocked as a result of past experiences.

What all this means is that we now have a number of positive experiences in terms of knowledge and wisdom, and that give us a degree of proficiency in the three worlds. Yet we still shoulder a heavy burden of material we have yet to understand, together with psychological garbage generated during the construction process itself. Our lack of proficiency stems from these parts of the ego, as does all our suffering and the limitations that we experience throughout our lives.

Think as we may that each individual evolves separately from all others, the truth is not so simple. Ultimately, all human beings are connected and each individual history will eventually play a larger role in the evolution of a more universal consciousness. Actually, Mankind is progressing collectively.

This feeling grows as an individual evolves. The pressure in our soul seems to grow stronger and forces us to continue with our quest, using all the means at our disposal. Until recently, the people who had felt this inner calling so clearly were very few and far between. Yet nowadays, the collective spiritual pressure of the soul, driven by all those who have already started out on paths to self-realization, has reached a level of such intensity that a growing number of people are feeling that inner calling to a more or less clear extent.

That is why we are seeing this "awakening of consciousness" throughout the world, as it gradually appears in all fields of human activity, be it in politics, social issues, the economy, medicine, or education, and in the growing public interest in a broad variety of activities that, to some extent, deal with personal growth and subtle realities. That "awakening" is experienced with varying degrees of consciousness, of course, but it is a sure sign that all Mankind is looking for a way out of the constriction of materialism. We're about to find the path to a higher level of consciousness and freedom.

When we do, we might notice that we feel less and less motivated by our own personal interests. When we access and connect with our soul's energy, the desire to contribute becomes our deepest and natural motivation to carry out that internal process. Spontaneously we strive to help others, create work in an original way, manifest love in a concrete way, through service to Mankind. We even do so at the cost of great personal effort, but with a free and joyful spirit of dedication, which lets the soul play a far more active part in manifesting the "Kingdom of God" on Earth.

This perspective is important, because it allows us immediately to avoid the danger of "spiritual selfishness", which could be expressed more or less thus: "I am concerned with my own growth, and all that matters is my own spiritual self-realization". This would contradict the very process of evolution and would hinder any further work. Yet we also have to take care to avoid "spiritual pride": "I am spiritually at a more advanced point than others, and have a great mission to fulfill to play in the world"; or "spiritual guilt": "I should be a better person". These distortions stem from the ego.

However, even these wrong attitudes contain some truth. In fact, working on our own spiritual transformation is, in a sense, the only path that we can take; you cannot take someone else's place and do their work for them, because everybody has their own path to follow, and the spiritual responsibility they have chosen for themselves. We can be an inspiration, an example and a model of support for others, but each individual has to move forward through their own personal efforts.

The time has come to underscore that all kinds of candidates are conditioned by the first and foremost principle governing true spiritual growth: the **purity of intention.**

The degree of purity of our intention and the righteousness of our personality's motivation will attract the attention of our soul, which in turn sends a wave of healing, transforming energy to our personality. This fact has been mentioned frequently by different Masters, when reminding in their teachings that we must clarify our reasons for finding the "right purpose".

A "pure" purpose is none too frequent but, when it occurs, it always leads to success. Our motivation may be selfish and personal or altruistic and spiritual. As far as spiritual candidates are concerned, it is a more or less intermingled motivation. Thus, power depends on the purity of intention and the intensity of our approach.

In fact, no matter what level we might have reached, or in what field of activity we might be involved, it is our intention, rather than our outward actions, that ultimately determines the outcome. This is true both of the material actions we take in our ordinary world and of the steps we take on our spiritual path. We can meditate ten hours a day, but if what we want ultimately is to obtain certain powers and feed our pride, or withdraw from the world, all we are going to do without realizing it is to intensify our unconscious patterns. Enlightenment will not come just because we have meditated; it is essential that we develop true self-knowledge lest we lose our Being in the illusion of "good intentions", which in fact stem directly from the unconscious part of our ego. The same applies to all the disciplines and techniques for inner transformation, and all methods of personal development and spiritual practices. Unless we strive, from the very outset, to understand how our ego works, we run the risk of reinforcing the wall of illusion and getting further caught up in the mechanisms of our lower nature.

Finding out how our ego works is a very demanding task, but sooner or later we have to face the facts, if we really want to gain access to the freedom and power of the soul. Clarifying our purpose as far as possible will give us the strength to tackle any task, but this clarification will be a conscious effort. Acknowledging our unconscious patterns of defense is a very useful way of recognizing the motivations that flow from the mechanisms of our ego.

At some point we will have to support our conscious intention by working at the unconscious level, where our most active motivations lie. What we think at a conscious level often has very little to do with our unconscious thoughts, which determine our life, provided they are not clear enough.

Our intention not only has to be clear, but also has to be strong.

Yet even if man can understand his potential, even in the clearest terms, this would not be enough to move even one step toward its realization. Realizing that potential entails feeling an all-consuming desire for freedom, and being ready to risk everything in order to achieve freedom.

If we wish to embark on a process of introspection, we need to be driven by a free and ardent desire. The soul does not force us to do anything at the personality level, and it's the personality that must consciously and freely decide to open up to the soul's impulse. Nobody is forced to take part in a process of transformation, and we can keep on living at the ego level as long as we want. There's nothing wrong with that, except that it's unsatisfactory and we keep on suffering. The choice is ours and only ours.

Here's where willpower comes into play. Following the spiritual path calls for determination and courage, because as mentioned before, when the soul manifests itself, the ego devotes all its energy to using its defense mechanism and the inner struggle can be fierce. Only an unbreakable will, reinforced by what a few call "faith", can help us to overcome the difficulties we face along the way.

Indeed, how much time and effort you devote to self-transformation and your willpower is directly related to your level of evolution. If you are inwardly prepared to take that step, to put aside your old structures and live more at the soul's level, you can devote plenty of energy to your process of liberation. Yet a less evolved person will not really be interested in this kind of work. Instead, they are more likely to keep on building their ego and experiencing their limitations, along with a limited joy and an inevitable suffering. They are unlikely to have any strong intention to undergo a transformation, because it is not the right time for that to happen.

Using intention as a motivating force for this transformation may seem simple, but it is not easy, because the ego does not intend to change or call itself into question. When somebody awakens their true Being/Self, they may experience internal conflicts that are not always conscious ones. What the Being/Self wants is to speed up the transformation process through a radical change in the mechanism of consciousness, while what the ego wants is to maintain the status quo.

Once an individual is aware of the work they have done and is willing to take part in this work in the context of the soul, methods become very effective. Which method is used does not matter, because what does matter is that a weak intention produces weak results, while a strong one produces powerful results. By the same measure of intention, an average method can produce good results, while a very good method will give excellent results. On the other hand, without a clear and strong intention, a very good method will not produce lasting results.

In a way, the issue at hand is freedom, albeit seen in another light. Indeed, if they key to the success of a process of internal work is not so much the method used to do so, but the will and the right motivation (purity of intention/intensity) of the individual to achieve their desired goal, this means that each human being is free and is fully responsible for creating their own result.

Chapter 3. Levels of consciousness

3.1 Levels of consciousness

Before beginning this section, it must be clarified that levels of consciousness should not be confused with the different dimensions of the Universe. Dimensions are energy worlds of different vibrational frequency, while levels of consciousness are levels of evolution of consciousness in the human kingdom.

The consciousness' energy field is invisible and non-linear, which is why it was never deemed worth studying, except by some enlightened Sages. Yet recent decades have seen some major scientific advances in the study of quantum physics, such as the Heisenberg uncertainty principle and the double-slit experiment, which have prompted scientists to start studying this field. Scientists found that simply watching an experiment changed the result -collapsing the electron wave function from potentiality to actuality; therefore, and for the first time ever, the subject of consciousness itself, and intention, became part of scientific debate and research.

Although philosophy and psychology had already explored the mental content of consciousness (the mind), they had not addressed what actually underlies the mind, namely *awareness*, by which mentalization could be subjectively discerned and experienced.

A unique quality of the field of *consciousness* is self-knowledge, which gives rise to the unique ability to "know". Without awareness, a human being is, but, paradoxically, does not know that it is.

Unlike one's IQ, one's individual level of consciousness, which exists from birth, can grow as a result of favorable factors, such as the influence of spiritual Masters and conscious individual work.

These factors have a biological influence on brain functions and hemispheric dominance, and also on neural patterns, connectivity and brain chemistry (remember **downward causality:** from subtle to dense). Thus, the IQ's importance may be overshadowed by developments in the level of consciousness, which in turn reflects the inherited tendencies, voluntary intent and different choices.

Each level of consciousness represents a predominant energy field as a result of its "attractor field", which acts in a similar way to magnetic or gravitational fields. They are progressive force fields, and any that represent a degree of energy above a certain level of consciousness –200 on the Hawkins scale or middle third level in the Schmedling model–, as discussed below, attract anything that is positive (true, loving and vital) and repel anything that is negative. Levels below this limit repel anything that is positive and attract anything that is negative, false and destructive. These energy fields, which had gone undetected until now, dominate and influence all human decisions very deeply: behaviour, perception, culture, religion and comprehension skills, as well as the range of emotional capacities and types of "temptations" that we experience.

It is important to realize the great extent to which understanding is limited at the lower levels of consciousness, equivalent to the difficulty of teaching the physics of quantum mechanics to small children or intellectually limited or educationally impaired people. For example, being "nice" seems normal for people above a certain level, while below it, it could be regarded as a weakness, almost as an insult, and therefore not effective as a communication tool.

Each level of consciousness offers a different view of what is real and what is of primary importance. Each level has its own ideals and perception of value. Levels of consciousness are not directly linked to IQ, but rather to the ability to distinguish the "essence" from the "appearance".

The structure of the human mind has been compared to a computer insofar as basically it resembles a computer's hardware, and its contents would resemble the software (Hawkins). In this context, the mind can be said to have little control over programming content, so the human being is both responsible for it and its author, and yet is innocent.

The brain's very physiology reflects the level of consciousness, as is shown in the following diagram:

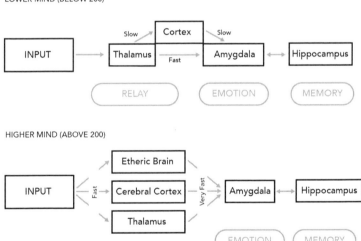

Figure 6. The brain's function and physiology. Taken from David R. Hawkins: Reality, Spirituality and Modern Man.

Below 200	Above 200
• Left-brain dominance	• Right-brain dominance
• Linear	• Non - linear
• Stress - Adrenalin	• Peace - Endorphins
• Negative emotions	• Positive emotions
• Less killer cells and inmunity	• More killer cells and inmunity
• Disrupt acupuncture meridian	• Balanced acupuncture system
• Disease	• Healing
• Negative kinesiological response	• Positive kinesiological response
• Track to emotions twice as fast as through prefrontal to emotion	• Track to emotion slower than from prefrontal and etheric cortexes
• Pupil dilation	• Pupil contraction

So the answer to the question "What is the purpose of life in this world?" mainly depends on the level of consciousness and on the brain's physiology. Broadly speaking, the higher the level of consciousness, the greater the ability to discern the truth, the essence and reality from illusion and from misperceptions.

In short, the subjective world of experience is a consequence of the level of consciousness that emerges from within, irrespective of external events. This means it is impossible to accurately determine the true reality of the world, because it is only experienced as it is perceived. When observed from the highest level of consciousness, the world is perfect as it is, as it offers all the opportunities and possibilities for evolutionary growth. Therefore, from this vantage point everything that happens is "perfect and necessary" for this purpose and the only valid option is to flow with manifestation.

We have already seen that understanding is a consequence of the context, and the level of consciousness itself offers the definitive context in which whatever seems to be dark, becomes obvious. This layer of attractor fields, according to the corresponding levels of consciousness, provides a new paradigm for recontextualizing human experience throughout time. Scales and levels of consciousness have been obtained from the fields of psychology, philosophy, quantum physics, the classic *"Great Chain of Being"* (Lovejoy 1936) and from Ageless Wisdom (Wilber, Hawkins, Schmedling, Marquier, Aurobindo, etc.).

Here follows a brief analysis of the Hawkins and Schmedling consciousness scales, and a closer look at the highest, or post-rational levels, which precede enlightenment.

LEVEL	SCL	EMOTION	LIFE-VIEW
Enlightenment	700 - 1000	Ineffable	Is
Peace	600	Bliss	Perfect
Joy	540	Serenity	Complete
Love	500	Reverence	Benign
Reason	400	Understanding	Meaningful
Acceptance	350	Forgiveness	Harmonious
Willingness	310	Optimism	Hopeful
Neutrality	250	Trust	Satisfactory
Courage	200	Affirmation	Feasible
Pride	175	Dignity	Demanding
Anger	150	Hate	Antogonistic
Desire	125	Craving	Disappointing
Fear	100	Anxiety	Frightening
Grief	75	Regret	Tragic
Apathy	50	Desire	Hopeless
Guilt	30	Blame	Condemnation
Shame	20	Humiliation	Miserable

Figure 7. Levels of consciousness scale. Taken from "Power vs. Force: The Hidden Determinants of Human Behaviour", D. Hawkins

As seen in Figure 7, and according to Hawkins, the consciousness is calibrated with a numerical value that indicates the predominance of an energy field, which, in turn, determines the perception.

In Hawkins' own words:

"It is very important to remember that the calibration figures do not represent an arithmetic progress, but a logarithmic progression. Thus,

the level 300 is not twice the amplitude of 150; it is 10 to the 300th power (10^{300}). An increase of even a few points represents a major advance in power; the rate of increase in power as we move up the scale is enormous.

The critical response point on the scale of consciousness calibrates at about 200, the level associated with integrity and courage. All attitudes, thoughts, feelings and associations below that level of calibration make a person go weak. Attitudes, thoughts, feelings, entities or historical figures which calibrate higher make subjects go strong. This is the balance point between weak and strong attractors, between negative and positive influence.

At the levels below 200, the primary impetus is survival, although at the very bottom of the scale, the zone of hopelessness and depression, even this motive is lacking. The levels of Fear and Anger are characterized by egocentric impulses arising from this drive for personal survival. At the level of pride the survival motive may expand to comprehend the survival of others as well. As one crosses the demarcation between negative and positive influence into Courage, the well-being of others becomes increasingly important. By the 500 level, the happiness of others emerges as the essential motivating force. The high 500s are characterized by interest in spiritual awareness for both oneself and others, and by the 600s the good of Mankind and the search for enlightenment are the primary goals. From 700 to 1,000 life is dedicated to the salvation of all humanity."

According to Hawkins, most people use their life experiences to elaborate and express the small variations of their level of consciousness present at birth; it's the rare individual who manages to move beyond their energy level. Awareness levels only increase by about five points, on average (Hawkins, *"Power vs. Force"*) in each lifetime. This is more easily understandable when we realize that what defines each person's level is the motivation-purpose-intent. Motivation proceeds from meaning/sense, which is an expression of individual context. So, success is limited by the context which, when appropriately aligned with motivation, determines the relative power of each individual.

Nonetheless, it's possible to make sudden positive jumps, leaping up even hundreds of points. If one can truly escape the egocentric draw of sub 200 attractor fields, consciously choosing a friendly, earnest, kind and forgiving approach to life, and eventually making charity toward others one's primary focus, higher levels can certainly be attained. Even so, great will is required. Consciousness evolves from selfishness to a transpersonal and unitive form.

In his magnificent book entitled *"Integral Psychology"*, Wilber says that moving from a stage of human development to another involves integrating the previous stage. For example, the current "mental age" of the rational mind's evolution must integrate the evolution reached in the previous era, that of the vital mind. This entails integrating the processing both of feelings and of meaning.

According to Hawkins, in the infinite field of unending potential —consciousness itself— lies an enormously powerful attractor field organizing innate human behaviour, or inherent to Mankind. Within that giant attractor field are other sequential fields with progressively less energy and power which, in turn, define behaviour by making patterns of conduct consistent across cultures and time, in other words, human history. Animal and vegetable kingdoms as well are also controlled by attractor fields of hierarchic power.

Another way of understanding levels of consciousness is by using the Schmedling scale.

This author starts by showing that anything can be divided and subdivided (for example, 1 meter = 100 = 1000 mm). Therefore any classification can be improved or enlarged. To simplify things, he suggests that there are three major levels of consciousness represented in the human population today (Figure 8)

LEVEL	PREDOMINANT INTENTION	CHARACTERISTICS	% POPULATION
2	GETTING	Dictatorship Government systems No technology generated Conflicts solved through physical violence	25%
Low 3	MOSTLY GETTING / RESPECTING SOME RULES	Democratic Government systems Technology is generated	50%
High 3	MIXTURE OF GETTING AND SERVING	Conflicts solved through verbal & mental violence	20%
Low 4	SERVING GROWING	Consensus Government systems Technology is generated, if intended	5%
High 4	SERVING	No conflicts to be solved	0,3%

Figure 8. Levels of consciousness according to the Schmedling scale

As may be seen, both this scale and Hawkins' essentially describe the same reality. Level 2 and Level 3 Low on the Schmedling scale is equivalent to levels 1 to 200 on Hawkins' scale. Level 3 High on the Schmedling scale is equivalent to levels 200 to 500 on Hawkins' scale and level 4 is equivalent to levels 500 to 999 on Hawkins' scale.

According to Schmedling, level 2 is that of physical violence, crime, terrorism, gangs, domestic violence, dysfunction, drug trafficking and so on. Although only 25% of Mankind operates at this level, those few make a lot of noise, cause most of the problems and are always in the news. It is the level of the law of the strongest, the law of retaliation –eye for eye–, war and the struggle for power. At this level, conflicts are resolved by physical violence – such as Al Capone–, who does not sue, but orders a murder. Governments are dictatorial and very little technology is generated, although whatever exists is bought and used.

Level 3 is where most of Mankind is right now. If you looked down from space, Earth would be considered a level 3 planet.

At this level, people still operate with the lure of personal gain: money, sex, relationships, power, toys, entertainment, pleasure of the senses, etc. People believe in rivalry and success, and devote most of their lives to achieving these goals. Man's rules and laws are codified and enforced under the rule of money, individualism and struggle within free competition. This level is characterized by reflection, discussion of different opinions and democracy to solve them. Physical violence has been transcended and conflicts are resolved by agreement or in court when an agreement is not possible. Systems of government are democratic but remain violent because they are governments of the majority over the minority. People try to vote wisdom because it is still not easy to recognize since minds cannot see essence clearly. Lastly, lot of technology is generated; it is not the same to go to New York or Tokyo as it is to Somalia, to give an example of the different levels of democracy and technology in one place and another.

At this level one finds many professionals from all walks of life who are not destructive to society –whereas level 2 people are–, but who have not yet turned their prevalent lifestyle into a change of consciousness towards nonlinear domains and have not made serving others their dominant intention.

Level 4 is where the major change in intention-motivation occurs and people begin to understand the order of the Universe. The intention-motivation changes from "getting" to "serving" because at this level people are "fuller" and feel less desire or need to "get" something in the external world. It is the first level where there is a change of polarity, and individuals realize that instead of fighting against the world, they must work on themselves.

At this level, there are no conflicts and situations are determined by the point of Law which is above any agreement, as will be discussed in the second part of this book. What conflict could Teresa of Calcutta possibly have with Gandhi? How would they solve it? Systems of government at this level are consensus governments, or Council of Elders, not elected but recognized.

At all scales of levels of consciousness, there is directionality. In general, evolution always moves towards more powerful levels. So even though the personality may move backwards, it does not do so in the consciousness archive which, as we saw, is incorruptible, thus ensuring that the soul moves upwards as it evolves.

The fact is that all souls will progress through these levels, which in themselves are impersonal and existed long before us. It is through intention-motivation and will that we can speed up that evolution, cooperating with the attraction of higher vibrational energies or Grace.

3.2 Happiness and level of consciousness

All consciousness research experts argue that there is a mathematical equation that everyone should know:

Happiness = Level of Consciousness

It is easy to see that what drives most people to make decisions is that they want to be happy. The old paradigm sought to convince people that they would be happy if they liked everything around them. Yet things around us always change and if we think of happiness in this way, we will always depend on what happens on the outside, which is beyond our control.

The New Paradigm shows that happiness only lies inside you. In other words, the source of happiness does not lie in events themselves, but in our attitude towards them. It is not in the "when" –"when I have money, when I graduate, when I find a partner"–, but in the "while", and depends on how connected we are to our inner source. The challenge is to be happy, irrespective of any external circumstance. The paradox is that the more we achieve this inner state, the easier our desires are fulfilled. It is as if the Universe responds to our inner attitude in this regard through synchronicities. In many spiritual traditions, this has been referred to as the "state of grace"; a state through which one feels a special connection to the creative power of the Universe.

The proposal therefore is to learn to find inner happiness directly and not through external events that are changing and ephemeral by nature.

Hawkins develops this idea in depth throughout his book, and in the following table shows how the general level of happiness is statistically directly correlated with the level of consciousness.

LEVEL	LOG	PERCENT
Enlightenment	700 - 1000	100%
Peace	600	100%
Joy	570	99%
Unconditional love	540	96%
Love	500	89%
Reason	400	79%
Acceptance	350	71%
Willingness	310	68%
Neutrality	250	60%
Courage	200	55%
Pride	175	22%
Anger	150	12%
Desire	125	10%
Fear	100	10%
Grief	75	9%
Apathy	50	5%
Guilt	30	4%
Shame	20	1%

Figure 9. Levels of consciousness and rate of happiness. Taken from "Spirituality and Modern Man", by D. Hawkins.

As explained earlier, evolution is inevitable in the long run. We have also seen how levels of happiness correspond to the levels of consciousness, and all that is at stake is how long we suffer during the process. It is just like university students, who know they have to complete their college education but our happiness is our responsibility, as it is a subjective journey of self-realization; it involves letting go of the ego and connecting with the Self, by whatever method or language we want to use. Connecting with the Self is not an intellectual, but an experiential matter. We will never attain permanent happiness through the objects in the world, but through the realization of our essence.

3.3 More detailed description of post-rational levels

What follow are some of the points of views, attitudes, motivations and actual practices that correspond to an individual who opens up to level 4 (Schmedling) or to levels 500 onwards (Hawkins).

• You start to see that everything that happens in the Universe is "perfect and necessary"; but it is from the point of view of souls' evolution, individually and collectively, but not necessarily, as we all know, from the limited viewpoint of our mind, which has its personal preferences. If everything is perfect and necessary, you start to understand that, in fact, there cannot be any problem. Each event is seen –without stress or resistance– as an opportunity to make further progress, otherwise it would not be happening, because the Cosmos is extremely efficient and does not waste energy.

• You develop an attitude of gratitude towards everything.

• You understand that you and only you generate external events, because they are manifested in relation to your needs for growth. So you can regain control by accepting full responsibility for your life and stopping blaming anything or anyone on the outside, as one does from the victim paradigm.

• Motivation changes from material success to conscious growth and serving others.

• You begin to clearly see that the Cosmos has a purpose and the only valid option is to fall in line with it because anything else would not only be ineffective but useless.

• You understand that because the evolutionary purpose of the Universe is not only individual but collective, each soul has a destiny and a mission in each physical experience. That destiny is the sum of experiences that a soul has to have in each lifetime for its own learning and evolution. These events are often difficult and trigger resistance and reactivity, yet have evolutionary value. The mission is what you contribute to everyone else's progression and is resolved easily, since it is merely the expression of old learned behaviours.

• You understand that every soul willingly accepts the initial script and set of circumstances that accompany each experience, which are ideal and related mathematically to the specific needs of evolution.

• You understand that, initially, all souls are created innocent and have to move through different hierarchical levels of understanding the truth until they add all the information about the Universe to their consciousness archive so they can finally merge with God, the final source and destination.

• You understand that forgiveness is not only a spiritual mandate, but the only option. You begin to see that there are two levels of forgiveness: one is superficial and another is profound. On the first, you still believe that something or someone "out there" has "done" something to you, but being who you are, you choose to forgive, which really means that you decide not to retaliate or fight back. Profound forgiveness, however, knows that nothing and nobody has really "done" anything to you, but rather that whatever happens to you has been triggered by your own evolutional needs and the external agent involved in manifesting this event is merely a tool of the Cosmos' evolutionary purpose for everyone's growth.

• You start to see that all your difficulties stem from the fact that your ego or lower mind puts up resistance against, or fails to flow with the universal plan for the soul's evolution. Your lower mind sees these events that happen as desirable or undesirable rather than neutral.

• You start shifting from self-identification with the body-mind to self-identification with the soul.

- You start to trust the flow of life. As a result, the ego feels less of a need to control external results, and inner peace increases.

- Since happiness is to be found on the inside, independently from external sources, the ego's need for approval and recognition also begins to fade. You realize that you are where you are on the evolutionary path and nobody else's good or bad opinion will change that fact, so you free yourself from dependence on others' opinions.

- You begin to understand that the Law of Evolution and the Law of Correspondence govern the Universe so actually it does not make much sense to fight to change external circumstances. Instead, you should work on changing yourself, so that, thanks to the Law of Correspondence, external circumstances will change effortlessly.

- You become better at sustaining higher vibrational thoughts in a voluntary and directed manner; these replace negative thoughts, which are physically heavier and one of their byproducts is negative feelings. In a way, one could say that the quality of our life will be the quality of our thoughts. At lower levels of consciousness, a high proportion of our thoughts arise involuntarily, because the mind works like a radio receiver tuned to the corresponding wave pattern.

- You begin to "surrender" your personal will or agenda to the will of the evolutionary purpose of "God". By doing so, your intentions are much more likely to manifest and you begin to verify the fact that synchronicities begin to happen frequently all around you.

- You also begin to spend less energy since all energy expenditure can be traced back to the failure to "surrender" to the Absolute's will. All human difficulties have their roots in the divergence between "my" will –preferences, attachments, aversions and so on– and the Absolute's will for the evolution of the soul (individually and collectively).

• You begin relying on your intuition. Human beings, as already explained, have four bodies –five if one takes into account the mystical states– for processing inputs. You can sense, feel, reason and intuit. We have seen that intuition is associated with the highest body in vibration.

Intuition is experienced as an ability to directly take in information, without going through the linear logical processes in which the rational mind is involved (A→B→C). It is the only tool with which we can experience –not just "know about"– nonlinear realities.

"Left brain" oriented people find it hard to trust intuition: it is not that they can't distinguish it from reason, but they can't distinguish it from instinct without some training.

People know very well when they are reasoning or thinking, if only by the fact that they use energy and get tired, and because it is a sequential process A leads to B, which in turn leads to C. But instincts appear in a much faster and direct way, as intuition does, grasping reality directly without any sequential process.

Mostly everyone understands the evolutionary advantage of reason over instinct, so most educational systems have trained us to "filter" our instincts through our reason, and most of us have learned that to use reason produces better results than not using it. Moreover, all scales of consciousness appear to show that living from reason is a necessary evolutionary step in the progression of consciousness than living from instincts and emotions.

Upon observation you learn that the best way to distinguish intuition (that can be trusted) from instinct (that should be filtered) is by the presence of a feeling of "peace and certainty" when understanding arrives through intuition, because it is manifested from a higher vibrational energy field or "attractor field" than reason.

Broadly speaking, here are some of the things to expect when you are growing in consciousness and begin to enter into these higher levels:

- You want to "serve" more and "get" less.

- You become less fearful, anxious or needy.

- Your mind becomes more "ungripped", and focuses less on materiality.

- You need less time to "let go" of stuff.

- People or things that used to bring conflict no longer do.

- You begin to have more experiences of the miraculous (synchronicities).

- Everything that happens is not seen as a problem, but as a gift, an opportunity to grow.

- You become more discerning but less judgmental –when you discern, you don't attach any emotional baggage as you do when you judge.

- Conflicts begin to resolve themselves.

- Intuition develops further.

- You become calmer and lose interest in activities or entertainment that you enjoyed before.

- You prefer to talk about growth and all other issues become less important.

- You don't get carried away by gossip as before.

- You start to not want to change people or things as much. You develop more acceptance.

- You perceive the world and everything in it as a perfect creation of God.

- Your emotional body begins to calm down.

- You're more interested in context than in content.

- You stop talking rubbish about things and people.

- You begin to need more quiet time by yourself.

- You flow more with the energy of Creation and learn to use it in your progress.

- You become gentler to avoid causing emotional damage to others.

- You learn to respect all living beings as God's creatures.

To end this explanation, there follows a description of how Hawkins analyses what happens at these levels of the scale, starting with his description of the previous level.

Energy level 400: Reason

Intelligence and rationality rise to the forefront when the emotionalism of the lower levels is transcended. Reason is capable of handling large, complex amounts of data and making fast, correct decisions; of understanding the intricacies of relationships, gradations, and subtle differences; and expert handling of symbols as abstract concepts becomes increasingly important.

This is the level of science, medicine, and of generally increased capacity for conceptualization and comprehension. Knowledge and education are here sought as capital. Understanding and information are the main tools of personal accomplishment, which is the hallmark of the 400 level. This is the level of Nobel Prize winners, great statesmen, and Supreme Court Justices. Einstein, Freud, and many of the other great thinkers of history also calibrate at this level.

The shortcomings of this level involve the failure to clearly distinguish the difference between symbols and what they represent, and confusion between the objective and subjective worlds that limits the understanding of causality. At this level, it's easy to lose sight of the forest for the trees, to become infatuated with concepts and theories and end up missing the essential point. Intellectualizing can become an end in itself. Reason is limited insofar as it doesn't afford the capacity for the discernment of essence or of the critical point of a complex issue.

Reason does not of itself provide a guide to truth. It produces massive amounts of information and documentation, but lacks the capability to resolve discrepancies in data and conclusions. All philosophical arguments sound convincing on their own. Although reason is highly effective in a technical world where the methodologies of logic dominate, Reason itself, paradoxically, is the major block to reaching higher levels of consciousness. Transcending this level is relatively uncommon in our society.

Energy level 500: Love

Love as depicted in the mass media is not what this level is about. What the world generally refers to as love is an intense emotional condition, combining physical attraction, possessiveness, control, addiction, eroticism, and novelty. It's usually fragile and fluctuating, waxing and waning with varying conditions. When frustrated, this emotion often reveals an underlying anger and dependency that it had masked. That love can turn to hate is a common perception, but here what was being talked about was addictive sentimentality, rather than Love; there probably never was actual Love in such a relationship, for hate stems from pride, not Love.

The 500 level is characterized by the development of a Love that is unconditional, unchanging, and permanent. It doesn't fluctuate its source isn't dependent on external factors. Loving is a state of being. It's a forgiving, nurturing, and supportive way of relating to the world. Love isn't intellectual and doesn't proceed from the mind; Love emanates from the heart. It has the capacity to lift and encourage others and accomplish great feats because of its purity of motive. Love is understanding and not a feeling, because if it were, it would be variable and fluctuating like all feelings.

As this level of development, the capacity to discern essence becomes predominant; the core of an issue becomes the centre of focus. As reason is bypassed, there arises the capacity for instantaneous recognition of the totality of a problem and a major expansion of context, especially regarding time and process. Reason deals only with particulars, whereas Love deals with entireties. This ability, often ascribed to intuition, is the capacity for instantaneous understanding without resorting to sequential symbol processing. Thus, apparently abstract phenomenon is actually quite concrete and comes hand in hand with a measurable release of endorphins in the brain.

Love does not take sides, and thus is neutral and global, rising above separation. It's then possible to be "one with another", for there are no longer any barriers. Love steadily expands the sense of self. Love focuses on the goodness of life in all its expressions, reinforcing positive ones and dissolving negativity by recontextualizing it, rather than by attacking it. This is the level of true happiness, but although the world is fascinated with the subject of Love, and all viable religions calibrate at 500 or over, it is interesting to note that only 0.4 percent of the world's population ever reaches this level of evolution of consciousness.

Energy level 540: Joy

As Love becomes more and more unconditional, it begins to be experienced as inner Joy. This isn't the sudden joy of a pleasurable turn of events; it's a constant accompaniment to all activities. Joy arises from within each moment of existence, rather than from any other source; 540 is also the level of healing and of spiritually based self-help groups.

From level 540 up is the domain of saints, and advanced spiritual students and healers. A capacity for enormous patience and the persistence of a positive attitude in the face of prolonged adversity is characteristic of this energy field; the hallmark of this state is compassion. People who have attained this level have a notable effect on others. They're capable of a prolonged, open visual gaze, which induces a state of love and peace.

In the high 500s, the world one sees is illuminated by the exquisite beauty and perfection of creation. Everything happens effortlessly, by synchronicity, and the world and everything in it is seen to be an expression of love and divinity. Individual will merges into divine will. A Presence is felt whose power facilitates phenomena outside conven-

tional expectations of reality, termed miraculous by the ordinary observer. These phenomena represent the power of
the energy field, not of the individual.

One's sense of responsibility for others at this level
is of a different quality from that shown at the lower levels: there's a desire to use one's state of consciousness for
the benefit of life itself rather than for particular individuals.
This capacity to love many people at the same time comes
with the discovery that the more one loves, the more one
can love.

Near-death experiences, characteristically transformative in their effects, have often allowed people to experience energy levels between 540 and 600.

As we look at the Map of Consciousness, it becomes clear that the calibrated levels correlate with specific processes of consciousness emotions, perceptions,
or attitudes, worldviews and spiritual beliefs. If there were
enough space, the chart could be extended to include all
areas of human behaviour. Throughout, the research results were mutually corroborating; the more detailed and
extensive the research, the greater their corroboration was.

3.4 Some examples of how human behaviour is manifested through the different levels of consciousness

Following this description of the levels of consciousness, it might help to understand them better if we describe
how the context that prompts human behaviour in different areas of life occurs. For the purpose of this exercise,
we have selected two fields of activity that matter to most
humans: work and sex. Now we will see how both are experienced from the different levels, taking the Schmedling
scale as a point of reference.

Work

• At level 2 of Schmedling's scale, work is always linked to physical violence and the people here are typically human or drug traffickers, terrorists, violent criminals etc.

• At the bottom of level 3, people who work do so for their benefit even if that means others lose and the rule of conduct is to do everything possible to get on without getting caught. They cheat, deceive and manipulate others, but no longer resort to physical violence to settle conflicts. People still lack a personal, internal ethical system to regulate their conduct, but instead think that "anything goes as long as I don't get caught". At this level, they still don't know that even if they are not caught here, the Universe does know how they have behaved and the associated consequences will be inevitable. This is where you find plenty of corrupt politicians and professionals, and people cannot be relied upon yet, striking up relationships out of self-interest.

At this level, bodily violence disappears –for instance, parliamentarians in civilized countries no longer get into fights when they argue–, though there is still some verbal and mental violence, both of which decline towards the top of this level. At the top of level 3, when working for your own benefit, which endures as an intention, you also seek other's benefit (win-win strategy). At this level individuals behave in line with personal ethical criteria. Conduct is not only controlled to avoid being punished, but in terms of what seems right. The intention of getting something blends with the intention of serving, which is the gateway to the next level. That's why it is common to see lots of people who not only work with the main aim of progressing themselves, but also use a relatively small part of their time or resources to help others, giving what they can spare to foundations, charities, etc. The top of level three is the first level where you can find people who are reliable, at least to a certain extent.

• At the bottom of Level 4, you no longer work to "make money" or for personal gain, but to help others, depending on how everyone understands that service. Here is where you find some missionaries, some members of charitable organizations, some priests, some spiritual teachers etc. Resources are used to serve even better and not, for instance, to buy a yacht. The best example is how Teresa of Calcutta used the money when she won the Nobel Prize. These individuals' energy, perseverance and persistence is what people at lower levels admire (they cannot do the same on account of the energy) draining internal and external conflicts in their lives. At this level, conflicts are not resolved through physical or verbal violence, but rather through consensus and flexibility.

This is where you start to let go even of mental violence, which is the last kind to go, through understanding, compassion, and the use of discernment instead of judgment. What's more, the two dominant intentions are personal growth and serving others. Broadly speaking, somebody is at the fourth level when their mind understands, above all other concepts, the lesson that the end does not justify the means and starts giving up violating spiritual principles in exchange for apparent short-term advantages in the form world.

• At the top of level 4, the motivation to grow gives way to the motivation to Be, and serving extends to all Mankind. Mental violence disappears and judging is replaced by discerning. The big difference between the two is that discerning does not involve any of the emotional baggage that arises when we judge so there is no aversion. It is hard to serve something or someone you dislike. Discerning is the right way, instead of judgment or relativism, both of which are not helpful for spiritual evolution. When you discern, you see and you assess, but there is no emotional or mental energy movement. The top of level 4 is where we enter Cosmic consciousness, which is examined in more depth in the chapter 5 of this book.

Sex

• At level 2, sex is always tied to physical violence. It is the world of rape, pedophilia etc. and if there is no violence in sex *per se*, there is around it, in other words, domestic violence in all its manifestations.

• At the bottom of level 3, sex is experienced genitally. It is the world of prostitution –without physical violence–, of "quickie sex", one-night stands, strings of short-term sexual partners, etc. It is no-strings-attached sex that mostly seeks genital pleasure.

• At the top of level 3, sex is still needed to maintain an energy balance, because one of its functions is energy recovery, and if it is missing, it shows. This sex is no longer so genital and people look for other things when they practice it like mutual growth, spiritual union, commitment, family, etc. It is usually a sex "with" strings attached and within a steady monogamous relationship.

• At this level, sex resembles nutrition to a certain extent because it does not lead to spiritual growth itself, but helps the body to be healthier and that helps growth processes. Everyone knows that "a healthy mind in a healthy body". It is in that sense that sexuality facilitates spiritual development at this level.

• At the bottom of level 4, sex can be practiced or not, as it is no longer deemed necessary and there is no need to recover energy as it is not lost in the first place. Internal or external conflict is what spends most energy and, at this level, there is hardly any conflict. If sex is practiced, it is by free choice and always within an even steadier relationship, as part of a strong spiritual bond. Purely sexual desire drops significantly in these individuals and great internal importance is attached to the freedom that this affords.

- At the top of level 4, sex no longer appears as an option to consider because nobody in their right mind would swap a mystical experience for sex.

3.5 Development lines and streams

This subject has already been covered by Ken Wilber in his book *"Integral Psychology"*, upon which much of this section is based. Wilber explains this idea as follows:

> *"Through the basic levels or waves in the Great Nest*[(*)] *flow some two dozen relatively independent development lines or streams. These different developmental lines include morals, affects, self-identity, psychosexuality, cognition, ideas of the good, role taking, socio-emotional capacity, creativity, altruism, several lines that can be called "spiritual" [care, openness, concern, religious faith, meditative stages], joy, communicative competence, modes of space and time, death-seizure, needs, worldviews, logico-mathematical competence, kinesthetic skills, gender identity, and empathy to name a few of the more prominent developmental lines for which we have some empirical evidence.*

(*)   More commonly known, and referred to further on, as the Great Chain of Being.

These lines are "relatively independent", so, for the most part, they can develop independently of each other, at different rates, with a different dynamic, and on a different time schedule. A person can be very advanced in some lines, medium in others, low in still others all at the same time. Thus, overall development –the sum total of all these different lines– shows no linear or sequential development whatsoever.

However, the bulk of research has continued to find that each development line itself tends to unfold in a sequential, holarchical fashion: higher stages in each line tend to build upon or incorporate the earlier stages, no stages can be skipped, and the stages emerge in an order that cannot be altered by environmental conditioning or social reinforcement.

If we allow for the fact that there are higher or transpersonal stages of development, and we call all of their parts post-conventional, then that would give us far broader stages or levels (sensorimotor, conventional, post-conventional and post post-conventional), through which their developmental lines proceed."

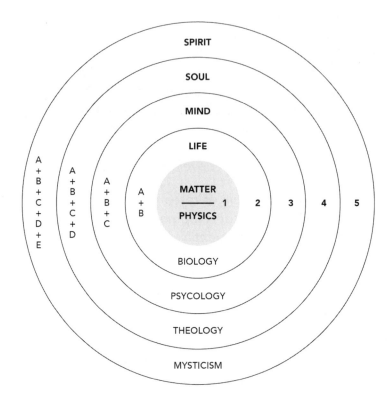

Figure 10. Taken from "Integral Psychology" by Ken Wilber.

These four broad levels are not more than a simplified version of the Great Nest of Being, of Perennial Wisdom, moving from body (sensorimotor) to mind (conventional and post-conventional) to spirit (post post-conventional).

In other words, the reason that most of the developmental lines proceed through a largely universal, invariant, holarchical sequence is that they are following the largely universal, invariant, Great Holarchy of Being they are following the general morphogenetic field so clearly suggested in the charts. The Great Nest is most basically the general morphogenetic field or development space. It simply represents some of the basic waves of reality that are available to individuals; and as different talents, capacities, and skills emerge in individuals, they tend to follow, in a general way, the contours of the Great Nest, they migrate through that development space. Again, it is not that these levels are etched in concrete or set in stone; they are simply some of the stronger currents in the great River of life... The individual potentials that emerge in human development tend to follow the currents in the great River of Life, they follow the waves in the Great Holarchy. This, at any rate, is what the preponderance of empirical evidence has consistently suggested.

INTEGRAL PSYCHOGRAPH

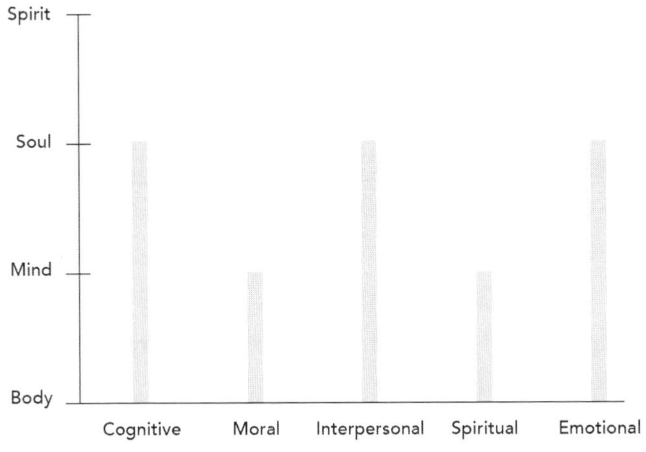

Figure 11. Integral Psychograph. Taken from Integral Psychology, Ken Wilber.

According to Wilber, all of this can be represented as in figure 2, which is called an "integral psychograph". The levels in the Great Nest are shown on the vertical axis, and through those levels run the various lines. (Of the two dozen or so lines, we give five as examples: cognitive, moral, interpersonal, spiritual, and affective. We have listed "spirit" both as the highest level and as a separate developmental line, reflecting the two most common definitions of "spirituality").

This does not mean that all, or even most, of the important aspects of development are hierarchical. In this system, each basic structure or wave actually consists of both hierarchy (or increasing holistic capacity) and heterarchy or nonhierarchical interaction among mutually equivalent elements. The relation between levels is hierarchical, with each senior level transcending and including its juniors, but not vice versa (molecules contain atoms, but not vice versa; cells contain molecules, but not vice versa; sentences contain words, but not vice versa), and that "not vice versa" establishes an asymmetrical hierarchy of increasing holistic capacity (which simply means that the senior dimension embraces the junior, but not vice versa, so that the senior is more holistic and encompassing). But *within* each level, most elements exist as mutually equivalent and mutually interacting patterns. Much of development —at least half of it— involves various types of nonhierarchical, heterarchical processes of competence articulation and application.

Thus, **holarchy** includes a balance of both **hierarchy** (qualitatively ranked levels) and **heterarchy** (mutually linked dimensions).

These levels and lines are navigated by the self. These three items —the levels, the different lines or streams and the self as the navigator of both— appear to be central to any model of integral philosophy and integral psychology.

It is important to point out that when you think about the self, you'll see there are two parts to this self that navigates the levels and streams. There's a sort of observing self (inner subject or watcher) and there's also an observed self (objective things that you can see or know about yourself, i.e. have blonde hair, weigh X number of pounds). The first is experienced as an "I", the second as a "me" (or "mine"). The first is called the "proximate self" and the second the "distant self". This distinction is important because during psychological development the "I" of one stage becomes a "me" at the next. In other words, the subject of one stage becomes the object of the next. The levels with which you identify with at one stage of development, tend to become transcended, or dis-identified with at the next, so you can see it more objectively, with some distance and detachment. As the locus of integration, the self is responsible for balancing and integrating all of the levels, lines and states in the individual. "

What happens in meditative and contemplative development is that the ego becomes the object of the soul, which is now the subject, and not its unrealized background.

As for attachment in the ordinary realm, it might not be the ego, but exclusive identifying with the ego, that is the problem. The ego is now my ego; it has changed from being "I" to "mine".

For anyone who is centered in the soul, the ego and the body and the world arise in the consciousness as objects in a healthy sense, and that person might say "I identify with none of them but they arise in my consciousness".

Finally, as the consciousness pushes on towards higher mystical levels, from the subtle onward (into the causal), the soul becomes object of the Self.

Chapter 4. Cognitive line development[*]

We first need to remember that the cognitive line is one of many developmental lines, not to be confused with the levels of consciousness, which include all developmental lines.

A single book cannot cover each and every one in enough depth, which is why only one of the lines is looked at in more detail: the cognitive line, which has such a bearing on the understanding of human beings.

On describing each stage of this line, parallelisms will be seen between how this line develops in the individual and in collective culture.

As will be seen, not only is each stage less self-centered than the previous one, but it also represents a steady liberation from the limitations of materiality. Materiality is densified energy, and is not negative *per se*, but is the least conscious of all the human body's parts.

Any advance in the cognitive line is a process of internal realization which, in turn, is the result of some kind of internalized personal experience. A process in which the previous view "dies" and a new way of understanding is "born".

The different stages of the cognitive development line are described below following the argumentation of Ken Wilber ("*Integral Psychology*", "Sex, Ecology and Spirituality") and Jim Marion ("*Putting on the mind of Christ*").

(*)   We will follow in this chapter the argumentation of Ken Wilber and Jim Marion in their books listed in the bibliography section.

4.1 Archaic stage

Individual

In newborns, this stage involves the child learning to distinguish its own body and emotions from its mother's. This stage usually continues until the child is 2 or 3 years old, is dominated by sensations and impulses, and is a very narcissistic stage.

Collective

Stone Age human beings were at this stage of archaic consciousness. They still had not developed the capacity to "understand" and their relationship with the environment was determined by their sensory/emotional experience.

4.2 Magic stage

Individual

Takes place between the ages of 3 and 7, and at this stage, children begin to believe in gods, fairies, elves, monsters, etc.

Children at the *magic* stage are still incapable of differentiating between what is in their mind and the reality of the outside world. For example, at this age children might believe that the sun follows them as they walk.

Collective

This stage of *archaic* consciousness was what tribal cultures of the past had. Religion was animistic, so for example they believed that the sky, thunder and other natural phenomena were "alive" and could be controlled through magic words and ceremonies.

4.3 Mythic stage

Individual

This runs from approximately 7 years of age up to adolescence, and is the first truly mental stage. At this stage, young children believe that the God in the sky can perform any miracle to meet their needs, just as their own parents could. A stage characterized by conformism, during it children see their culture as true and undeniably the best, and their country as the best in the world. There is no point talking to children at this age about ideas such as diversity and tolerance.

Instead, their minds are filled with ideas such as Santa Claus (or the Three Kings or Wise Men in Spanish culture), etc. who will look after their needs if they are "good". In this case, being good means joining one's peer group and sticking to its conventional rules. If they come across others who follow different rules, they feel a need to reject them and defend their own principles, because such rules threaten their own sense of "self", which is anchored in a certain set of beliefs. Individuals believe that happiness and salvation are only to be found within their group, and that all is lost outside that group. Members of many sects, in which the individual consciousness (one's own freedom) is replaced with a collective consciousness (what the group says), which is considered to be the "will of God" that is to be obeyed without question, are most likely to be at this stage.

For example, adults who haven't moved past this mythic stage find it important to impose their own religion on everyone and ensure that governments enact laws in accordance with their beliefs. This implies eliminating all "dissidents," whether by conversion or other methods, for their own good. They regard anyone who adheres to other beliefs as being intrinsically "evil" and try to save them from "hell". Anybody who dies trying to do so will be rewarded by their God with a direct ascent to "Heaven".

In the Middle Ages, the power wielded by certain individuals at this stage triggered events such as the Spanish Inquisition and the "Holy" wars, and today, nearly 600 years later, this could be the stream of thought responsible for Islamic Terrorism.

Individuals who have not got past the mythic stage cannot think globally, and instead tend to focus solely on their own family and religious or ethnic group, and on their nationalistic concerns. This is a rigid and separatist stage.

Collective

Many believers of the "major" religions were historically at this stage.

Such religions were universal, but only in the sense that anyone could belong to them without having to have blood ties, as was required at the (magic) tribal stage, through their acceptance of its doctrines, rules, beliefs, etc.

The mythic culture gave rise to the great empires, all of which would have liked to "conquer" the whole world. However, although the mythic stage represented a step up from the previous (magic) stage, it also has its limitations. In christianity, for instance, many people were only capable of understanding the message of Christ at a mythic stage and that problem has continued within Western society until today. This was also the case with the message of Eastern Spiritual Leaders.

4.4 Rational Stage

Individual

This is the prevalent stage in the current "civilized" world. It is the next stage of the human being who continues to evolve, in other words, who is not stuck at the mythic stage. As a general rule, anyone who manages to reach this stage only does so in adulthood. That is why the teenager must learn to reason above the rules, norms and roles accepted at the mythic stage.

Reaching this stage lets the individual think abstractly and contains many sub-stages. For example, thinking in "clichés" is common at the lowest sub-stages, and you can still fall into "isms" when a pattern of thinking captures your attention to the total exclusion of others.

For example, an individual at the mythic stage would think that a person who opens up to rationality is "losing faith".

At this stage, for the first time one understands that the rational rules of science are not limited to any one religion or belief system, but rather are universally applicable. Rules and conventions of the cultural environment can be analyzed and assessed, other potential worlds can be imagined, etc. People at this stage become more tolerant, compassionate and inclusive, and less judgmental, fearful and aggressive.

Collective

The rational stage is currently predominant in our world (Universities, Governments, Science, Technology, Philosophy, Medicine, etc.). Yet not all political or religious leaders have reached it; some remain at the mythic stage, albeit less and less thanks to educational advancements.

Remaining at the mythic stage leads to fundamentalism, whereas the major spiritual achievement during the two thousand years following the birth of Christ has been Mankind's move to the rational stage.

4.5 Vision-Logic

Individual

This is the highest of the three mental stages (mythic, rational and vision-logic), and is typical of the thought of many of today's artists, professionals, scientists and philosophers. Characteristic traits include personal identification with the abstract mind and the capacity to "see" something from many points of view or different perspectives.

The concern of anyone at this stage is global, because they can analyze problems holistically, beyond what is possible at the national or societal stage as a whole.

This stage is seen as a threat by people who are still at the mythic stage.

Upon reaching the vision-logic stage, the mind frees itself of "isms" as it is able to understand many different perspectives, which is why it can produce ideas, works of art, philosophy and literature with a global reach. Individuals at this stage have the skills required to negotiate treaties between countries and create global systems through international law, communications, markets, etc.

At the rational stage, you can fall so in love with an idea that you can live the rest of your life in your head. This does not happen at the vision-logic stage, which is the stage of the integrated personality, and the first where the body, emotions and mind can come together. People can access a global view, and seek the good of all Mankind rather than of just their religious or political group.

At this stage, there is a quest for tolerance, and one can appreciate different philosophies and perspectives, which are regarded as being more complementary than antagonistic; and people defend each individual's inalienable freedom to make moral choices. People at this stage do not usually have problems finding creative work to do.

When an individual approaches the end of this stage, they begin to transcend the mind itself and to see the mind as an object. Right then, they start being able to see themselves as "witnesses" of the body, emotions and mind. That "witness" is another part of us that can observe the three inferior bodies and which starts "breaking away" from our personality in space-time. That is how one enters the first stage of Cosmic/Mystic/Unitive Consciousness: the psychic stage.

Collective

In terms of cultural evolution, our immediate future as Mankind is going to be the vision-logic stage, even though most people on our planet are now trying to settle into the rational stage.

Currently, human beings with vision-logic are reaching Government positions in many fields that no longer solely require intellectual creativity but also common sense and practical wisdom.

The vision-logic stage is inclusive and focuses on the whole; it does not worry the rational stage, but is terrifying for the mythic stage. Yet in the end, vision-logic will prevail, because the creative growth of the Universe cannot be stopped.

4.6 Psychic stage

At this stage, the individual no longer identifies with the rational mind, but instead with the internal witness that is capable of observing the mind. This witness is the part of the person that is beyond space/time.

Individual

When somebody reaches this stage, they become aware of the "information" that they receive, above and beyond what they get from their five senses. They have "awakened" that part of their consciousness that is eternal and is subject to neither space-time nor materiality.

A deeper world, expanding into infinity, opens up before them. Other authors, such as Ralph Waldo Emerson, have called this stage "nature mysticism". In it, the individual begins to open up to the "Cosmic consciousness"; concerns are no longer focused on the world, but rather the Universe. Individuals begin to glimpse their oneness with everything; they connect, or resonate, with their interior "self" and their intuitive capacity speeds up.

Unlike the world of the body and personality, this psychic world exists in another dimension of higher frequency vibrations which our senses cannot capture.

Certain telepathic and other abilities, such as the capacity to know what is on a person's mind, begin to appear at this stage. People who have reached this stage can go into any meeting and immediately "know" what is happening and each person's stance. They can easily capture the "energy" of anywhere they go and can clearly "see" what others feel.

At this stage, individuals no longer think that "they have a soul" but rather that the soul has become their "self". It is the soul that has the person; and it is seen as the very part that gives life to all other bodies. "My soul is what I am".

For the first time ever, individuals starts to be more interested in what is going on inside themselves than in the world outside, and become more skilled at understanding what is happening inside themselves. People at this stage become more contemplative, hardly ever depend on others' opinions, teachings and values, and become more sensitive to the messages of the soul.

This does not mean that people who reach the psychic stage shrug off the material world, as each stage is necessarily built upon the preceding stages. On the contrary, people usually become more creative and efficient in the world of form, though sometimes, at the beginning, they can get a feeling of "allergy" when they descend into it, which then slowly disappears.

Collective

This was the highest stage reached in the ancient world (Greece, Rome, etc.), and was the stage of the first christians up until degeneration imposed the mythic vision in this religion.

Lower-level disciples cannot understand spirituality and focus more on religious forms, until long after they have stopped being useful.

The physic stage can be prostituted, one example being the New Age current that sometimes returns to magical states or idealizations of primitive societies, or low-level "channeling" (of energy), etc.

From the psychic stage, nothing is said which is truly incompatible with the basic teachings of the major religions, even if it is expressed from a different angle.

One important question about this stage is: Where do people who open up to this stage go to receive guidance and support? Contemporary religions can only provide the resources necessary to provide this service if their own spiritual leaders have reached these levels of consciousness.

4.7 Subtle stage

Individual and collective issues will be addressed together in this and all following stages.

Saint John of the Cross was perhaps one of the thinkers to best explain the move from the psychic stage to the subtle stage, within the group of Western mystics. Nagarjuna also did this in the East. Their accounts are very similar. Saint John said:

> *"God feeds and nourishes the soul when it has already fervently decided to be at His service."*

At this stage the human being completely "detaches" from bodily needs (survival, sex, etc.), and spends a lot of time in prayer or meditation. Internal joy develops very intensely. At this stage, people stop fighting or acting to develop themselves, leaving such development in the hands of God. The mind is no longer as active and "goals", even spiritual ones, disappear as such. In the East, this energy is called *Kundalini* and when awoken, whether naturally or by a Spiritual Master, the cosmic/mystic experience appears.

People who experience this stage say that anything else pales in comparison to the exquisite sensation of internal joy. Reaching it involves letting go of all negative emotions and mythical or rational beliefs. Otherwise you might have isolated experiences, but will not manage to stay at this stage. Literally, those emotions or beliefs act as a counterweight that holds you back from the ascent.

The vibrational power of this stage lets you get rid of all the "garbage", without engaging in the introspection required at previous stages to let go of negativities one by one. This vibration is much more powerful than psychotherapy because it has the power to "clean" even anything in the subconscious that the individual did not even realize that was dirty. Furthermore, it is a much deeper clean.

People's capacity at this stage to influence the outside world through thought and prayer is huge. Thanks to God, psychic power is given to us in proportion to each of our levels of consciousness, love and responsibility, and is not available to individuals who are not as spiritually developed.

This is the last stage where there is still a certain degree of identification with the personality and Saint John of the Cross saw this stage as the second of the 3 mystic stages (psychic, subtle and causal).

People who reach it feel a strong impulse to write or explain to others how they too can reach this stage. One has to be careful not to forget about one's own personal growth and devote too much time to serving others. A balance has to be maintained to reach the next stage: causal.

At the subtle stage, one starts to receive "information" from the non-physical beings that exist at the highest vibrations. Profound realizations appear and there are non-predictable moments of ecstasy during which someone could become "dysfunctional" from operating normally in the world of form.

At this stage, individuals are aware of the synchronicities that appear in the world, settle into a routine of the miraculous and count on it in their daily life, and it is useful to have the help of a "Teacher" because if not, it might seem like you are losing your "sanity".

The phenomenon known as the "dark night of the soul" may also show up in this stage in preparation for the final ascent to the causal stage. That is how Saint John of the

Cross referred to it in the West, while Trungpa Rinpoche, in the East, called it *"the night of hell"*.

4.8 Causal stage

At this stage, life as a personality disappears. The world is observed with a different and astonishing tint, and it is clearly seen that the origin of "sin" is ignorance:

"Whoever is born of God doesn't commit sin, because his seed remains in him" (John 3, 9).

The Bible says:

"God is the light and object of the soul. When it is wrong and is focusing the energy on other things, it is blind. Although the Light of God is shining it is not seen because of ignorance" (Ecclesiastes 51, 26).

This stage also includes the idea that no soul shall be lost; that all questions can be answered by looking deep inside oneself; and it also includes the Law of Sacred Times: that is, that God does not reveal his mystery until we become correspondent with it. "Becoming correspondent with" means having completed an internal task, as a result of which you might, or might not, need to experience certain situations that foster your soul's growth

This is the stage from which Saint Paul spoke when he said that he was no longer him, but rather that Christ (the "Christ" Consciousness) was living in him.

People at this stage are already free of physical, emotional and mental addictions and live at all times in the present, detached from the battles and anxieties of daily life.

So the causal stage is characterized by an enormous internal peace. People have to re-learn how to translate pure intuition into ideas, words or images that can be understood by others. They frequently seek solitude and meditation and the only option which seems to be viable is working for the benefit of other souls.

It is not that they feel indifference or negligence in their actions but rather a great capacity to "be" in the moment and for emotional detachment when carrying out activities that were previously emotionally "addictive". Expectations are lost and external actions do not provoke any kind of reaction or resistance.

The Hindu spiritual leader Paramahansa Yogananda explained it like this:

> "The Universe is a materialization of the thoughts of God, and the verisimilitude of life in our ordinary experience prevents us from believing or seeing that life is no more than a Cosmic dream. We need to develop our mental capacity to understand that the Universe is nothing more than the thought of God and that, like any dream, it is structurally evanescent."

And he goes on to say:

> "Suffering is no more than observing a "movie" with emotional involvement."

Another feature of this stage is that there is no longer any interaction with others egos. There is no interior polarization, and so no discussion or attempt to win arguments.

Furthermore, as there are no longer any neurotic projections, people can be seen as they truly are and can act properly as a result. There is a "space" here between what happens and an individual's reaction to it. Silence is regarded in a special way, because it is seen to be deeper than verbal communication. One acquires a "contemplative" look. The presence of God is creative and people who have reached this stage see themselves as co-creators with God.

Yet dangers also lurk at this stage. Remaining detached from worldly matters can get out of hand and make one unbalanced. As everything is seen as divine, knowing that God manifests everything in the Creation can trigger a certain degree of "disinterest" in the world. One cannot forget that formal manifestation also matters, otherwise it would not happen: God is efficient and does not waste energy. So whatever happens does so because it has to happen (if not, it wouldn't happen) and it matters. Not understanding this can hinder one from moving to the final stage: the non-dual stage.

4.9 Non-dual stage

This represents the end of division between Creator and creature. It is the stage from which Jesus was speaking when he said:

"The Father and I are one."

Meister Ekhart in the West, and Chogyan Trungpa and Yogananda in the East are some examples of people who have reached this "beatific vision" stage, as it is described by some christian mystics.

This is the end of the cognitive evolution of the human conscience, and from here the soul continues evolving but with experiences associated with non-physical beings.

If the previous causal stage is characterized by a deep inner peace, this non-dual stage is characterized by an intense joy or "ecstasy". This stage cannot be reached without first renouncing all polarity.

One might say that this is not only the last stage, but also the framework in which all stages develop until one reaches this one. This is the final "surrender".

Ramana Maharshi, the great Hindu mystic wrote about this stage:

"The world is illusory.
God ("Brahman") alone is real.
God ("Brahman") is the world."

The first two lines can represent the causal stage while the third is non-dual (the combination of non-form with the world of form). God transcends all worlds, and includes all worlds.

At the non–dual stage, the world is no longer seen as taking one form or another and, in any case, in no way can it be described using linear concepts or language. The world is seen "directly" with no "filter" or "glasses" of any color which have inevitably existed up until this stage.

If you want to reach this stage, you have to empty yourself altogether to be filled with God. Even the positive-negative, good-bad polarity has to be overcome to reach this stage. The elements are seen as complementary in Unity, the All.

All material creation has one sole purpose: that souls evolve to reach this stage.

The legitimacy of Law, ethic or logic of the physical plan is not denied at this stage, provided that we remember that these rational disciplines are dualist (and therefore inherently imperfect) and we acknowledge the supremacy of consciousness and internal wisdom above anything else.

Chapter 5. Consciousness and its manifestation: three possibilities

To understand this whole question of levels of consciousness once and for all, it might be useful to look at it from a different viewpoint. This chapter describes three broad levels of the manifestation of consciousness in the animal and human world.

Consciousness manifests itself at three levels or stages:

- Simple consciousness

- Self consciousness

- Cosmic/uniting/mystic consciousness

Simple consciousness is possessed by animals. It is only inmanent and has no access to transcendence. In this consciousness one cannot get outside oneself and look at oneself as a witness.

Self consciousness is the predominant level in humans today. With it, you start accessing transcendence because this consciousness is inmanent and transcendent at the same time.

At this level, not only are you aware of your body or the trees "out there", but can also recognize you are a separate entity from the rest of the Universe and begin to observe your own mental states and processes as objects in consciousness, just as anything else is observed.

Somehow humans can get outside themselves and say "I think that what I thought is "true", I know it is "true" and I know that what I know is "true"".

Complex language is closely linked to the consciousness of self. It is the objective system built upon the subjectivity of this consciousness. They are like two sides of the same coin.

Cosmic/uniting/mystic consciousness is a development beyond that of self consciousness, just the way the latter is a development beyond simple awareness. The previous two remain but Cosmic consciousness includes and transcends (see the explanation about the holonic nature of reality and the properties of holons in chapter 6 of this book).

The Cosmic consciousness is a uniting, non-fragmenting (as is the consciousness of self) and comprises life and the order of the Universe.

Explaining this consciousness through language is no easy task. Language, as already seen, is more prepared for dealing with the consciousness of self because it uses concepts. Cosmic consciousness is beyond mental concepts.

Apart from this intuition of unity, consciousness provides intellectual enlightenment which, of its own accord, places the individual on a new level, or rather, in a new dimension of existence. It could be argued that it makes human beings who possess it into a new species.

Indeed, the traditional classification into three levels —plant world, animal world and human world— may already be insufficient and we could say that a classification with five levels might be more instructive:

• Plant world

- Animal world without the second layer of the brain, i.e. without emotional capacity: insects, some birds, amphibians, reptiles, etc.

- Animal world with emotional capacity: dogs, horses, dolphins, etc.

- Human world with simple consciousness and consciousness of self: centaurs, the centaur is half man, half animal and is used to describe less evolved humans who still use much of their animal part, instinct and emotions, in addition to rationality.

- Human world with Cosmic consciousness.

Other signs of Cosmic consciousness are moral elevation, internal pleasure, almost physically "tangible" peace, the sense of immortality, understanding of the perfection of divine Creation in its entirety and of the purpose of the Universe, the loss of mental dualism and also of fear, which is the opposite of Love.

Only a personal experience of living with this consciousness can explain effectively what this is. Failing that, we can study the writings and testimonies of those who have attained it to approach an understanding.

Today the expansion of this consciousness in human beings is accelerating in line with the purpose of the Universe (creative evolution), and more and more people are expected to become part of it. Here it is worth recalling the idea of morphogenetic fields and the critical mass to be reached in order for the change to occur at a wider level in the mass of Mankind. Pope Benedict XVI expounded upon this idea in *"The Salt of the Earth"*, explaining how a small number of advanced people could act like "yeast in the dough".

This is the consciousness of supra-rational intellect; i.e., intuition and not concept.

To see this in more detail, remember that there are four stages in the intellect:

- Perceptive mind;

- Receptive mind

Both perceptive and receptive minds are are part of the simple consciousness.

- Conceptual mind, which includes the two previous ones and adds something new: the "Consciousness of self" concept.

- Intuitive mind, i.e. Cosmic consciousness.

This is the mind that enables unrestricted perfect expression of the soul in the material world. It has a higher vibrational level than the previous three.

Thus, instinct and emotion are pre-rational; concept is rational and intuition is post-rational.

Cosmic consciousness does not see the Cosmos as a dead matter governed by rigid laws without any definite purpose, but rather as something spiritual, immaterial and deeply alive; it understands that no evil can exist in Creation because God does not let it get out of hand. It also comprises the learning processes of the Universe, which are not the same as "evil".

Many things that anyone who has a Cosmic consciousness understands may seem absurd and incomprehensible to the consciousness of self, more rooted in the material reality perceived through the senses and rational mind.

The birth of Cosmic consciousness is very similar to that of self consciousness over and above simple consciousness. In the highest manifestations of self consciousness, the mind gradually takes on increasingly complex and numerous concepts, and suddenly –when conditions are favorable to manifest this potential–, the fusion of some of these and their moral elements takes place. The result is a special intuition, and people settle into the intuitive mind or, in other words, Cosmic consciousness.

The mind develops uniformly. The receptive mind is composed of many perceptions. A concept arises from many receptions and intuition is constructed from a large number of concepts.

Someone with Cosmic consciousness will use consciousness of self –still available to them, as is simple consciousness– to function at a practical level in life, and to communicate through language but always illuminated by this new light.

Access to this consciousness is not arbitrary; it is a "gift" available to all that is accessed when one becomes correspondent on receiving it. It does require a developed and perfected personality in the consciousness of self, which involves a degree of peace acquired as a precondition for its emergence as a general rule.

This does not mean that there can be no exceptions in the Universe because in it anything is possible, as seen in Saint Paul. If the historical account is true, Paul was in the consciousness of self with a lot still to perfect, and was thrown off his horse by a flash of light that apparently left him blind for a few days. On getting up again he had already entered the high levels of Cosmic consciousness.

With the knowledge we have today about the workings of the Universe, we could speculate that this ray of light was an illumination that had the effect of artificially and suddenly increasing the vibrational frequency and the corresponding manifestation appeared (the Cosmic consciousness) without going through the usual process of evolution.

Also, what might seem unfair with previous knowledge, can now be understood, because we now know that there is neither luck nor arbitrariness in the Cosmos, but rather exact mathematical correspondence. Like everything else, this was also "perfect and necessary", or it would not have happened. We also know that the future has as much causative power over the present as does the past, so we can assume that the future dedication of St. Paul, which God knew but not us, may have made him somehow correspondent with the "jump". Furthermore, this is not the only similar case known in history.

People with Cosmic consciousness have a special, remarkable magnetism, perceivable by others. Their presence changes the energy field for everyone and their high vibrational energy is very contagious, more so than the flu.

With the emergence of this consciousness, some lower mental faculties, such as the sense of sin, fear of death, desire for wealth, power, etc., are eradicated.

Cosmic consciousness is the first opening of the internal Kingdom of God which the Gospel talks about. Those who access it experience a series of physical transformations: others often tell them that they are "radiant". A large decrease in physical diseases occurs, and the aging process slows down.

It should not be assumed that having entered Cosmic consciousness one is already infallible. Somehow, the people who are open to it for the first time, go back to being a little "child-like" in the sense that they leave the "known" world of before, and open themselves up to a new stage where a great deal has to be learned again. This is the meaning of the evangelical mandate about becoming like children to enter the Kingdom of Heaven.

Humans have not yet developed the mastery of this new consciousness, except for a small number of isolated individuals throughout history.

Even at this level we must distinguish wisdom from ignorance, as we have had to do at previous levels. What happens is that in Cosmic consciousness everything goes much faster, in the same way that when we launch a rocket into space, the largest amount of energy is needed at first but when the rocket picks up speed and leaves the atmosphere, the engines can be shut down because there is less resistance.

This level, like everything in the Universe, is a process, and moves along roads of very fast successive purifications. Once it is attained, there will still be room for improvement, as there is in a dysfunctional personality in the consciousness of self. Although in Cosmic consciousness there is a total or almost total disappearance of the "ego", the absence of ego must also be integrated.

The power of Cosmic consciousness can only be used when aligned with the purpose of the Universe, and disappears if the intention is contaminated. The moral elevation typical of this level does not allow any other option to appear as possible or attractive This, the mystic, St. Augustine was well aware of when he uttered his famous phrase: "Love and do what you want". That is, position yourself in Cosmic consciousness and thence nothing "bad" can be done.

Another important point is to know that nobody accesses this level of consciousness through orthodoxy alone.

The way in is not by obeying rules of behaviour, no matter how strict they are. On the contrary, until man rises above orthodoxy and conventions, he cannot enter this level.

The entry requirements are inner peace, the intention to serve, the courage to open oneself up to a different internal psychic experience –opening oneself up to Grace, to the attraction exercised by high vibrational energies over the thickest–, opening up the heart, and humility to become like children and relearn.

Those who study this subject claim that no case has ever been found of people accessing this level when the main purpose in their lives was only material gain. It appears that the key does not lie in great faculties in the previous consciousness, of self, but in the use we want to make of these powers. The intention is the engine that propels entry into this consciousness.

Nobody in the consciousness of self can understand what happens at this level, just as nobody still at the simple consciousness can understand someone who has reached the consciousness of self. Yet someone at the Cosmic consciousness level can understand the previous two, and therefore this is the only one which can adapt to them.

The wisdom of consciousness of self does not serve much purpose for the person who has entered into Cosmic consciousness. In turn, what seems obvious to Cosmic consciousness can sometimes be disconcerting, confrontational and absurd to those who continue to be in the consciousness of self.

From Cosmic consciousness the experience of human beings on Earth is seen as necessary for the development of their spiritual being.

Another feature of this level is the search for periods of silence and recollection. It is as if things of the previous world no longer held any interest or not as much as before. One focuses more on what led to the way in: "purity of intention, peace and desire to serve".

God always provides the (internal and external) tools to anyone who is willing to be of service with the right intention: the Universe shows us the Law. This trust has been observed throughout history in great spiritual leaders, who used to embark upon their exploits with hardly any resources whatsoever, knowing that these would "appear" at the appropriate time.

Another feature of this level is that marriage or a love relationship, as conceived from the consciousness of self, becomes meaningless. People at this level usually do not have a partner and, if they do, only focus on the growth and freedom of their partner; it is impossible at this level to feel possessiveness, jealousy or dependence. Sex is no longer necessary, though it is possible as a free choice, in which case it is committed, exclusive, stable and always within a strong spiritual connection.

It seems, therefore, that we can think of the existence of three different worlds:

• **World of natural action:** it is not permanent, either in its essence or its properties.

• **World of spiritual understanding:** it is permanent in its essence but variable in its properties.

• **Divine world or world of Love:** it is permanent, both in its essence and in its properties.

For the first time in the history of Mankind, Western science has begun to study the features of the Cosmic consciousness with a scientific method, the knowledge of which has, up to now, been reserved for Mystics.

It should also be noted that between the borders of consciousness of self and the beginning of Cosmic consciousness there may be a kind of "nebulous" area where Cosmic consciousness can shed more or less light until one is in it completely. Personal experience in this "nebulous" phase is like having one foot in the consciousness of self and the other in Cosmic consciousness, and leaning on one foot or the other, depending on the particular time and what we are fixing our attention on. In these incipient stages of new consciousness, given the appearance of any minimal stress, one goes back to the foot of self-consciousness.

We must understand that the mind in the consciousness of self can believe in God but cannot know Him; that knowledge is reserved for the minds established in Cosmic consciousness. A step is taken from a God based on faith or beliefs, to a God verified in Creation and experienced through His presence in everyday life. A good way to facilitate the appearance of this conscience is to invert the flow of energy of mind by turning it inwards rather than focusing one's attention on the external world. This exercise will enable the mind to become a centre of perception capable of grasping the truth by direct perception, without relying on fallible senses. The truths about the Kingdom of God lie beyond our senses and beyond the reflections of the rational mind. They can only be grasped by intuition, in other words, by awakening intuitive knowledge or pure understanding of the soul.

The miracles of wisdom that illuminate the mind are even higher than the miracles through which nature is affected.

If everyone had Cosmic consciousness, everyone would agree on the fundamental philosophical and religious issues being discussed today. However, other questions would arise at another level and there, there *would be* debate.

From Cosmic consciousness it is understood that God is both the substrate where everything happens and the goal of evolution. God is both transcendent (goes beyond the limits of Creation) and inmanent (present in all Creation). If not seen that way, one can fall into a reductionist pantheism or unreal transcendentalism. Pantheism is the result of reducing or collapsing the spirit into what has been created. Using the example of Plato's cave and the shadows, it is like confusing the shadows in the cave with the light that projects them from outside. Moreover, radical absentee transcendentalism does not adequately understand the presence of God in Creation.

From the Cosmic consciousness, God is seen as one who has no second. Nothing exists outside God. Isaiah said:

"I am God and there is nothing else."

If there was something outside God, that would limit him, as then it would be "One outside a second and not One without a second".

In Cosmic consciousness there is no condemnation, sin, evil, or death. This can be confrontational for the consciousness of self but it is clear to Cosmic consciousness.

St. Paul summed this up very appropriately:

"The law of the spirit of life, which is in Christ Jesus, has set me free from the law of sin and death" (Romans 8, 2).

Another important issue to mention when describing Cosmic consciousness is the fact that when it appears, it always brings certain physical changes in the body and brain. Some or all of the following symptoms always come together with this change in consciousness:

• A sensation of brightness both on the outside and inside. People perceive their surroundings and even their own interior bathed in a more intense brightness.

• An overwhelming sensation of awe and wonder.

• An unshakable conviction about the reality of the experience.

• A sensation of infinity and unbounded knowledge

• A certainty of immortality itself.

• A substantial strengthening of the immune system.

• Intellectual enlightenment.

• Appeasement of the emotional body.

• A clear, vivid feeling of an encounter with the supreme intelligence of a divine and omniscient being.

Whether or not the experience includes visions, it brings about far-reaching changes in the individual's personality and their observation channels. A new area of perception opens up inside them, where consciousness begins to perceive itself. It is wrong to think that the altered states of consciousness that are attained by taking LSD and other substances have anything to do with genuine mystical experience. Although the latter cannot be explained with concepts and language, it resembles a combination of grace, beauty, harmony, peace, grandeur, rapture, surprise, happiness and Love, all with sufficient intensity to paralyze the mind due to the impact of ecstasy. In contrast, experiences induced by substances may be exciting, but often are more misleading than inspiring and not integrated into the personality; instead they drive the ego towards distorted perceptions, and tend to create addiction rather than transformation.

When a genuine mystical experience occurs, it has a significant effect on the mind that involves a transformation of the individual's life; it leads to an unshakable belief in the existence and presence of God, even in the most skeptical minds.

The false notion that people of different traditions –christians, buddhists, hindus, sufis, jews, etc.– have different kinds of mystical experiences has triggered confusion in this matter and has historically limited the writings of researchers to one tradition in particular. Further research is required in this field, focusing on what mystical experiences of different traditions have in particular and what they have in common. What is certain is that the brain, mind and nervous system of everyone who has experienced this process became far sharper, with a subtler kind of intelligence to which more ordinary brains and minds cannot respond.

Mankind's progression towards this type of consciousness is just as predestined in its evolutionary path as was the emergence of the consciousness of self after simple consciousness.

As it becomes clearer that all religious ideas and concepts, as well as all rituals and forms of prayer, owe their existence to an evolutionary impulse that lies within human beings, Mankind will get better accustomed to a certain mental state. We will start to grasp the laws governing this spiritual process and abide by them just as normally as we now follow rules of bodily hygiene. Humans will realize, better and better, that the spiritual world is governed by its own laws, just as the world of matter has its own.

Chapter 6. Integral philosophy and psychology[*]

On writing this chapter, the author has chosen to try to sum up the ideas of one of integral psychology's leading figures, Ken Wilber, about two key aspects of that philosophy; the holonic nature of reality and the four quadrants of manifestation.

6.1 The holonic nature of reality

Some of the patterns that appear to be necessary for evolution from matter to life to mind have already been identified by the integral approach.

Reality is composed of wholes/parts or "holons". Arthur Koestler coined the term "holon" to refer to an entity that is itself a whole and simultaneously a part of some other whole. A close look at reality and its processes soon shows that all things are part of something else. They are wholes/parts, i.e., holons.

For example, an atom is something complete and in turn is part of a molecule. Every molecule, apart from a complete reality per se, is part of a cell and so on. None of these entities is only part or only a whole but rather a whole/part, or a holon. The fact is that somehow, everything is basically a holon.

In their two thousand-year old philosophical dispute, atomists and wholists ask one another: What is ultimately real, the part or the whole? In fact, the answer is: neither, or both, at the same time. Actually, there are only wholes/parts in all directions.

---

[*]   In this chapter we will follow the presentation of Ken Wilber in several of his books listed in the bibliography section

A subatomic particle is itself a holon. So is a cell, a symbol, an image or a concept. So the world is not composed of atoms or symbols, but of holons.

These are just some of the properties that all holons have in common:

Since each holon is a whole/part, it could be said to have two "tendencies" or "impulses", because it has to maintain both its wholeness and its partness.

On the one hand, it must maintain its own integrity and identity, autonomy, organization and function. If it fails to preserve its own identity, it simply ceases to exist. So one of the characteristics of a holon, in any field, is its agency; its ability to maintain its integrity against environmental pressures that would otherwise destroy it. This is true for atoms, cells, organisms, ideas etc.

Yet a holon is not only a whole which has to preserve its identity, but also part of some other system or whole, so besides having to maintain its autonomy as a whole, at the same time it has to be part of that "something" else. Its very existence depends on its ability to fit into its environment, on the success of its communions as part of other wholes; and this is true for atoms and molecules, animals and humans.

So every holon has not only its own identity, it also has to fit within its communions as part of other wholes. "Communion" refers to certain spiritual links or connections, but here this term is applied to all kinds of essential connections in the dynamics of holons. If an error occurs in any of its two impulses —in maintaining its agency or its communion— it is simply erased, it ceases to exist.

If a holon does not maintain its agency and communion, then it can break down completely. When it breaks down, it does so into its subholons: the cells are broken down into molecules, which, in turn, break down into atoms etc. What is fascinating about the decomposition of a holon is that it tends to dissolve in the opposite direction to which it was organized.

So, we have an agency and communion operating "horizontally" at any level, while "vertically", at a higher level, there is self-transcendence and, at a lower level, self-dissolution. Holons are subject to several "pulls" in their own existence: the attraction of being a whole; that of being a part; being pushed upwards and pulled downwards. In other words: agency, communion, transcendence and dissolution.

Another feature of holons is that they "emerge". Evolution is a process of self-transcendence which always goes beyond what went before. And thanks to that emergence, new entities come into being and exist.

This is one reason why a holon cannot be reduced to its most basic components; the entirety of a holon cannot be found in any of its parts.

Many scientists and thinkers agree that self-transcendence is integrated within the fabric of the Universe. Overall, it seems that we love the Spirit, creativity and holons.

Another feature is that when holons emerge, they do so holarchically. "Holarchy" is another name for natural hierarchies. When holists say "the whole is greater than the sum of its parts", this means that everything is at a higher level of organization that the parts themselves, which is why it is higher up in the hierarchy (or holarchy).

Yet another feature is that each emergent holon transcends, but in turn includes its predecessor. For example, the cell goes beyond its molecular components, and yet also includes them; molecules transcend but also include atoms, which transcend and include particles, and so on.

On transcending, the "heaps of parts" become wholes and, in the inclusion, the parts are accepted, united in a community and a shared space that relieves them of the burden of being a fragment.

Evolution is a process of **transcending and including:** transcending the heart of the spirit-in-action; it is the ultimate secret of the evolutionary impulse.

One could say that everything lower is contained in the upper levels, but not vice-versa; that is, not everything in the upper levels is in the lower ones, which is what invariably establishes a hierarchy.

For example, even if the biosphere were destroyed —which would entail the end of all forms of life— the "physiosphere" would still exist. But if this were destroyed, the biosphere would immediately disappear too. This is because the biosphere transcends and includes the physiosphere, and not vice versa. The physiosphere is at a lower level of structural organization than the biosphere. Similarly, the "noosphere" is higher than the biosphere. This is what being more or less organized means. So, the physiosphere forms part of the whole that is the biosphere, while the latter, in turn, is part of the whole of the noosphere. Therefore one might say that the physiosphere is more fundamental than the biosphere, but less significant than it in evolutionary terms.

Size or scope should not be confused with depth, which is given by the number of levels in any holarchy, while size refers to the number of holons at a level.

The fact that evolution produces greater depth and less spans at the highest levels may be rather confusing, but the reason is that the higher transcends and includes the lower. For instance, there are fewer molecules than atoms, so there will always be less of the higher and more of the lower, without exceptions.

The Spirit is both the highest "level" in the "holarchy" but also the frame or "ground" on which the entire holarchy is written.

Human identity can certainly be expanded to include the All —let's call it Cosmic consciousness— in a mystical union. Individual identity expands towards the Spirit and therefore embraces the Cosmos it transcends everything and is all-inclusive. And that is good. Yet the number of people who are actually aware of that supreme identity is very, very small. In other words, this great depth is actually very limited in breadth. As always, the deeper, the narrower.

However, in that experience, conscious identity is indeed an identity with All, with the Cosmos; and in it, all beings, high or low, sacred or profane, are actually seen as perfect manifestations of the Spirit, exactly as they are.

So, the maximum depth is the end unity with the Absolute.

Yet this understanding does not occur equally in all beings, even though all beings are manifestations of the Spirit. This realization is the result of an evolutionary process of development and transcendence.

"Web-of-life" theorists usually focus on the equality of beings and lose sight of the holarchy of the making. They think that because both an ant and a monkey are perfect manifestations of the divine —which they are— then there is no difference in depth between them; but this idea is, in fact, reductionist.

We want our environmental ethics to respect all holons without exception, as the manifestations of the Spirit they are, but at the same time, pragmatic distinctions must be made about the intrinsic value of each being. So, it is much better to kick a rock than a monkey, much better to eat a carrot than a cow; and much better to subsist on grains of cereal than on mammals.

Another feature of holons is that their emergence has directionality. Therefore, evolution has a direction: a principle of order in chaos, as they say; in other words, a drive towards greater depth. That means that chance does not exist, but depth emerges, so the intrinsic value of the Cosmos increases with each manifestation.

Evolution has a broad and general tendency to move in a certain direction (*telos*): towards an increasing complexity, differentiation/integration; organization/structuring and relative autonomy. These are some of the scientifically accepted directions of evolution. This does not mean that no regressions or dissolutions occur —as mentioned earlier—, dissolution is one of the four abilities of any holon. Nor does that mean that all short-term development must follow these instructions. As Michael Murphy says, evolution meanders more than moving forwards in a straight line. Yet in the long term evolution has a broad telos (direction and purpose), which is particularly evident with increasing differentiation e.g., from an atom to an amoeba, and from the amoeba to a monkey.

All these scientific descriptions can be summarized as follows: **the basic impulse of evolution is to increase depth.** This is the transcendent thrust of the Cosmos: to always go further, yet including what went before, increasing its own depth. The greater the depth of a holon, the too greater its degree of consciousness.

Consciousness and depth are synonymous. All holons have some degree of depth, which increases with evolution, meaning that consciousness increases. No matter how much depth atoms have, molecules will have more; similarly, cells are deeper than molecules, plants are deeper than cells, and primates are deeper than plants.

There is a spectrum of depth, or of consciousness and evolution makes it gradually manifest itself. Consciousness develops increasingly, boosting its ability to be conscious of itself. Thus it steadily manifests itself with greater intensity.

Since depth is everywhere, consciousness is everywhere. It is simply what depth sees from within. Therefore, since **depth and consciousness** are everywhere, so too is the Spirit. And as depth increases, consciousness awakens and the Spirit develops more and more. In other words, to say that evolution produces greater depth is simply to say that it develops a greater awareness.

This can be summed up very simply: as evolution goes "beyond" what we had before, and because it must "encompass" what happened before, its very nature is to transcend and include. Therefore, it has an inherent directionality, a secret impulse towards increasing depth, increasing its intrinsic value as the consciousness does.

6.2 The four quadrants of manifestation

The integral view has identified the problem of material reductionism that dominated the old paradigm and has found a simple way to reverse it.

All previous systems fit or fall into four general categories. Over time it has become clear that these four categories represent the interior and exterior of the individual and the group.

In the diagram below, which represents these categories, the top half of the diagram is individual; the bottom half is communal or group; the left half is internal (subjective, the consciousness); and the right half is external (objective, the material).

	INTERIOR	EXTERIOR	
INDIVIDUAL	A "I" Personal Meaning Sense of Self STRUCTURALISM	B "IT" Body and Behaviour MEDICINE	**INDIVIDUAL**
COLECTIVE	C "WE" Culture and Shared Values HERMENEUTICS	D "ITS" Institutions Systems and Processes SYSTEMS THEORY	**COLECTIVE**
	INTERIOR	EXTERIOR	

Figure 12. The four quadrants of manifestation

Thus, the **upper left-hand quadrant** represents the interior of a person; the subjective aspect of consciousness or individual consciousness. The entire upper left-hand quadrant includes the full spectrum of consciousness as it appears in an individual, from bodily sensations to mental ideas in soul and spirit. The whole psychograph is a graphic in this quadrant. The language of this quadrant is of the "self": first-person accounts of the inner stream of consciousness.

The **upper right-hand quadrant** represents the objective or external correlations between inner states of consciousness. Without worrying for now about the exact relationship of the inner mind with the objective brain, we can simply note that the two are at least closely correlated with each other. Researchers studying this quadrant focus on the mechanisms of the brain; the neurotransmitters and organic computations that support consciousness (neurophysiology, cognitive science, biological psychiatry, etc.). The language of this quadrant is the "*it*" (it-language): the third person who records and relates the scientific facts about the individual organism.

Yet individuals never exist alone: every being is a being in the world. People are always part of a group, which has "interiors" and "exteriors". These are in the lower left and right quadrants, respectively. The **lower left-hand quadrant** represents the interior of the community, or values, meanings, worldviews and ethics that are shared by a group of individuals. The language of this quadrant is the language of "us" (we-language): the second person or "I-Thou" language, which involves mutual understanding, justice and goodness. In short, "how you and I will make sure we get on well". This is the quadrant of culture.

However, this does not exist only as imaginary ideas in interiors. Just as the individual consciousness is somehow anchored in the world of material and objective forms –like the brain–, all cultural components are anchored in institutional, material and external forms that belong to the **lower right-hand quadrant.** These social systems include material institutions, geopolitical formations, and the forces of production. Because these are objective phenomena, the language of this quadrant, like the objective individual, is the "it" (it-language).

Since the upper and lower right quadrants are objective its, they can be treated as a general domain. This means that the four quadrants can be summarized in the *"Big Three"* of I, we and it; or the aesthetics of "I", the morals of "we" and the "it" of science.

In other words, the four quadrants are actually the foundation of the modern differentiation of the value spheres of art, morality and science. Where pre-modernity had tended not to differentiate the Big Three clearly, modernity has done so and made each of them free to go their own way. This differentiation was part of the dignity of modernity, allowing each domain to pursue its own truths, surprising, far-reaching discoveries; discoveries which even the harshest critics agree with and which establish a clear, differentiating line between modernity and pre-modernity.

Yet there is something which most definitively differentiated both stages. The differentiation of the Big Three was taken too far in their dissociation, and this made an imperialist science dominate the other spheres and claim that they did not have any inherent reality themselves. Thus, knowledge was reduced to "scientism" or scientific materialism and to a one-dimensional vision of Man and disenchantment with the world. The mind, soul and Spirit were left behind.

Therefore, it seems that pre-modernity had at least one great strength that modernity lacked: it recognized the **Great Chain of Being,** which is basically a general map of the higher human potentials. But pre-modernity also had at least one major weakness: it did not completely differentiate the different spheres of value at any of the levels of the Great Chain. Thus, among other things, objective scientific research into the spectrum was hampered; specific cultural expressions of the Great Chain were taken as universally valid; and moral precepts recommended for all remained linked to those limited cultural expressions.

The outstanding work thus seems to be to take the strengths of pre-modernity and modernity and jettison their weaknesses.

One possible valid goal could be to integrate the enduring truths of pre-modern and modern approaches to psychology and consciousness. As explained earlier, the essence of the vision of the pre-modern world is the Great Chain of Being, and while the essence of modernity is the difference between the value spheres of art, morality and science. Therefore, to integrate pre-modern and modern, we would have to integrate the Great Chain with the differentiations of modernity. This means that each of the levels of the traditional Great Chain needs to be carefully differentiated according to the four quadrants. This would respect both the central thesis of ancient spirituality –that is, the Great Chain– and the core claim of modernity that is, the differentiation of value spheres. And it could provide the basis to move towards a more integrative psychology.

This integration can be represented in a very simple way, as in the figure below, which displays each different level of the Great Chain according to the four quadrants.

Yet unlike modernity, which denied the highest levels, the diagram includes all the levels in all four quadrants, ranging from body to mind, soul and spirit. Furthermore, unlike pre-modernity, it includes all quadrants in each of the levels, instead of indiscriminately merging them.

Figure 13. Taken from "A Brief History of Everything," Ken Wilber.

Therefore, the objective of integral psychology is to coordinate and integrate research results at all levels and in all the quadrants. The essential point of the comprehensive approach is that, for a complete understanding of any quadrant, this has to be analyzed in the context of all the others.

This integration, "all levels, all quadrants" was denied to pre-modernity (which was all levels, but not all quadrants) and also to modernity (which was all quadrants, but not all levels).

Modernity, in its understandable desire to correlate all the "metaphysical" supernatural realities with the "empirical" realities in this world (a legitimate program, since all the events on the left-hand side have, indeed, correlations on the right-hand side), inadvertently "collapsed" all the interiors into exteriors, thus breaking the vital harmony.

A comprehensive approach of the Cosmos would consist of researching all the levels and lines in all the quadrants, without trying unreasonably to reduce any of them to the others.

It is noted that all entities or holons in quadrants on the right have a "simple location". Both they and their extensions can be observed through the senses, in rocks, villages, organisms, ecosystems, planets, etc. Yet none of the holons in the quadrants on the left have a simple location. We cannot see feelings, concepts, states of consciousness, instances of internal enlightenment, cultural values, and so on running around the outside world. None of them exist in physical or sensorimotor space, but in the emotional, conceptual, spiritual space, the space of mutual understanding, of shared values and meanings, etc. Although they have correlates in the objective, physical world, they cannot be "reduced" to them without completely destroying their essence.

There follows a brief summary of some of the principles that can explain the high and low points of the manifestation of consciousness, which are necessary for cultural development in accordance with the holistic approach.

As consciousness is evolving and manifesting itself, each stage solves or appeases the problems of the previous stage, but adds the problems of the new stage. As evolution, in all domains, operates through a process of differentiation and integration, each new and more complex level contains problems that are not present at previous levels.

The more stages there are in evolution, the greater the depth of Cosmos, the larger the number of things that can go wrong.

So, evolution inherently involves new possibilities, wonders and glories entering each stage, but they are always accompanied by new fears, problems and disasters. Any balanced account of history is a chronicle of the new wonders and new disorders that have developed in the evolution of consciousness.

Precisely because evolution proceeds through a process of differentiation and integration, something can go wrong at every stage the deeper, the Cosmos, the more the disorders that may occur. As already seen, one of the commonest forms of evolutionary pathology occurs when differentiation goes too far in the dissociation, both ontogenetically (in terms of the birth and development of the individual) and phylogenetically (as regards the birth and development of the species). In human evolution, for example, one thing is to differentiate mind and body, and quite another is to dissociate them: one thing is to differentiate culture from nature, and quite another to dissociate them. Differentiation is the prelude to integration, while dissociation is the prelude to decomposition.

Human evolution —like evolution everywhere— is characterized by a number of important distinctions, which are absolutely normal and totally crucial to the development and integration of consciousness. For instance, an acorn becomes an oak tree due solely to differentiation. Yet at each stage, these distinctions may go too far in dissociation, turning growth into cancer, culture into nightmare, and consciousness into agony. Any balanced account of history is a chronicle not only of the differentiations necessary for the evolution of consciousness but also of pathological dissociations and distortions which have occurred too often.

It is also worth underscoring the **difference between transcendence and repression.** To say that evolution proceeds by differentiation and integration is to say that it does so looking for transcendence and inclusion. Each stage includes its predecessors and then adds its own defining and emergent qualities: it transcends and includes.

Yet sometimes, and pathologically, the higher dimension does not transcend and include, but transcends and represses, i.e., it denies, distorts, interrupts. Every new and higher stage has exactly this choice: to transcend and include, protect, integrate, honor and respect, or else transcend and repress, deny, alienate, oppress.

A distinction must also be made between **natural hierarchy and pathological hierarchy.** During the evolutionary process, what is "whole" at one stage in time, becomes "a part" of the whole of the next level: whole atoms become part of molecules, whole molecules become part of cells, whole cells become part of organisms. As seen, each and every element in the Cosmos is a whole/part, a holon, which exists in a nested hierarchy or holarchy, and increases in fullness and holism.

Yet what transcends can repress and natural hierarchies can degenerate into pathological hierarchies, of dominance. In these cases, an arrogant holon does not wish to be both whole and part, but only wants to be everything. It does accept being part of something bigger than itself, or participating in the fellowship of its fellow holons, rather it intends to dominate with its own agency. Thus, power replaces communion; domination replaces communication; and oppression replaces reciprocity.

Furthermore, **higher structures may be dominated by lower impulses.** Tribalism, when left to its own devices, is relatively benign, simply because its resources and technologies are more or less harmless. The problem is that the advanced technologies of rationality, when kidnapped by tribalism and its ethnocentric impulses, can be devastating.

6.3 Does psychological development have to be completed before starting spiritual development?

The answer to this question depends, once again, on how the terms are defined. If spirituality is explained as a separate line from development, the answer is "no", because spiritual development occurs alongside, not above, psychological development. Yet if spirituality is defined as a peak experience, the answer is also "no", because this can happen too without any great psychological development. Yet beyond that, the answer becomes a bit complicated.

Firstly, what many theorists mean by "psychological development" are actually the personal stages of development (pre-conventional, conventional and post-conventional), and what they mean by "spiritual" is the transpersonal stage (post-post-conventional). If these definitions are borne in mind, and noting any line of development, the psychological must generally be completed before the spiritual can arise in a stable form; this is simply because, as research suggests, there can be no post-conventional without the conventional first, and so on.

However, —and this is what has confused many theorists— because the lines of development can evolve independently, an individual may be spiritually very advanced (transpersonal or post-post-conventional) on one of the lines, and yet still be in a very low-level personal or psychological state (conventional or pre-conventional) in others. For example, a person may be at a transpersonal level of knowledge (perhaps achieved through contemplative development), and still be at a personal or psychological stage (conventional or pre-conventional) of moral development.

Therefore, according to these definitions, even though the spiritual comes only after the psychological on any given line, spiritual development can occur before, together with, or after, any type of psychological development; precisely because the lines themselves are relatively independent. A person may be at a pre-conventional stage on one line, a post-conventional stage on the other, and a post-post conventional on the other three which, by these definitions, means being at two psychological levels and three spiritual levels. The conclusion drawn is, therefore, that psychological development generally does not have to be completed before any kind of spiritual development takes place.

Chapter 7. Religion and spirituality in the New Paradigm

Here again we will follow the arguments made by Ken Wilber on one of his essays on this subject.

Though some might believe that spiritual practice does not necessarily entail going through different stages, what is certain is that true spirituality involves certain practice. This is not to deny that, for many people, beliefs are important; faith or religious mythology is also important; it is simply a question of adding what is the testimony of the great yogis, saints and sages of the world have made very clear: true spirituality must also involve direct experience with a living reality, revealed immediately and intimately in the heart and consciousness of individuals, and fostered by diligent, sincere and prolonged practice.

Even if we think of spirituality as a peak experience, these can often be induced, or at least incited, by various different forms of spiritual practice, such as contemplative prayer or intensive meditation. All these actions can open us up to a direct experience of the Spirit, not just beliefs or ideas about it.

Authentic spirituality is not about translating the world differently but about transforming consciousness.

Too often, in the translation of the mystical traditions of the East and the christian ones of the West to Western language, their characteristic immense depth is flattened out; their radical demand is diluted; and their potential for revolutionary transformation is impaired.

Religion has always played two very important but, at the same time, very different roles; one of them acts as a way of creating meaning for the separate self/ego: it offers myths, stories, tales, narratives, rituals and rebirths which, taken together, help the separated "self" to give meaning to its experience, to endure the slings and arrows of outrageous fortune. This function of religion does not usually much influence the level of consciousness of a person; i.e., it does not achieve a radical transformation. Neither does it offer a complete release from the separated self. Rather, it consoles, strengthens, defends and promotes that ego. As long as the separate ego believes in myths, performs rituals, utters prayers or embraces dogma, then the ego fervently believes that it will be "saved" either now or in another life in which an eternal wonderment is ensured.

However, secondly, religion has also served the function —usually in a very small minority— of radical transformation and liberation. This function does not fortify the separate ego, but transcends it completely. In short, it does not pursue conventional strengthening of consciousness but rather a radical transmutation and transformation in its deepest depths.

In short, the **difference between religion and enlightenment** lies in that the former is primarily directed towards the realm of duality (good-bad, grace-sin, salvation-condemnation), while the latter is directed at non-duality. The ego must be transcended and seen as the illusion it is. Being a "good person" is praiseworthy and great spiritual progress; yet, by itself, it does not bring enlightenment. An advanced understanding of the nature of consciousness is also required. One must understand the difference between duality and non-duality and how to transcend it. Enlightenment is not a new belief, but the transcendence of all belief. And, like all transcendence, it does not exclude belief, but includes and transcends it.

These two functions of religion can be explained in various different ways. The first of them —creating meaning for the ego— is a type of horizontal movement, while the second —which consists in transcending the ego— is a type of vertical movement, higher or deeper, depending on the metaphor. The first is called **translation;** the second, **transformation.**

With translation, the ego is simply given a new way of thinking or feeling about reality, a new belief perhaps holistic instead of atomistic, related to forgiveness instead of with blame; perhaps relational rather than analytical. The ego learns to translate its world and its being in the terms of this new belief, language or paradigm, and these new and enchanting acts of translation alleviate or diminish the inherent fear in the heart of the ego, at least temporarily.

However, with transformation, the process of translation is challenged, undermined, and eventually dismantled. With typical translation, the self (or subject) is given a new way of thinking about the world or objects; but with a radical transformation the ego observes and delves into itself, and literally chokes itself to death.

True transformation is not a matter of faith but of the "believer's death"; it is not a matter of translating the world but of transforming it; not trying to find solace but infinity on the other side of death. The ego does not content itself, rather the ego is shattered.

Both functions are significantly important and totally indispensable. Individuals are mostly not born already "enlightened", but instead are born into a world of errors and suffering, hope and fear, desire and despair. And they start, very early on, to learn different ways of translating their world to make sense of it and give it meaning.

As much as we would like to transcend mere translation and find true transformation, translation itself is an absolutely necessary and crucial function for most of our lives. Whoever cannot or does not know how to translate properly, with a good deal of integrity and accuracy, falls rapidly into severe neurosis or even psychosis; for them, the world ceases to make sense and the boundaries between the ego and the world are not transcended but rather begin to fall apart. There is no achievement, rather a collapse; there is no transcendence, but disaster. In this sense, the role which organized religion has played throughout history has been extremely important, and still is.

Yet at some point in our maturation process, translation itself, no matter how adequate or safe it is, simply ceases to console. New beliefs, new paradigms, new myths, new ideas ... none of that will work. The only path that makes sense is the **transcendence of the whole being.**

Still, the number of individuals who are ready for such a path has always been, and probably always will be, a minority. For many people, any kind of religious belief will fall into the category of consolation: it will be a new horizontal translation that creates some kind of meaning in the midst of the monstrous world.

To a great extent, the service of religion is to provide legitimacy to the ego for its beliefs, paradigms, world views, and its way in the world. This function of religion has been the most important of all religious traditions of the world.

The basic glue that holds ordered societies together as a whole should not be "played with frivolously". The reason why is that, most of the time, when the glue (the translation) dissolves, the result is not progress or liberation, but personal and social chaos.

Where translative religion offers legitimacy, transformative religion provides authenticity. For the few individuals who are ready, an increasingly insistent appeal is made for a transformative opening, genuineness, a true enlightenment and liberation. And, depending on your capacity for suffering, sooner or later you will respond to that call.

Transformative spirituality does not seek to bolster or legitimize any present worldview, or console, at all, but rather intends to provide genuineness, breaking with the establishment and what the world takes as legitimate, shattering the mundane. This spirituality is, in short, revolutionary.

These facts lead to several conclusions:

First of all, and broadly speaking, it is true that the East has produced a greater number of people who have genuinely attained self-realization. However, the actual percentage of the population in both the East and West who have devoted themselves to true transformative spirituality is, and has always been, small.

That means, unequivocally, that the rest of the population, at most, is involved in various types of **translational, horizontal religion** that only legitimizes. They are involved in magical practices, mythical beliefs, material prayers of petition, rituals, and so on. In other words, they only get involved in translative ways that serve to give meaning to the separate "self", a function which is the principal social agglutinating factor of all cultures to date.

The matter is quite simple, in fact: radically transformative spirituality is extremely rare anywhere in history and in the world.

So it is better to accept the indisputable fact that true transformative spirituality is one of the most precious jewels of all human tradition precisely because, like all jewels, is exceptional.

Although we are deeply convinced that the most important function we can perform is to offer true transformative spirituality, the fact is that much of what we have to do, within our ability to practice "decent" spirituality to the world is, in actual fact, to provide a "milder" and "more useful" "translation". In other words, even if we practice or offer a truly transformative spirituality, much of what we have to do first is to give most people a better way to "translate" their condition. We should start first with helpful translations, before we can offer true transformations. The reason is that if the translation is too fast or too abrupt, the result is once again not progress release liberation but collapse.

In addition to offering authentic and radical transformation, we must also be sensitive and responsive to the benefits of lower and translative practices. Therefore, this position requires a "comprehensive approach" of global transformation, an approach that honors and incorporates transformative and lesser translating practices encompassing the physical, emotional, mental, cultural and community aspects of the human being in preparation for definitive transformation.

A comprehensive approach to spirituality combines the most valuable parts of the horizontal and the vertical, of the translational and transforming, of the legitimate and authentic; therefore efforts must be focused on a balanced and healthy view of the human situation.

All excellence is elitist, that is evident. And that includes spiritual excellence. Nonetheless, this is a case of elitism to which all are invited. Spirituality, like everything else, is a matter of all quadrants and levels, so it is important to understand that both spirituality and religion will have to offer a pre-conventional, conventional, post-conventional and transforming version of Christ, Buddha or Krishna.

For example, in the **upper left-hand quadrant,** psychologically speaking, an individual needs to move from ethnocentric to geocentric beliefs. This is a difficult transformation, from a role-based identity into a person-based identity. Yet, at the same time it allows the individual to adopt a post-conventional approach, a morality that takes the world as a centre, not just an ethnocentric morality that mentality of "us-versus-them". For a person with a christian background and faith, the "leap" consists in realizing that Jesus Christ may be my personal savior but that others may find a different road to the same salvation, because the Holy Spirit speaks to men and women in different ways, in different languages and in different countries. Jesus was asked about those who did good, but were not in his group and he said: "Do not forbid them, for those who are not against me, are with me". In other words: those who do not scatter, harvest.

At the same time, in the **lower left-hand quadrant,** the individual needs to feel that their religion supports a truly universal or catholic Jesus, and not a mere ethnocentric creed. How this is institutionalized in the **lower right-hand quadrant** will help determine the behaviour –to be found in the **upper right-hand quadrant**– that is appropriate for a person of faith in the post-modern world.

Most of the translational approaches to the New Paradigm recommend using holistic thinking. Yet cognitive development has already been seen to be necessary, though not sufficient, for spiritual development. You can practice a holistic thought and, at the same time, be less advanced in other areas of development, such as egocentric and emotional impulses, narcissistic inclinations, etc. Thinking holistically will not be enough, despite being a great help, to transform one's inner consciousness; because to do so, we must address the internal stages of growth and development.

Humans evolve towards high levels of consciousness on going through a series of important internal transformations. It is also true that you can sit on a meditation mat for decades without ever seeing anything similar to the stages of Spiral Dynamics. However, you can study Spiral Dynamics and never have a mystical experience.

Bearing both in mind, it is essential to make progress in understanding the role of religion and spirituality in the world of the New Paradigm.

Spirituality is an important and natural dimension of the human psyche and the spiritual quest is legitimate and fully justified human behaviour. However, it should be noted that this applies to genuine spirituality based on personal experience and does not provide support for ideologies and dogmas from organized religions. To avoid misunderstanding and confusion which, in the past, has led to similar discussions, it is very important to make a clear **distinction between spirituality and religion.**

Spirituality is based on direct experiences of dimensions of reality, mostly invisible, which only occur or become visible in holotrophic states of consciousness. It requires no special place or persons officially designated to mediate with the Divine. Mystics do not need churches or temples. The context in which they experience the sacred dimensions of reality, including their own divinity, is provided by their bodies and nature. They may indeed need a support group of fellow seekers or the guidance of a teacher who is more advanced in this journey inwards.

Organized religions tend to create hierarchical systems. When this is the case, true spiritual life continues only in the mystical branches and monastic orders of the religions involved. A profound mystical experience tends to dissolve the boundaries between religions and reveals deep connections between them, while the dogmatism of organized religions tends to emphasize the differences between the different faiths and generate antagonism and hostility.

The great mystical traditions have accumulated extensive knowledge of human consciousness and spiritual realities in a manner similar to how scientists acquire knowledge about the material world. This is a methodology for inducing transpersonal experiences, systematic data gathering, and intersubjective validation. Spiritual experiences, like any other aspect of reality, may be subject to thorough and open research, and can also be studied using the scientific method (provided we understand that we are referring to science in its broadest sense, not to analytical-empirical science, as will be explained in the next chapter).

Scientific research of consciousness has provided convincing evidence of the objective existence of the reality of the imaginary realm, and thus the main metaphysical assumptions of mystical vision have been validated.

The conflict between religion and science reflects a misunderstanding or a fundamental lack of comprehension between the two. As already noted by Ken Wilber, there can be no conflict between science and religion if these two fields are understood and practiced correctly. If apparently there is a conflict, it is likely to be "false science" and/or "false religion". The apparent inconsistency is due to the fact that both sides seriously misunderstand the other's position and probably also represent a fake version of their own discipline. The same God who gave us religion, gave us reason and, as he is the truth, if there were any opposition between the two, we would have lost God, and also the truth.

Mystics could be regarded as inner scientists, as scientists of the mind. Traditional scientists seek to understand any phenomenon through careful observation; they suppress any data which is "distracting"; they also reduce the "noise" to a minimum and control the factors which could disrupt their observations. They then make deductions from their observations and share their findings with others to see if they corroborate them.

Mystics do the same, but in the realm of the mind. They try to minimize the noise of mental distractions by withdrawing attention from sensory experiences, calming their mind and focusing on aspects of consciousness which usually go unnoticed by ordinary mortals. They have also shared their findings; not in scientific journals, but in the many spiritual teachings and discourse that abounds in every culture.

These scientists of the mind have observed the arising and passing of thought. They have looked to the source of their experience, to the very essence of mind. There they have discovered a profound connection with the basis of every being. The sense of being someone individual –that feeling of "I-ness" that everyone knows so well but finds so hard to define– turns out to be not so unique after all. It is simply the feeling of being aware, and something we share with everyone else. The light of consciousness that I know as me is the same light that you know as you–the same light shining in a myriad of minds.

Once again, genuine spirituality is transforming and not translative. The aim is to succeed in uniting with reality. The mystic is a person who believes in and aims to achieve such a union. Being a mystic is experiencing the soul, in other words, the source, the essence, and presence of transcendent reality.

Spirituality is the domain of consciousness, which embraces the observer, the observed, and the observation process. In an updated language, this is how *Vedanta*, the deepest branch of Indian spirituality, defines itself:

> *"Spirituality is the essence of every faith but it is not contained in any faith."*

As Rumi says:

> *"Love is in all religions, but Love has no religion."*

In its manifestation as an individualized soul, the Spirit progressively develops its power of knowledge through the successive stages of evolution: as a subconscious response in minerals, as sensitivity in the plant world, as sensitive and instinctive knowledge in animals, as intellect, reasoning and introspective intuition still relatively undeveloped in humans and as pure intuition in man installed in mystical consciousness.

"Being reborn", as spiritual Masters invite us to do, means much more than becoming a member of a church and being baptized in a ceremony. Mere belief does not guarantee the soul a place in "Heaven", but instead needs to achieve communion with God now. Human beings become angelic on Earth and not in "Heaven". At whatever point somebody ceases their spiritual progress due to the onset of death, it will be from that same point that they will continue their successive purifications. To put it another way, it is from that same point that the consciousness archive should keep on being filled with understanding of truth.

7.1 Is greater convergence between religions possible today?

Undoubtedly, more than ever, we have knowledge that can lead to greater convergence between different religions. This knowledge comes primarily from new science and a better understanding of Cosmic consciousness.

The truth is, in itself and for itself. Even though it may be expressed in different ways by the "isms" of different faiths, these can never exhaust it. Truth has different expressions and can only lead to the direct experience of the Absolute, the only reality. The human seal of denominational affiliation has little importance. It is not belonging to a particular creed or a particular culture that gives us salvation, but entering the Kingdom of God within us.

All of the world's truly revealed religions are based on intuitive knowledge. Each has an exoteric or external particularity and an esoteric or inner essence. The exoteric aspect is its public image, constituted by moral precepts reasoning, rules and customs. The esoteric aspect consists in certain methods that focus on the real communion of the soul with God. The exoteric aspect is intended for the multitudes and the esoteric for those who decide to embark upon a personal transformation. It is the esoteric aspect that leads to intuition and direct knowledge of reality.

New science

Obviously, nowadays no religion could postulate that the Earth is flat. If this happened, it would suffice to show a "picture". With the picture, there would be little further discussion. Faith, the system of beliefs, is only necessary when we have no external verification of the fact. If there is, faith must be in accord.

There is a point in the last Apostolic Exhortation (*Evangelii Gaudium*) by Pope Francis (2013), which is very important and can help us to better understand this issue. It is point 243, which states:

> "The Church does not intend to stop the admirable progress in science. Instead, it rejoices and even enjoys recognizing the enormous potential that God has given to the human mind. When the development of science, maintaining academic rigor in the field of its specific objective, a certain conclusion becomes evident that reason cannot deny; faith does not contradict it. Nor can believers pretend that a scientific opinion that they like, and which has not been sufficiently proven, acquires the weight of an article of faith. But sometimes some scientists go beyond the formal object of their discipline and overreach themselves with statements or conclusions that go beyond the field of science itself. In that case, it is not reason which is proposed, but a particular ideology that closes the path to genuine, peaceful and fruitful dialogue."

That is, when science proves something that cannot be objected against through reason, faith can never be in contradiction with that. Yet it also says something else very important, namely that believers need to know that any scientific principle which still lacks sufficient demonstration, even if one likes it, is not strong enough to change any position or dogmatic truth.

If the Universe is said to be holographic, and the author personally thinks it is, and this will become fully demonstrated in a few more years, this statement stills lacks the strength required by point No. 243 of the Pope's Exhortation.

Downward causality, with the rigor point 243 requires, might be scientifically proven. This is the information that minds must accommodate, which takes time because established patterns have to be broken. If the mind does not understand what this means, it will be a limitation to apply the tools discussed in the second part of this book.

Science increases its knowledge without stopping, so there are more and more topics where "pictures" can be shown, as it were, that demonstrates an argument's strength. In this sense, religions must accept scientific knowledge as it develops, as common to all. It is important to note here, however, that science will never reach full understanding of the mystery of God and the Universe because it does not have the tools to do so; nevertheless it will increasingly advance in its discoveries, and provided that it always acts within its sphere of application, religions will be unable to differ from each other on these points.

Insisting on this idea, all religions should agree about recent scientific discoveries: the new cosmic vision, levels of consciousness, downward causality, the development of the cognitive line in humans; the various manifestations of consciousness; the multidimensional Universe, etc. Each religion can and should offer their characteristic view of transcendence, and of the most effective spiritual practices, but always placing this above and based upon available knowledge; never below or instead of it.

Not only does scientific knowledge progress, but religious knowledge too. Now we laugh at what 14th century scientists and religious figures said about many beliefs which we have now gone beyond. And one could imagine those who will come after us laughing at the way we oppose things which in fact are different perspectives of the same truth, things which are often complementary.

Teilhard de Chardin, said of himself:

"As I speak there are many things that can be true and many things that can create discord, but I continue with the idea of the Gospel of not pulling out the tares lest I also take the wheat."

In other words, a doctrinal truth improves if how it is told makes it easier to understand. As it happens, at the beginning of the 20th century it was said that the first passages of Genesis were historical according to the statement of the Pontifical Biblical Commission, as a doctrine. So catholics had to believe that man came from the form that God made of mud, among other things. Yet a few years ago, Pope John Paul II recognized this language was that of a myth, nothing more than a metaphor applied whenever one cannot speak rationally of a mystery. Thus, a truth is revealed, in this case a doctrinal truth, like the Creation (now better understood as emergence or continuous creation) from a shape similar to a story. The Pope also added that the theory of evolution was something more than a hypothesis. Finally he also said that the Biblical Commission was not doctrinal.

The evolution of doctrine is observed in many fields. Suffice it to see the joint statement on the act of faith of catholics and protestants, changing everything said at the great Council of Trento, and retouching all of its disciplinary or cultural elements. Many more cases could be found in all religions.

In short, a system of beliefs is established to ascertain the truth, but what matters is the truth *per se*. If one has to choose between beliefs and truth, it is better to throw away the beliefs (the crutches) and keep the truth. Yet many of us still prefer beliefs, because the education we receive solidifies our ways of thinking and prevents us from seeing. In many areas, not only in the religious sphere, people do not accept the truth because it is hard to let beliefs go. In religion, this phenomenon is called "fundamentalism".

In any case, one has to be sympathetic to these forms of "petrification" of beliefs learned through education; that clinging to what was thought to be true. Yet in the end, one has to endeavor to choose truth, because God is truth, not belief. God "is" the truth. And this can be verified through its result: inner peace.

The Cosmic consciousness

Historically, very few individuals have reached this level. Their writings have been known and studied, so we know about their experience. But recently Western science has also begun to research this region of knowledge, applying its methods, and our understanding of it has been deepened significantly.

When this manifestation is studied in more depth, the conclusion reached quickly is that this new consciousness is "unitary" and "uniting". As explained in Chapter 4, if all humans were already at this level of consciousness, many of the current discussions between religions would cease; not so much because their conceptual differences would blend in with each other, but rather because we would realize that they are not so important. Also because we would understand that the value of unity is more important than being right or not about a particular concept.

Humans compete unconsciously for the energy that we have opened ourselves up to: what flows between us. By opening ourselves up to Cosmic consciousness, this competition ceases immediately because we aware of the problem and find another inexhaustible source of energy that we can use without fear of it running out.

Something that is understood quickly, on studying levels of consciousness, is that problems arising at one level are only resolved at the next, and they are resolved because from the next level one realizes that there was, in fact, no problem, because problems are always in the mind and not "out there".

Cosmic consciousness manifests itself in everyone equally and with the same developmental stages, regardless of their previous concepts or religious faith. It does so the same way in a buddhist as it does in a christian and, when it appears, the conceptual differences lose much of their meaning because, among other things, this consciousness is post-conceptual. We have to understand that the difference between the thought and teachings of Christ and Buddha is virtually non-existent when interpreted from Cosmic consciousness and that such differences only begin to appear when interpreted from the consciousness of self.

Both are different in their dogmas, in their ways of seeing God and eternal life. But they share the good heart, the idea of life after death, and many other elements. A christian knows, by faith, that in Christ the Divine Truth, the Word of God, is revealed. Although this is overwhelming, we can never fully possess it, rather we have to let ourselves be possessed by it. Yet returning once more to this example, when Jesus is told of people who baptize, or do good works, and he is asked whether "we should forbid them," Jesus says, "he who is not against me is with me; those who preach salvation and heal should be allowed to do good works". Thus, he establishes a pattern of "diversity" and "respect" in these ways of knowing or interpreting the truth, without showing any kind of intolerance.

We can therefore conclude that with the help of science and if a greater number of individuals from different religions enter the Cosmic consciousness, convergence between different beliefs is inevitable in the near future. Moreover, this convergence will help bridge many of the divides that exist between human beings today. Also, one can delve into the deepest religious traditions and see that they all tell us not to fall into the exclusivism of "neither yours nor mine", but to build together in inclusive forms of the "et et": "yours "and" mine", "this "and" that"; it is the "not only but also", because the truth can be seen from many perspectives: scientific, religious, anthropological, philosophical, mystical ... like the faces with which a cubist painting breaks down a figure. Yet that is not the truth; they are only perspectives. If we made absolute one of them, we would distort the truth that keeps them all in harmony.

The truth is a set of aspects; something measureless; a whole which is never reached completely, but which we aspire to for its knowledge. Therefore, assertive –not exclusive– dialogue helps us to go hand in hand with others in the knowledge of truth, which is ultimately God.

Chapter 8. Verification(*)

8.1 The three eyes of knowledge. No more category errors

Any attempt to find a comprehensive paradigm ought to combine the knowledge of empirical-experimental science with those of biology, psychology, philosophy and spirituality. As the famous physicist Wheeler once said, no physical theory that only deals with physics will ever explain physics.

Empirical science is inductive, instead of rational and deductive; it uses logic and deduction, but subordinates them to empirical induction, which is why the method of empirical science is based on measurement. Where Aristotle classified, Galileo and Kepler measured. Psychology is considered empirical science if it can "measure" patterns. Therefore positivist psychology, which studies behaviour, is considered empirical science and psychoanalysis is not.

The first problem we would have to solve is the connection between a holistic paradigm and empirical science. Could we find validity criteria in philosophy, psychology and spirituality?

St. Bonaventure in the West and Nagarjuna in the East, among many other authors, asserted that there are three "eyes" through which human beings can acquire knowledge, namely:

- The **eye of the flesh,** *cogitatio* or *sensibilia*.

- The **eye of reason,** *meditatio* or *intellegibillia*.

(*)   For a more detailed description of the ideas included in this chapter please see *Eye to Eye* from Ken Wilber listed in the bibliography section.

- The **eye of contemplation,** *contemplatio* or *trascendalia*.

This terminology is christian but is also to be found in Eastern philosophy.

It is important to understand that each higher eye includes and transcends the lower one. For example, the eye of reason partakes of the world of ideas, concepts and logic; the mental field includes and transcends the sensory field (*cogitatio*). As Schumacher said, we see not only with the eyes of our senses, but also with our mental equipment. So, mathematics is not an empirical but trans-empirical knowledge. The same applies to logic: nobody has seen the square root of a number through the eyes of the senses. Whitehead held that the mental sphere is necessary and *a priori* for the manifestation of the sensory realm, and this is what spiritual mystical traditions mean when they say that the "gross" arises from the "subtle", which in turn arises from the "causal".

The eye of contemplation is to the eye of reason as the eye of reason is to the eye of flesh. Just as reason transcends flesh, so contemplation transcends reason. The eye of reason is trans-empirical and the eye of contemplation is trans-rational.

Thus, a higher eye cannot be reduced to nor explained in terms of a lower eye. Each eye is valid and useful in its own field, and commits a fallacy when it attempts, by itself, to fully grasp higher or lower realms that fall outside its scope. For example, with the eye of contemplation we can see that everything that exists is "one" but not that the molecule of water is H_2O. When an eye attempts to usurp the realms of the other two, it makes what we call a category error and both religion and philosophy have been guilty of this in the past. For instance, in 535 B.C., the christian monk Cosmas wrote a book called *"Cosmic topography"* in which, after studying the Bible literally, he concluded that the Earth was a flat parallelogram. Dogmatic theology has made these errors in the East and West alike by failing to understand the category problem. Mankind had neither understood nor separated the "three eyes".

Empirical science later made the same error stating that what is real is only that which can be perceived by the senses or its extensions. This view of things gave rise to materialist reductionism.

Returning to St. Bonaventure and Nagarjuna, all valid knowledge of any of the three eyes is known to follow a basic structure formed by three components:

• **Proposition or Instruction:** internal or external instructions that basically say "I you want to know this, you have to do that".

• **Illumination:** seeing with the appropriate "eye".

• **Confirmation:** sharing the vision with others who are using the same "eye". When the vision is shared, it receives communal confirmation.

To acquire this knowledge, the eye doing the work must be a trained eye. For example, mathematical knowledge must be confirmed among individuals who have trained that eye in that discipline. If someone refuses to train an eye, their views on the relevant scope would be irrelevant; this was the case of the monks who refused to look through Galileo's telescope. St. Augustine said that contemplative eyes have to be trained in order to attain direct knowledge of divinity.

Confirmation in the world of the eye of reason is even more complex than in the eye of the flesh because we all have basically the same senses, but have a different mental setup. For instance, there is no empirical-scientific proof of the meaning of a literary work such as *"Hamlet"*. Something like that has to be interpreted from *intelligibilia* and not from *sensibilia*.

All knowledge is experiential in the end, as empiricists say, but is not only based on sensory experience, as they also hold. Herein lies the confusion. Both *sensibilia* and *intelligibilia* and also *trascendalia* can be experiential, but rational or contemplative knowledge cannot be reduced to sensorial knowledge as empirical scientists claim.

Even within the field of empirical science, we need to understand that its language is mathematics, and therefore we can ask ourselves: how valid was our knowledge of the Higgs particle before it was experimentally proven in the Geneva particle accelerator? Until that accelerator was built, there was no device powerful enough to observe that particle, and yet all of modern physics was built on its existence. Scientists knew that it existed on account of their mathematical equations.

Does this mean that the truths discovered by the three eyes using the three structural steps of all valid knowledge can be referred to as scientific knowledge?

The answer is: it depends on what we understand as scientific. If it is taken to only mean empirical-analytical knowledge that can be experimented with the senses or their extensions, then mathematics, psychology, sociology or philosophy would not be science under this definition. Yet many recent and current thinkers, such as Piaget, Wilber, Whitehead, Habermas, Gadamer, Bateson and many others, have abandoned pure empiricism as a valid definition of scientific knowledge.

So scientific, in the broadest sense of the word, could be used to refer to any knowledge open to experiential observation and communal confirmation. If this were so, we could talk in terms of *"sensibilia* sciences" (physics, chemistry, geology, etc.), *"intelligibillia* sciences" (philosophy, psychology, sociology, etc.) and *"trascendalia* sciences" (zen, vedanta, christian mysticism, etc.). We just have to be careful not to refer to empirical-sensory sciences.

Part II: Living from de New Paradigm

Introduction

When you come to understand the paths that the latest research in many disciplines of current knowledge are taking and, at the same time, you investigate the teachings of Eastern and Western mystic wise men of the past, a new vision of reality starts forming in your mind.

From this point onwards, the task is to start living one's very existence in line with the new context. What is challenging is how to start practicing that new vision, and what internal changes you have to tackle. You can let yourself be guided by your inner teacher; another possibility is to learn from others who have already trodden this path.

In this respect, I myself had the good fortune to gain access to information from different sources; but especially to an extraordinary one: the one that Gerardo Schmedling provided in his *"Magic of Love"* workshops. It is the fullest, and best-structured information I have managed to find so far on these topics. I have witnessed, both in myself and in many others, just how far this information facilitates training, and, therefore, growth.

The information that readers will find in this second part of the book is based mainly on that source, on other similar ones and on my personal experience. When I opened myself up to those teachings, my mind had already understood everything explained in Part I, which is why I quickly grasped its relevance and how perfectly it fits in with the New Paradigm that is emerging about the nature of reality.

The contents of Part II are as follows:

Chapter 1 addresses the Laws of the Universe. These are the immutable principles that govern how the Universe functions and determine manifestation. These laws are described in hierarchical order. Nothing can happen outside the Law, so knowing about them is the key to growth.

Chapter 2 describes how these Laws work in everyday life, and provides some keys for recognizing their presence.

Chapter 3 provides an overview of the multidimensional Universe and explains the role that Grace plays in our growth. It also analyses the issue of "miracles" and how they work within the New Paradigm.

Chapter 4 explains that how everything that happens is perfect and necessary from the standpoint of the soul, even though it does not seem the same to the ego. We have to try to develop the "science" of "Acceptology" to achieve inner peace.

Chapter 5 analyzes the change of thought that can be confronted in the light of this new information. This chapter describes the dematerialization of thought, personal identification with the ego or soul, and human beings' ability to stand as a witness and not as a subject of thought itself. It also examines how the new understanding of the levels of consciousness helps to resolve personal and social difficulties.

Chapter 6 broaches the fundamental issue of taking responsibility for one's own growth, through the science of "coming to terms with life", and tries to define what is life and what is death. Readers will see that death does not exist as such, and is only a change of experience. The destiny and mission that everyone brings to physical experiences are also defined.

Chapter 7 discusses how to manage and understand relationships from the point of view of this new vision and the universal Laws. We will try to analyze the real cause of the difficulties in human relations and offer some solutions to this problem.

Chapter 8 focuses on abundance, and the internal values that we need to access it. Readers will see that abundance is the natural characteristic in the Universe, and how to transcend certain internal blockages that make it harder to experience.

Chapter 9 analyzes service as an action and as information. It explains how to train properly for service and looks at the problem of personal suitability in the light of these new tools, to avoid making the mistakes of the past and not confuse disposition with suitability.

Chapter 10 touches on the theme of integral spiritual practice in the New Paradigm. Growth is seen to rest on three pillars: the right information, training with that information and managing energy. This chapter goes on to explain how prayer and meditation boost internal energy.

Chapter 11 describes the difference between knowing about God and the personal realization of God.

Chapter 12 discusses whether it is necessary or not to have a Teacher to help in the process.

Chapter 1. Laws of the Universe

All events, both individual and collective, are governed by mathematically precise laws, as the material world does not function on pure fate. Behind every occurrence there is a Law. Nature does not respond to the fate or whims of an emotional God.

Those individuals who become aware of and verify these Laws that shape our lives will be able to achieve alignment with the evolutionary process of the Universe and transcend the dualisms that plague our world: justice/injustice, guilty/innocent, good/bad luck, and many others. These dualist concepts run against the principles of the Universe and, therefore, do not help us to maintain inner peace.

Laws of the Universe can be defined as the "immutable principles that govern the universal order and processes of creation, manifestation, functioning and understanding of the Universe". The Law is not individual, but rather universal. Yet, what is completely individual is the understanding of the Law. As an individual, if I do not understand the Law, I cannot follow it, with the result of this lack of understanding being all that which does not function. The Laws of the Universe resemble the laws of physics in the sense that they can be measured. They produce the same result every time they are applied. Once you learn how to apply them, you will always be able to attain specific and invariable results. The Law is witnessed by way of its results; these Laws aren't beliefs, but rather verifiable truths.

Human law can be defined as "the variable decisions that govern the territorial, economic and social order of human institutions".

The key difference between these laws is that human law changes over time and can be repealed, whereas Laws of the Universe never change.

Everything that is manifested falls under these Laws, as nothing can occur beyond them, otherwise the Universe would fall out of order. The fundamental question in this regard is: how can violence, intolerance, selfishness and hatred be part of these Laws? These questions can only be answered when the process of the evolution of consciousness is understood. Behind every event, no matter how unpleasant it may appear or how difficult it is to accept, there is a purpose based in Love. What makes understanding difficult are learned intellectual limitations. No question lacks an answer; the Laws will always provide an explanation for any and all human experiences.

The following is a summary of some precepts of the Laws:

• Everything within the Law functions well and flows on its own.

• Everything I need for my growth can be found within the Law and will be given.

• Everything I want but do not need falls outside the Law.

• I need everything that life gives me and I want everything I do not have.

• When I want and obtain something, it is because I need it.

• What I have is valuable, and if I do not value it I am destined to lose it.

• What I want but do not need is the cause of all suffering.

True strength does not stem from willpower, but rather from understanding. Willpower without understanding may have the appearance of "working," but eventually this illusion will disappear. Take for example Forrest Gump, the film character, who was running non-stop and then one day asked himself: "Why am I running?," and he simply stopped running. Understanding is the source of inner energy. This energy is eternal and originates from profound understanding, a divine component of humans, which can only be activated once the individual understands that all problems are only perceived as such in his mind and that they cannot be blamed on anything external. It's important to highlight this, as it's a fundamental idea.

The second step involves setting out on a profound process of intellectual reprogramming involving the assimilation of new information. This process can also give way to the creation of substantial energy; if you are able to understand, this will trigger an internal change that will make significant space for energy.

Freewill is the ability to make decisions and to make mistakes in the process of understanding and verifying the existence of the Law. These mistakes are not outside of the Law, but rather form part of the educational process. The Law is understood by observing its results. There is neither reward nor punishment in the Universe, only results. If they are satisfactory, they flow with the Law. If they are not, they violate the Law, whether consciously or not.

If the Law is not accepted, suffering cannot be avoided, and anything that is not understood cannot be accepted. And yet, ignorance of the Law does not absolve you from its results. In order to escape from the system of beliefs, that is, the ego, you have to make mistakes, observe the results of the Law, understand how it works, and ultimately flow with it.

The Law operates in two ways: It governs the manifestation and operation of the Universe; and it governs the understanding of the manifestation and operation of the Universe.

In the first way, it descends onto matter and produces the manifestation. The second way provides a process for recognizing the Law and understanding the Universe; this makes way for an ascent accompanied by the overcoming of material limitations and the freeing from all processes based in ignorance. As Teilhard de Chardin once said,

"Everything that rises, must converge."

On the other hand, the Laws have two basic functions: The superior Laws govern Creation and the inferior Laws govern the understanding of Creation.

One possible way to explain these Laws would be as follows:

The seven Laws of the Universe –from most to least powerful– are:

Superior Laws:

    1. Law of Love

    2. Law of Manifestation

    3. Law of Polarity

    4. Law of Evolution

Inferior Laws:

5. Law of Correspondence

6. Law of Harmony

7. Law of Nature

These Laws can also be displayed in a triangular structure corresponding to their hierarchical position:

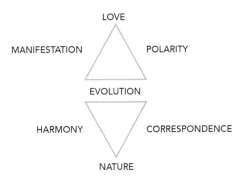

Figure 1. The seven Universal Laws

The Law of Evolution integrates both triangles and is responsible for the manifestation of the superior Laws in the inferior Laws. All universal processes are permanent, eternal, constant and immutable. Those individuals that work through the Laws in their development process will be those that change or transform.

As previously stated, the three superior Laws –Love, Manifestation and Polarity– regulate the process of creation of the Universe, whereas the three inferior Laws –Correspondence, Harmony and Nature– regulate the verification and understanding of the existence of these Laws. The Law of Evolution fills the gap between the two groups of Laws with the aim of generating those "learning" processes which all human beings must go through.

Hierarchically superior Laws influence inferior Laws, but not the other way around. Superior Laws operate on a higher level both as regards information and vibration. For this reason, they can influence lower laws. Each Law has its own precepts which help us to understand what they govern.

The Laws will be described below, starting with the inferior Laws

1.1 The Law of Nature

Precepts of the **Law of Nature:**

- All natural manifestations require proper conditions.

- All natural cycles have specific functions.

- All violations of the Law incur the relevant consequences.

- All living organisms need proper nourishment for survival.

- All living organisms are aware of this Law at an instinctive level.

- All living organisms have a specific function.

The Law of Nature is horizontal and unfolds at the level with the densest vibrations (the material world). It cannot operate vertically on the other laws; it manifests through the four material kingdoms mineral, plant, animal and human.

This Law leaves no room for imperfection or impairment and it destroys all that is weak. If this were the only Universal Law, Darwin would have been right. Any deviation from this Law affects the original flawlessness of nature, a process which superior laws allow in order to enable verification of the Law's existence. Violations of the Law of Nature provoke, among other things, sickness, malformations, hereditary defects, weakened immune systems and infections.

The Law of Nature operates when individual instincts are followed, which are a form of "mind" of nature. Instinct is the basic natural human behaviour controlled by a part of the brain called the reptilian brain (limbic system).

Basic instinctive functions include: procreation (mating) and the maintenance (goods, desires) and defense (survival) of life.

The Law of Nature acts through constant reproduction, natural selection and depredation. It works on binary code and although it has a lot of "strength," this Law has less information than other Laws.

With regard to the Law of Nature, it's important to point out that without a physical body it would be impossible to have a mental field containing the personality. The physical body plays a fundamental role in sustaining the mind, developing the personality, and making comprehension possible; it's like the "clothing of God," that is, experiential bodies or biological entities, designed by God for a purpose.

1.2 The Law of Harmony

The Law of Harmony is the integration of the parts of a whole, and of the whole into a superior body. Its precepts are the following:

• The world responds to and gives back everything that you put out.

- Only understanding ensures that destruction will not be possible.

- All that which is attacked defends itself.

- Events should be controlled; people should not be controlled by events.

- The best teacher is learning by example.

In order to demonstrate how the world responds to and returns what is sent into the Universe, I will share the story my friend, Lluciá Pou, tells about the echo of life:

"A father and his son were hiking up a mountain. The morning dew had dampened the Earth and the child slipped and fell to the ground. A shout of fear and pain broke the silence: 'Aaaahhhhh!!' To his surprise, a voice from somewhere on the mountain repeated his cry. Curious, the boy shouted: 'Who are you?,' to which he received an identical response. The boy, angry, shouted to the mountain: 'Coward!,' and the hidden voice responded with the same word. Confused, the child asked his father: 'Who is answering me and why is he mocking and insulting me?' The father, smiling, shouted to the mountain: 'I admire you!' And it was these exact words that the mountain returned to him. Finally, the father unveiled the secret to his son: 'People call this an echo, but it's nothing more than life itself, which gives back all that you think, say and do."

That same idea is expressed in St. John of the Cross' quote:

"Where there is no love, put love and you will find love."

The Law of Harmony is the Law of universal order. It organizes the operation of everything in existence. It is static in relation to the organization of processes and dynamic as regards the sequencing of such processes. This Law manifests in everything that co-exists without destruction. It can be seen in the interactions of different species and the establishment of the cycles of the Universe as well as in tolerance, socialization and any other event where energy seeks equilibrium.

The Law of Harmony is transgressed where there is dissatisfaction, stress, anguish, limited resources, difficulty in relationships and emotional conflicts. This Law manifests in everything that survives, co-exists and is not destroyed. It can be seen in all events where a force or energy intervenes in search of balance.

The key technique for Harmony is respect, which is expressed by accepting and supplementing personal experiences with those of others. The Law of Harmony has been ingrained in the instincts of mammals, (where emotions and feelings of pleasure and displeasure are generated), in intellectual memory (as concepts of beauty, aesthetics and art) and in psychological memory (where human beings record their defenses to trauma and the personality's different expressions of enjoyment and harmony).

1.3 The Law of Correspondence

The **Law of Correspondence** includes the following precepts:

- Every situation is a learning experience.

- Every circumstance is generated from within.

- All events happen to whom they are meant to happen.

- That which is necessary for personal growth will always be available (but not necessarily that which you want).

- Only that which needs to happen, will happen.

- You are always in the mathematically appropriate place.

This Law governs the universal order. It determines the arrangement of time, space, location, acts and the function of all living beings. It controls everything that occurs and the specific characteristics and interactions between each experience to make way for the learning process. Only that which must occur, does occur and nobody can experience something which was not meant for them.

It is useless to act against this Law, as the Law will block all that which is not in line with it. Human beings have unlimited inner freedom, with the exception of those limits imposed by personal internal restrictions; however, their external freedom is limited. For example, if you attempt to shoot someone who is not meant to be shot, the pistol will jam.

The Law of Correspondence determines who, what, when, where and how an individual's personal destiny and mission will unfold. This Law also determines the baseline conditions for each person —their parents, place of birth, country, ethnicity and other genetic conditions—, which are appropriate for their life experiences. When an individual grows in consciousness, this Law will change the events in order to tailor them to the new experiences needed for the individual learning process. Once the required levels of experience and the appropriate characteristics and locations for a certain function or learning process are in place, the Law of Correspondence produces the necessary circumstances so that what is meant to happen can manifest and occur. All human beings, without exception, are in the perfect place to learn exactly what brought them to the physical world. Human beings are always carrying out a dual-purpose in accordance with the Law of Correspondence: to learn and to teach.

When a person has nothing left to learn from the place and circumstances surrounding him, and when such person is not helping others in the same place and circumstances to learn, that person will move on to a new place with different circumstances, which will be appropriate and suitable, for continuing to develop his consciousness. The process by which life experiences are replaced with increasingly advanced and satisfactory experiences can be compared to a student who completes high school and is accepted at a university to continue learning at a higher level. This program is necessary and appropriate for some students, and we would never consider placing students based on individual learning needs as unfair.

The Law of Correspondence is encoded in the mind of destiny —as individual experiences related to the personal need to learn— and in the mind of consciousness —as the capacity to teach and serve—.

1.4 The Law of Evolution

The **Law of Evolution,** which operates between the superior and inferior Laws, can be expressed through the following precepts:

• Experience alone will open the way for a full understanding of the truth.

- Human beings are confronted only by those situations which are necessary for understanding and transcendence.

- Individual levels of consciousness increase only through proper transformation.

- The soul's need to learn and understand, in accordance with the Universe's evolutionary plan, is the sole reason for the physical existence of human beings.

Whenever one of these Laws is transgressed, the transgressor immediately suffers the consequences (as results) and falls under the Law of Evolution, which allows minor Laws to be violated as a learning experience until the individual is ready to voluntarily respect and obey such Laws.

The Law of Evolution determines which learning processes the individual must go through. It manifests in difficult situations, in all that which is interpreted as a problem, in the unpleasant and recurring circumstances which are faced, and in suffering in general, which is nothing more than mental resistance to what "is". Resisting the Law does not serve to resolve problems, but it is useful in that it brings limitations to light.

Essentially, the Law of Evolution exists so that human beings can learn how to be happy under any circumstances, to have eternal peace, and to serve without limitations. The three inferior Laws may sometimes be violated —for example, starting wars, plagues, pollution, violence, hatred, etc.—, that is, the Law accepts that it is in disequilibrium and gives rise to circumstances that go against the other three Laws because it is only in this way that existence of the Laws may be verified, that is, by acting against the Law and exploring the negative results of such disequilibrium.

One way to tell where we stand in the understanding of the Laws of the Universe is to observe the results which we obtain in life. In this regard, three internal and four external results should be considered.

The internal results are:

    1. Happiness

    2. Peace

    3. Service

The external results are:

    1. Relationships

    2. Health

    3. Abundance of Resources

    4. Adaptability to the environment

The Law of Evolution works through a mechanism that pits opposites against each other: it triggers disagreement of ideas, beliefs, cultures, customs, feelings and emotions; it considers disequilibrium and seeming nonsense as being within the Law; it creates circumstances that go against the inferior Laws, acting as an "anti-law" before those laws it contradicts Nature, Harmony and Correspondence. It is only by acting against the Law that its existence can be discovered, similar to the way in which it is only possible to know what a current is by having swum against a current. In other words, a force may only be measured through the resistance of such force.

Evolution is realized through two types of contrasts:

Inverse: appears when actions are taken against the Laws of the inferior triangle. Its results include sickness, war, suffering, resistance, etc.

Harmonic: appears when actions are taken in line with the Law or when a person observes the manifestation of a higher level Law and follows such observation.

The aim of the Law of Evolution is to verify what is not, what does not work, what is not true, and what is a mere belief, in order to transform it into wisdom. Ultimately, the Law aims for each and every person to pass from a state of "I am not," which is a state of ignorance, to a state of "I am," which is a state of wisdom, making the person impervious to all outside influences.

Within the evolutionary process that allows individuals to pass from one level to the next there are three different types of people acting within the parameters of the Law. These persons can be divided into three groups: the **good,** the **bad,** and the **wise.**

The **bad** is a person that has yet to develop the sentiment of kindness: he doesn't worry about other people's problems nor does he attempt to remove them from their learning experiences. This is someone who is completely ignorant of the Law. Meanwhile, the **good** has already developed feelings towards his neighbor, having traversed a more advanced evolutionary path; however, he is also unaware of the Law and, without knowing it, attempts to interfere in the learning experiences of others. The **wise,** on the other hand, is an individual that is no longer ignorant and has understood the Laws. He respects the experiences of others and is always available to serve, giving advice at the appropriate time; the wise does not place blame.

Each of these three figures serves an extremely important role within the evolutionary process of human beings. The **good** is part of the harmonic contrast, the **bad** provides an inverse flowing contrast, and the **wise** is neutral. The effect of the **good** on the **bad** is to provide him with more harmonious options for living and to facilitate the development of his feelings. The human relations of the **bad** are generally not satisfactory; he has a contrasting effect on the **good,** enabling the latter to recognize the Law, as the sentiments of the **good** often lead him to violate it. The function of the **wise,** on the other hand, is to provide an example and teach; he does not become unnecessarily involved in the activities of the **good** or the **bad,** as both should undertake their own learning, and he is always successful in his own actions and human relations.

As regards those processes which fall under the Law of Evolution, the actions of the bad's matter more than the good's actions, because the former creates an inverse flow contrast so that the good can recognize the Law.

This process is similar to what takes place between innocence, ignorance and wisdom. The innocent doesn't know –he lacks information–; the ignorant believes that he knows –he finds himself in the positive/negative and false/true duality– and the wise knows that he knows –he understands the Law and flows with it–.

The way in which this Law interacts with individual destiny and mission is described below:

The Law of Evolution is programmed in the mind as destiny, as those experiences that must be lived in order to understand the Law, and in consciousness, as the Law that has already been understood, which allows the individual to carry out his life mission. The Law is understood by taking advantage of your destiny as a learning opportunity. **Destiny** includes anything that requires an effort, to varying extents, to be achieved. **Mission** is whatever the individual is drawn to achieve, whatever they can do best and most easily and whatever they identify with most closely.

It matters more in life to fulfill your destiny than to complete your mission, because fulfilling your destiny lets you learn what you don't know and understand the Law, which at the same time advances the development of consciousness. The mission, on the other hand, while making it possible to teach others what you already know and to maintain high inner energy, does not contribute as much to the development of consciousness. Destiny supports learning, growth, and the mission to serve. Hence, there is no fate or luck in the circumstances surrounding the life of each human being.

By understanding the principles of the Law of Evolution, processes and events of everyday life on Earth as well as the rationale behind social, physical, economic, religious and political differences among human beings can be better understood. Instead of talking about injustice, we begin to refer to the applicability of experience, individual destinies and the varying needs of each individual.

It becomes clear after a certain level of wisdom is reached that mistakes of omission or excess must be avoided; a mistake of omission involves not doing that which you are meant to do and a mistake of excess involves doing more than you are meant to do. Both cases fall outside the margins of the Law.

Based on the foundations of the Law of Evolution, it's clear that people are neither good nor bad in absolute terms; everyone acts in the way they know and believe to be best and they fulfill a function within the order of the Universe in accordance with their level of ignorance or wisdom.

1.5 The Law of Polarity

The **Law of Polarity** controls the interaction between masculine and feminine poles in the Universe, from divine creation to the most complex matter, passing through spiritual, human, animal, plant, mineral and atomic levels of the Universe. The Law makes it possible for the manifestation to materialize in what we call creation, causing movement, dynamism and universal evolution.

The absolute dimension —which refers to the absolute in-manifested, just as with beings of non-physical or spiritual worlds—, is characterized as androgynous, that is, it contains both masculine and feminine poles simultaneously; in this way, it is fundamentally neutral. Such beings, therefore, may express themselves with either of their polarities in accordance with the function to be fulfilled at any given time.

This Law functions primarily through the attraction of opposites. The proton and the electron are attracted to each other and create atoms; masculine and feminine give birth to new life; the smooth complements the rough; the soft the hard; the bright the dark; the difficult the easy; the long the brief; the tall the short; the action the result. The Law of Polarity gives rise to diversity and interactions that produce the experiences needed to understand the Universe and the perfect laws that govern it.

1.6 The Law of Manifestation

The **Law of Manifestation** allows the preexisting or unmanifest to be manifested in all that which is created, from the most subtle to the densest. It forms the origins of every thought, every idea, every word, and every work, and in general, of everything which exists or occurs. The Law of Manifestation is also called "the first emanation of God".

Anything that did not already exist in the unmanifest cannot be imagined, thought, or believed. As part of the absolute and preexisting information of the Universe, any process deemed "creation" is merely the result of the manifestation acting on polarity. It is not a new creation.

In this context, the concepts of time and space refer solely to the dimensions within which the processes of learning and understanding are carried out as regards the laws governing the perfect order of the Universe. Evolution processes completed at inferior levels have a beginning and an end and they can be measured in time and space. However, beyond the tenth dimension, the past and the future, the before and the after, are seen simultaneously.

1.7 The Law of Love

Love is the source of everything that transpires and understanding it frees us from all events.

The children of God, from the moment they are created by from the Father, are in a state of innocence; that is, they do not yet possess any information about the Universe or the laws that govern it. The Father creates the Universe to serve as a "school" for his children, to confer upon them all information existing in the Absolute. Creation of the Universe fulfills the Father's promise of love towards his children by enabling them to encode all of the Universe's information as well as the laws governing it in their innocent consciousness and, in this way, become one with the Father.

Based on all of the above, it can be concluded that everything is manifested by the Father's love for his children and that everything exists and happens because of love; and that, when this is understood, the individual is freed from all evolutionary processes. The material world is no longer needed for experimenting with the laws because all have been understood and all experiences within the physical world have been transcended; all missions of love and service have been fulfilled. Thus, a point is reached where the unmanifest and manifest, nothing and everything, form a unit that no longer must go through any experiences because it has transcended everything and it "IS" for all eternity the same essence as the Father, living in the absolute dimension.

The Law of Love, by virtue of being a superior Law of the Universe, manifests through the other Laws which govern the specific processes for evolution and the development of consciousness. This superior Law governs all processes of descent and ascent. Everything which occurs in the Universe occurs because of Love.

The Law of Love can be identified in everything that is eternal, perfect, pure, peaceful, joyful, harmonized and happy, regardless of anything else happening around it and of whether it clashes with an individual's beliefs. Love does not form part of the ideas, beliefs, thoughts, feelings and fears experienced by human beings, but rather refers to a psychological understanding and permanent awareness.

Living in peace and joy is to live in Love. Respecting the experiences of others and being ready to serve them not subject to any conditions is to express Love in human relations.

Chapter 2. Practical Application of the Laws to everyday life

The old saying, "The leaf in the tree moves not but by the will of God," refers to the existence of superior laws which act on the material world.

Up until now, culture has not taught us how to recognize the signs through which the Law is manifested, and what we usually refer to as "bad luck" is actually the result of unconsciously violating the Law because we do not know it exists or how it works.

Yet there are certain signs in everyday life that we can learn to recognize in order to turn destiny into mission. To do so, we need to be aware of the "Laws of life", which are related to the seven Laws of the Universe. Some of them may be described as follows:

2.1 The Law of Warning

Life gives us advance warning about upcoming hardships that can be avoided. This warning can be recognized when something is blocked and does not flow under any circumstances. It is subtly manifested in simple details that emerge as various sequential "reminders".

This sequence may involve something as simple as an untimely phone call that make you run late, followed by a flat tire and, then, a blocked road. What appears to be "bad luck" is actually a warning.

Learning how to recognize warnings requires attention to recurring details even when seemingly unrelated to the situation. Only the person that the warning is intended for can interpret it, as they are best placed to understand the relationship between the warning and the intended action. There are always signs along the way that show us in advance whatever each of us are not meant to experience.

The Law of Warning is directly related to the Law of Evolution and indirectly related to the Laws of Correspondence and Harmony, as the purpose of the Universe is for human beings to enjoy the learning process with the least amount of suffering possible, albeit not bypassing necessary experiences.

2.2 The Law of Opportunity

A person who has failed is considered to be living outside the Law, whereas a successful person lives within it, but both are unaware of their situation. A wise person lives his life consciously in accordance with the Law. On the other hand, when what one thinks, says and does is inconsistent, there will be disorder in the universal flow and everything will be blocked.

Opportunities are the exact opposite of warnings, but, just like warnings, we can also recognize them through small and subtle details. Seizing an opportunity means pursuing what has been decided with all available energy. There is no lack of opportunities, just people who are unable to seize them.

The other extreme of this would be a person who, for example, finished their Law degree and after having spent some time looking for a job as a lawyer, still had not been offered any job. Finally, he had to accept a job as a waiter in order to make ends meet. However, he was enthusiastic and put his best efforts into the job, and within a few months he was promoted to manager of the restaurant; a few months later, the owner opened a new establishment and offered him the opportunity to run that restaurant; and a few years later, he started his own restaurant. He now owns a restaurant chain with more than 300 establishments and is a millionaire. He managed to seize this opportunity because he was enthusiastic and gave the best of himself to the job which, despite not being the one he was looking for, life offered him. From that point forward, the Universe showed him the Law.

The Law of Opportunity is directly related to the Law of Correspondence and indirectly related to the Law of Harmony.

2.3 The Law of Two

The Universe will block any attempts to alter processes under the Law of Evolution. The Law of Two enables people to fulfill the Father's will in their daily life, and is manifested through a binary system: Yes/No.

"Yes" is shown through everything that is provided and "No" in everything that is blocked. This Law answers questions posed through action, as life does not respond to inertia. People should ideally assume less in their lives and, instead, make use of their ability to ask the Universe. You can flow even without being a fortune teller; by submitting to the divine will and not asking for anything, life will offer multiple alternative courses of action, any of which will come under the Law. Life makes opportunities available to persons who initially refuse to put in the work. At the same time, life does not respond to mere prayer and meditation unaccompanied by action. Prayer serves to flood the mind with peace and raise vital energy, but you still have to make an effort after the fact to take advantage of opportunities.

Although at first we should direct our questions towards activities that we want to carry out, if after a certain period of time that path does not open up, we should begin to ask questions aimed at other pursuits that we had not first considered. For instance, if you have started up a business but you have yet to make a profit, you should set yourself a trial period of, say one or two years; if the business fails to take off within that period, this can be considered life's answer that the business was not right for you. By using what we have and enjoying whatever life gives us, we fulfill the Father's will.

Using "want" as a tool for asking questions is healthy, and if you get a positive answer then you will know that it was not simply a desire, but rather a need.

This Law is directly related to the Law of Harmony.

2.4 The Law of Three

Some expressions exemplifying this type: "Constant dripping wears away even the sturdiest rock" and "If at first you don't succeed, try, try again" are, in part, true. However, we may end up paying a high price in terms of energy spent on matters that contribute correspondingly little to growth experiences. So we need to learn to distinguish between perseverance and stubbornness.

To avoid error through lack of perseverance, the wisest course of action is to make at least three attempts down the same path, but no more than seven so as to avoid falling into stubbornness. There are no good or bad jobs, work or places, just activities that are right for some people and not for others.

The Law of Three is "the Law which streamlines the use of vital energy". Every individual has a specific function in life. If we are persistent, we spend the right amount of energy, get results and make headway, albeit slowly; on the other hand, stubbornness implies spending more energy than you produce and unsuccessfully. In these types of decisions, pride, that is, insisting on doing one thing over anything else, and the ego, or the need to "get what's mine," are both factors.

People who do not flow with the Law have not clearly identified their appropriate function. They want and insist on doing what they enjoy. Life is formed by a cyclical and variable wave; it's not a straight path. A "cycle" is the space between two points on the wave, which may be a job, business, relationship, etc. This is where the expression "God draws straight with crooked lines" comes from, an expression which could be slightly altered in light of the latest information to read: "God draws straight with straight lines, which we perceive as crooked". In this way, we can see the efficiency of the divine as well as our own limitations.

This Law is directly related to the Law of Harmony and the Law of Correspondence.

2.5 The Law of Communicating Vessels

Only someone who has, can give. Anyone who does not have, can only receive. People sometimes complain about human "vampires" that steal their vital energy, and it is in fact true that certain people, jobs and situations can "suck the blood" out of someone else; all human beings unknowingly compete for other's energy until they manage to generate and save their own energy.

The laws of physics are related to the Laws of life. For example, if you mix cold water with hot water, you'll get lukewarm water. If several glasses of water are connected at the bottom, the level of the liquid in each glass will be the same. Positive always flows towards negative, just as energy always travels towards lower energy levels in order to reach equilibrium.

A person's mental balance depends on their vital energy levels. People who are apathetic, depressed or sad have low energy levels. When a high-energy person interacts with a low-energy person, the former's energy flows towards the lower energy, leaving them feeling exhausted but not knowing why. Every person, business or place with low energy acts as a potential energy "thief". As the saying goes, "He who leans close to a good tree will be blanketed by good shade".

Everyone is personally responsible for protecting their own vital energy. If we allow our energy to become destabilized, we will no longer have access to our centers for understanding and wisdom. If we decide to give our energy to someone or something, we have to learn to do so consciously rather than automatically. The most common way that vital energy is lost is through mental and emotional conflict; it rises and falls according to how thoughts, feelings and emotions are managed. The most harmful "vampire" is not external but rather internal, and this is what we call the ego. Perhaps when Jesus drove all the merchants out of the temple He was also referring to removing everything that feeds on our inner energy.

We have to learn how to replace feelings with a better tool: the understanding of Love. For example, an involuntary and automatic expression of affection may be positive, but it could just as easily turn into an aggressive explosion at any time; acting from instinct or feeling is a double-edged sword. Only from a place of understanding and training in Love may non-automatic feelings be voluntarily expressed at all times. Nobody would ever voluntarily express negative feelings. Human relations should not be based on shared suffering, but rather on peace and harmony. The best way to attain high energy is to express happiness.

This Law is directly related to the Law of Polarity, which controls energy levels for creativity.

2.6 The Law of Cause and Effect

Every human being receives the effects of whatever he causes. There is no such thing as good or bad luck, only effects of a cause. There are no idle words, no thoughts without effects and no actions without results.

The brain is structured by thoughts in a manner similar to that of others with similar thoughts. This structure gives rise to physical and emotional manifestations and specific behaviours, which are then perceived by others. In this manner, it forges a direct relationship so that we ourselves also experience whatever we do to or desire from others: the whole Universe is connected and intertwined.

2.7 The Law of Saturation

Deliverance begins where suffering ends; the information needed to grow in wisdom is made available when the individual is ready for internal change. The Law of Saturation breaks through the resistance to change, preventing the stagnation of spiritual growth, as every process needs a certain amount of time to mature. The mind becomes saturated when it verifies that although all processes of struggle and suffering are useless in practice, you must endure suffering in order to overcome suffering through attaining wisdom.

2.8 The Law of Generation

Everything that happens in life is generated by the individual himself. This is the great human capacity to create; every individual co-creates his destiny and mission, and he is always working to build his future. Anything that is created in the mind —consciously or subconsciously— is manifested as reality, as all creations are first manifested as a thought or idea and then later translated into action.

The idea that individuals should internalize and identify with the best of life is a spiritual growth technique taught by the Gospel in the phrase: "But seek first the Kingdom of God and His righteousness, and all else shall be added unto you". A person's surroundings are the mathematically exact result of his inner state; these "additions" or connections are external. Knowing this ultimately makes it easier to understand and use these teachings in everyday life.

Enjoying the learning process will facilitate growth and the transformation of destiny into mission. Besides, anyone interested in spiritual growth already has a relatively developed consciousness; otherwise, they would have no interest in such growth.

This Law is directly related to the Law of Manifestation and it operates in both ways. The sequence this Law follows is like this:

Mental conception towards life generates an internal outlook on life. This outlook prompts specific thoughts and feelings that are then translated into external behaviours which, in turn, lead to verifiable results. Once verified, we gain wisdom and understand life better. This sequence demonstrates that as our conception of life begins to change, so does everything outside us. The process is a feedback-driven cycle.

2.9 The Law of Compensation

All actions and services entitle us to be compensated. This principle of action and compensation together with symbiosis govern the proper equilibrium. This Law indicates that every interaction —human or divine— tends towards efficiency, as all relations have a healthy and mutual interest in being supplemented and obtaining mutual benefits.

For instance: in a parent-child relationship, the parent provides love, support, safety, guidance, education, etc., and in exchange their child will compensate them in their old age or when otherwise required. In the teacher-student relationship, the students provide the teacher with economic compensation for his teaching so that he can support himself and continue providing educational services. The buyer-seller relationship is also efficient when both sides benefit equally, ensuring that the commercial activity is secure for all clients.

2.10 The Law of Sharing

Universal information is handled hierarchically and always flows in the same direction: from more to less information, such that each level of the hierarchy teaches the level below. Information provided should be useful and timely, and it should first be verified that such information may be shared. Furthermore, it's important to keep in mind that what is known is, in fact, wisdom; on the other hand, whatever is believed to be known is ignorance, and whatever is unknown is innocence.

Information is not provided properly unless requested or where we make a mistake of omission or excess. In contrast, when the information or permission to provide such information is requested correctly, it is properly provided. Providing incorrect information will cause our destiny to be chosen for us, whereas providing information from wisdom is the greatest service of Love.

People further develop their mission by teaching, effectively and timely, what they know. Furthermore, bear in mind that the truth is not a belief, but rather a verified understanding.

2.11 The Law of Affinity

All beings of similar character tend to convene in the same place. The best always associate with the best. Everything that we choose to feed internally produces situations, people and places in line with that energy.

2.12 The Law of Empty Spaces

All empty spaces will be filled with something new. With the exception of the Absolute, everything in the Universe is replaceable; nothing and no one is essential. So, anything that leaves our life and mind will be replaced with something new. This means that everything outside the spiritual realm is temporary, and people are never alone: the feeling of loneliness is no more than a mental limitation.

We have to learn how to remove from the mind – and closets– everything that we no longer use in order to make room for the new. When we open ourselves up to removing the ego, we make space that can be filled with wisdom.

2.13 The Law of Understanding

Life never repeats a destiny situation that has already been understood. Therefore, faced with any event, it's important to ask ourselves: "What can I learn from this?" The ignorant hide their inabilities behind their aggression and flee from the best opportunities that life offers them. They blame others for their own results and criticize and judge anything that is different from them. They complain about what they have and suffer because of what they don't have. They are unaware that there is no good and bad in the material world, but rather everything is neutral. There are only perfect and necessary processes.

By analyzing the "drama," the ignorant can come closer to understanding. Although nobody experiences anything which they are not meant to experience, they will keep on suffering from the drama if they confront the situation from a place of feeling and ignorance instead of from a place of understanding; don't forget that feeling is a part of the ego.

This Law is directly related to the Supreme Law of Love and the Law of Evolution.

In reality, all of the Laws of life form part of the Laws of the Universe, but the former are closer to human beings. The seven Laws of the Universe act constantly and simultaneously. The Laws of life are either used or not depending on whether the person understands those Laws, but ignorance of the Law does not mean that the individual is not covered by the Law.

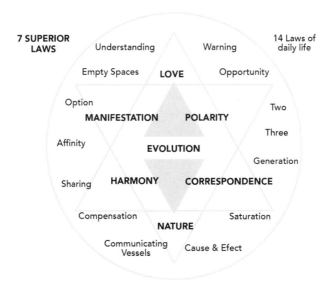

Figure 2. The fourteen Laws of life versus the seven Universal Laws

Chapter 3. The higher dimensions and human relationship with them

One of this book's aims is to make it easier for minds to understand the idea of multiple dimensions and how human beings might be connected with them. To achieve this it may be useful to draw up a tentative "map" —and others that are different may be equally valid— of how the multidimensional Universe operates. Any map, in this sense, is a mind map, and therefore some sort of classification or division will be necessary. If one meter is equal to 100 centimeters, which in turn are equal to 1,000 millimeters, it follows that any classification is modifiable. In this chapter we will discuss how a Universe of 40 dimensions might operate.

To do this, it is first necessary to understand the concept of *dimensional variable frequency wave*. This requires a number of concepts to be defined:

Transmission waves

Dimensional variable

Dimensions of physical matter

Non-physical dimensional planes

3.1 Transmission waves

Existing knowledge about the laws of physics tells us that both sound and light are transmitted through space by what science calls "sound waves" and "light or electromagnetic waves". Transmission waves possess three specific characteristics that define them: speed of propagation, wavelength and vibratory frequency.

The **speed of propagation** refers to "the speed at which the waves transmit information from the Universe". This speed varies depending on the circumstances; for example, sound waves are propagated through the air at 340 meters per second, and light waves at 300,000 kilometers per second. The thought waves of the Self are propagated instantaneously (zero time) to anywhere in the Universe; that is to say, thought moves at the absolute "speed" of the essence of the Self, where time and distance meet at a single point, the value of which is equal to zero. In other words, when travelling at infinite speed from one point to another, it takes "zero" time to get there.

The **wavelength** through which information is transmitted is variable, and matches "the distance between the crest of one wave and the crest of the next". The possible variations in the wavelengths existing in the Universe range from zero to infinity. The decrease in a transmission wave's length is inversely proportional to the increase in its vibratory frequency; the shorter the waves and the higher the vibratory frequencies, the greater the transmission power. The transmission wave of thought has unlimited range, because the wavelength can be reduced to zero, thereby increasing the vibratory frequency to infinity.

The **vibratory frequency** is "the number of oscillations per second experienced by a signal travelling through a wave, moving laterally within the height of the wave". When the vibratory frequency becomes infinitely rapid, the wavelength is reduced to zero, at which time the Unmanifest Dimension of the Self is reached.

The following example of a sound wave and its cycles per second illustrates these concepts:

Where the wavelength (distance from one crest to another) is 34 m:

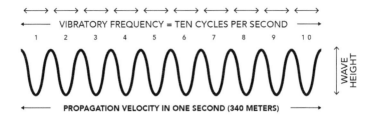

Figure 3. The wavelength

To make it easier to understand, the elements that make up transmission waves are expressed as equations:

Speed = Length x Frequency

Length = Speed ÷ Frequency

Frequency = Speed ÷ Length

3.2 Dimensional variable

Although synchronicity and the connection of thought belong to a non-material world, we will try and explain these concepts here with the example of waves and their vibratory frequency.

Transmission waves travel through the Universe adapting their propagation speed and varying their wavelengths and their vibratory frequencies in inverse proportion according to the different transmitters, different states of matter and dimensional spaces that they encounter on their path.

When waves are propagated at a speed faster than light, they enter the dimensional planes where time and space start to contract in accordance with the acceleration, shortening of the wavelengths and increase in vibratory frequencies. These changes are known as the *dimen-*

239

sional variable. Thought can come into contact through the dimensional variable with all the planes and dimensions from dimension 0 to the dimension of the Absolute. To understand this better, we can use the example of the two extremes of the Universe, which science calls the Big Bang and the Big Crunch. The Big Bang has been generally accepted by the majority of astrophysicists, while the Big Crunch is one of a number of hypotheses.

The **Big Bang,** "the great explosion that brought an expanding Universe into being" was the greatest possible condensation of matter, where:

Speed = Zero

Length = Infinity

Frequency = Zero

When the speed is equal to zero, any distance, however small, has a value that is equal to infinity. Any movement is cancelled out; therefore, the frequency is also equal to zero. This could be expressed as follows:

Speed of Propagation = Infinite length x Zero Frequency = Zero.

In other words, a wave of infinite length is equal to zero movement. In such a situation, the electrons make contact with the protons and the explosion occurs; there is no space or movement (Dimension Zero).

The Big Crunch, "the great contraction or end of the universal expansion" is, supposedly, the greatest possible expansion of energy, or Absolute Single Frequency, where:

Speed = Infinity

Length = Zero

Frequency = Infinity

When the speed is infinite, any distance, however great, has a value that is equal to zero, and the frequency rises to infinity, as a result of being inversely proportional to the wavelength. This could be expressed as follows:

Speed of Propagation = Zero length x Infinite frequency = Zero.

In other words, a wave of zero length is equal to zero time. In such a situation, the ends of the wave make contact, time and space are reduced to zero and there is no longer any beginning or end (Absolute Dimension).

3.3 Dimensions of physical matter

Physical matter is what is called the "physical or three-dimensional plane" –length, width, height–, plus the time dimension. This can manifest in three states –solid, liquid and gaseous–. According to Einstein, the highest speed of propagation within the three dimensions is the speed of light.

3.4 Non-physical dimensional planes

Beyond the speed of light, time begins to contract and distance loses value. When time reaches zero – the speed of thought–, distance also equals zero; at that moment the absolute dimension of the Self is reached –a dimension without time or space–, which is called Nothingness, the Unmanifest Whole, or the State of the Eternal Present.

The concept of **pre-existing Universe** means that the information for everything that exists and happens in the Universe has always existed in Dimension 40, also called the Unmanifest Absolute. The Absolute is located in an atemporal dimension, so we cannot speak of before or after, but of the State of the Eternal Present, where past and future can be observed simultaneously. The states where time can be measured are lower dimensions, where learning experiences take place. These happen in the three physical dimensions and the six mental dimensions, where the processes of learning and understanding take place. That is to say, only up to the ninth dimension can we speak of time and space, and of before and after.

Variations within the non-physical dimensional planes are classified into:

- Mental Dimensions: mental plane

- Spiritual Dimensions: spiritual plane

- Absolute Dimension: unmanifest plane or dimension of the Self.

In the **Mental Dimensions,** the mental plane would cover six dimensions, starting at the fourth and ending at the ninth. Personality, feelings, ignorance and understanding belong to the mental plane.

As for the **Spiritual Dimensions,** the spiritual plane would comprise 30 dimensions, starting at the tenth and ending at the thirty-ninth. Human consciousness is developed between the tenth and the eighteenth. Immortal beings begin at the nineteenth.

The **Absolute Dimension** or unmanifest plane is Dimension 40 or the "single dimension of the Self". The original information about everything that exists is to be found in the unmanifest plane.

In total, then, there would be 40 dimensions of the Universe, as we said at the beginning of the chapter, and they would be classified in the following manner:

One Absolute dimension

Thirty spiritual dimensions

Six mental dimensions

Three physical dimensions

To locate the dimensions within human characteristics, one could say that the brain, as part of the physical body, is in the third dimension; the dense mental body is located between the fourth and the fifth; the light mental body between the seventh and the ninth; the consciousness of human correspondence is located between the tenth and the eighteenth dimensions. All of the dimensions of the Universe are represented in the human being.

3.5 Grace

The process of spiritual development cannot take place without the help of Grace. Human beings are helped from higher vibration dimensions to enable them to dissolve their ignorance (ego). The ego cannot be transcended from the ego alone. It is truth that dissolves ignorance, ignorance does not transcend itself.

If a person has religious faith, they will understand Grace as a divine gift that comes to them with redemptive assistance. If they do not, they may understand Grace as the "energetic attraction" that the higher dimensions —with the highest vibration— exert over those of lower vibration for the fulfillment of the Universe's purpose. However, one understands it, Grace exists.

This new information brings benefits for both types of persons. It helps the first, the person with faith, to confirm their belief externally and to offer information to more types of minds whenever requested; and it helps the faithless person to "spiritualize" their thoughts and to begin to use that help.

Grace is a constant, permanent attraction, that is available to everyone. Its strength is not limited by whoever conveys it, but by its recipients' mental blocks. Imagine a hot air balloon: once it is full of hot gas, it tends to rise; this is prevented by staking it to the ground. Grace would be like the hot gas, a "force" that drives human beings to rise. Attachments and mental limitations would be the stakes in this example.

3.6 Personal experience of the miraculous. Acting in the New Paradigm

What is a miracle? According to St. Augustine:

"Miracles are not contrary to the Laws of nature but only contrary to what we know about the Laws of nature."

He was right. To be more precise, we could say that miracles appear to be outside the known Laws of nature: but they are not outside the Laws of the Universe, otherwise they would not occur.

In the Gospel, Jesus made these two statements: "Greater things than these you will do" and "If you had faith, you could move mountains". Other spiritual Masters have said and done similar things.

Any being from the nineteenth dimension upwards, according to the previous model or "map" –you may call them "angels", "archangels" or "immortal masters", or whatever you want, because how they are named is not going to change what they are and it does not matter to them— can, in the world of matter, perform much greater actions than turning water into wine or moving a mountain. When it comes down to it, whether it is water or wine depends on how the electron wave function "collapses".

The soul's evolution in the human kingdom does not end until it learns how to manipulate matter. That happens at approximately the sixth level of human consciousness, on the Schmedling scale. At that level of vibration, one has enough energy and information to manipulate matter. Until then, Consciousness collapses the electron for the person, so that they can have the appropriate experiences of destiny. Matter is not manipulated from matter, but from the subtle level. As with everything else, being able to "perform" miracles depends on the level of consciousness and its related vibratory frequency.

Miracles are not performed from the ego, and they are not personal. They occur when the miracle worker becomes one with the energy of the universal source and becomes the perfect instrument for that energy to transform matter. Miracles come from that source, not from the instrument. They occur "outside" the perception of the senses, and therefore they are not recognized, or they are discounted as "luck" or something fortuitous. However, there is scientific research into miracles such as those at Lourdes, the stigmata, the incorruptibility of the bodies of some saints and mystics, etc. Until now there was no context available in which to recognize them and understand them better. Carl Jung suggested the term "synchronicity" to refer to them. Being certain that they exist and surrendering to the Source appears to facilitate their manifestation (Lynne Mctaggart, *The Intention Experiment*).

The following paragraphs describe a possible context from which this may be better understood: when the level of consciousness is around 570 on the Hawkins scale —by way of attempting to place it at some approximate point which the human mind can understand—, many phenomena that cannot be explained through logic or cause and effect analysis, begin to occur. In some way they accompany the personal spiritual field, and occur more because of the field itself than by volition. In Sanskrit literature these are called *siddhis*, and they refer to mystical or supernatural powers that cannot be explained using linear logic.

These *siddhis* begin to appear sporadically but become more frequent as spiritual development increases, until eventually they are continuous. They can produce inexplicable transformations, physical healings and other similar phenomena. The *siddhis* are not under "personal" control; they are emanations of the spiritual field. The events are the manifestation of nonlinear power plus intention, which activates the linear potentiality.

With the increase in the level of consciousness, the miraculous becomes the new reality in which what, in appearance, is impossible manifests without effort, as though it were orchestrated.

This lets people change their mind about their actions. They learn to act by concentrating on the process and "letting the results go", which contributes enormously to remaining at peace. When taking action, only the process can be controlled: "Did I do my best? Was my intention pure? Did I prepare myself well? Did I use wisdom tools? This is all that we can do, and what determines whether or not our actions are within the Law and, therefore, help the person to evolve.

When it comes down to it, the results are always in the hands of the Absolute. It may happen that the individual acts with the intention of achieving an evolutionary change somewhere; but the Universe may need to delay that change to facilitate unfinished processes of evolution. Understanding this idea releases the person from frustration. It is therefore necessary to learn to act "letting the result go", that is to say, to act in peace. Whenever there is any intention to control the result of the action, it will come with a certain degree of anxiety.

Another aspect that helps growth is to act "as if"; if we want to be light, we must start to act as light does. Even if we have not yet achieved the inner level to which we aspire, acting "as if" that level has been achieved will make things much easier. When wondering what to do in a given situation, it helps to ask oneself: "What would Jesus, or Buddha, or Gandhi do in the same situation?" It is obvious that we are not them yet, and we should not feel guilty for not being able to act like them, but we can always ask ourselves that question. The answer will show us the work that is yet to be done, and will bring clarity to our mind.

In the Gita, when the battle of Kurukshetra began, Krishna said to Arjuna:

> "Let not the fruits of action be thy motive, neither let there be in thee any attachment to inaction."

When we are going to take action we should remember that there are two inner energy places from which we can do things: the place of "I choose to do them" and the place of "I have to do them". It is possible to ascertain quickly, in our own lives, that "I have to" expends a large amount of vital energy. It also produces an energy blockage at some level, as a result of which it will be more difficult to obtain good results. However, when we act from "I choose to do it" no energy will be expended and the results will be satisfactory, because we are acting from the energy place that flows with the Law.

When attempting to break habits or negative patterns, "I choose" is also much more helpful than "I have to". It takes a lot of energy to break away from these situations; otherwise, the force of gravity will win. Becoming accustomed to placing intention continually behind something will increase the possibilities of manifesting it, and as this becomes evident we will become more confident about continuing to do it.

Chapter 4. Everything that happens is perfect and necessary

As explained in the first part of the book, there is downward causation. It is worth remembering here the words of the Gospel: "Even the very hairs on your head are all numbered". We have also seen that every human being is a soul undergoing a learning process, and the operation of the Laws of the Universe has been set out.

A powerful idea may be derived from all of the above: everything that happens is "perfect and necessary" or else it would not happen since the higher dimensions do not make mistakes and they are efficient; however, this is true for the soul's evolution, and not necessarily for the ego's preferences. In fact, it may be said that all of the stress in a human being is caused by the divergence between the Universe's plan for each individual and whatever everyone devises for themselves.

Once we better understand how the Cosmos works, it is easy to realize that the Absolute's will is always going be fulfilled, while the human being's will is only going to be fulfilled when it is in line with the former. As such, being prepared to flow with God's will is not only a piece of spiritual or religious advice aimed at ensuring some reward after death, but rather, and in practice, the only intelligent way of living life. By flowing and accepting no life energy is spent, which leads to peace, which is the doorway into the higher faculties of consciousness.

But even accepting the idea that it is necessary to flow with the Laws of the Universe, it is worth asking: How can we know which plan is destined for each of us, that to which we must conform? Indeed, we don't get a telephone call to tell us. However, the answer to this question is easy with current knowledge: we just have to observe what is happening out there; that is the divine will.

By taking this idea further, we could develop a new science of acceptance, which could be called "Acceptology". On the pages that follow, we analyze the form that this could take.

4.1 Acceptance, reality and inner peace; the problem of suffering

The suffering, pain and anxiety that most Mankind experiences right now have been a constant in the different civilizations that have existed to date. Perhaps the response to the question of what causes such widespread suffering is simple: everyone struggles to adapt the reality of life to their own ideals, thereby failing to understand the function of the present reality.

Human beings always have a fundamental purpose: to find total satisfaction in their lives. This general purpose rests on one specific ideal, that each person develops in their personality and which, like a powerful inner force, drives them to work in their own interests or other people's interests, in line with their own ideal. Most people assume that, by fulfilling their desires and satisfying what they call their "needs", they can obtain satisfaction, happiness and peace in their lives. Yet the truth is that it will only help them to realize that, as soon as they achieve one goal, new challenges will immediately emerge. Their initial purpose will never be achieved in this way, because people still fail to realize that their particular ideals are contrary to their general purpose.

Some people seek to pursue their ideals through suffering and sacrifice for others, but they fail to put a stop to the pain, since there will always be people to suffer and make sacrifices for. Other people devote themselves to one of the many religions, philosophies and spiritual schools; however, the differences between them result in confusion, and they can often take any path as the only truth, denying the validity of the remaining options. Likewise, some people seek personal fulfillment through science, but they always find new unresolved problems and mysteries which science cannot explain. Other people try to achieve their goals through power, fame and money, although once they have obtained all of these, they discover that they have not achieved either the satisfaction or the peace that they were longing for. Another possible path is that of politics; nevertheless, it is riddled with heartache, disappointment and opponents. Finally, some people, driven by their inner ideal, attempt to change social structures, by fighting against injustice; however, this objective will never be satisfactorily achieved, since the differences between human beings and injustice will always exist, making the fight never-ending.

All of a human being's ideals are valid and necessary when it comes to establishing a reference which makes it possible to recognize universal order and the existence of the Universal Laws. But once we manage to understand how the Universe is organized, ideals turn into something obsolete, become an obstacle to inner peace and limit our ability to reach higher levels. They only lead to a fight against the Laws, and to a repeated confirmation of their existence.

For this reason, Acceptology (the "science" of acceptance) is a discipline aimed at people who do not need to develop the functions that were necessary and inevitable in the primitive levels of human civilization. It is the complement of wisdom, since just as Acceptology makes it possible to recognize the order of the Universe, wisdom makes it possible to monitor it, such that both together complete evolution.

Science is about knowing, about having knowledge of the world that is certain, well-founded, exact and reasoned; it is based on observation and experimentation of material phenomena, with the aim of discovering the immediate laws which govern them. It also uses hypotheses and theories, always based on real and irrefutable facts, which can be misleading in terms of their evaluation, but never in terms of their result. Acceptology wholly fulfills the parameters proposed by science as applied to the study of people's behaviour. It is a fact that when someone cannot accept something, the consequence is always inner conflict and suffering. It is not a belief, it is knowledge: it involves understanding exactly what the causes and motives of the human behaviour are, and how to obtain a specific result out of certain types of conduct.

Humans beings may decide to cease in their vain attempts to adapt reality to their own concepts and ideals (man's will) and can accept that the present reality fulfills a specific purpose (will of the Father). They may also accept that it is not they who modify reality, but the Law, and that this happens only when the present reality no longer fulfills the function of teaching human beings the Law of the Universe. Accepting the truth breaks the spell of suffering and liberates the energy for action, thereby generating a new reality.

External reality cannot be changed, because it exists due to its alignment with the interior of the individuals who experience it. However, when individuals change inside, they generate a new reality. This is achieved on understanding and accepting that the external reality is the result of the internal experience; when individuals decide to change that experience, the intention itself has an influence on the reality, transforming it.

Acceptance triggers an extraordinary process: accepting reality leads to permanent peace, liberates the individual from suffering, accumulates and increases life energy, and this all serves to activate the higher faculties. Suffering serves no practical purpose. The human being is here to grow in enjoyment, not in suffering. Suffering can be equated with fever: this is a sign of physical infection and suffering is a sign of an infection of the mind which manifests itself in something that the individual is failing to understand and accept, something that the individual is resisting; and we already know that whatever you resist, persists. Being happy does not require anything from the exterior, the only thing that is necessary is a specific understanding and inner mental attitude.

Yet people cannot develop internally without sharing their life experience with the world, with other people and with external situations, those which let them distinguish between the truth and falsehood; see what works and flows well with life and what hinders life and does not flow. This internal recognition of external situations is the tool for personal development, which is nothing more than constant interaction between internal individuality and external community.

A highly evolved being replaces ideals with the wisdom of the knowledge of the Laws that govern and organize the Universe. Idealizing implies not accepting reality, since if you accept it idealization is not necessary. We idealize something that is not present in reality; on the other hand, accepting means understanding that everything that happens is perfect and necessary.

Reality is here where we can experience it and act upon it. Consciousness can manifest itself in every dimension, and something can happen in all of them. Reality is that which happens in the place where the consciousness is present and we have the capacity to act.

Reality does not depend on the senses; rather it is entirely independent of the individual. It does not matter what he does, sees, thinks, understands or does not understand, since none of these elements modifies reality. Reality cannot be changed. However, what happens inside an individual when faced with reality can be modified.

This leads to two possible conclusions:

• Reality is independent of the individual.

• Reality cannot be changed. Yet what happens inside the individual with respect to reality *can* be changed.

One way that human beings spend or waste most energy is when fighting against reality, imagining that this is something different to what it is. A Master is absolutely immune to any external situation and no longer uses his free will, because he regards this as primitive and obsolete; it is a tool for making mistakes, and errors are necessary for recognizing Laws and developing inner wisdom. Yet a Master follows the Law to the letter and no longer needs his free will. Nevertheless, this does not mean that he has lost it, simply that he has decided to exercise his freedom to follow the will of the Absolute.

Anything that one cannot accept, be it the death of a loved one, a financial loss, a physical limitation or an illness, immediately generates suffering. This is a verifiable reality, it is not a belief.

When we are suffering in the face of any eventuality, it is a good idea to ask ourselves: What am I not accepting that is generating this suffering? The pain is directly proportional to whatever cannot be accepted and, furthermore, it does not modify anything externally, only our inner state.

Not being aware of reality prevents you from enjoying it. Instead of experiencing what is happening right now, sometimes the mind is somewhere else, so we don't make the most of what is happening around us, and yet we cannot act in that elsewhere either. Imagine you're attending a lecture, but you're worried about your son at school. You're not making the most of the reality taking place during the lecture, but you can't help your son because he's somewhere else, so worrying serves no purpose. As such, you would not be focused on reality.

Reality serves to show human beings what they have inside. Through this, people can experience inner transformations, change concepts and achieve acceptance, reaching a permanent state of inner peace. Reality shows us what we must learn and what we have already interiorized.

People can take three possible attitudes towards reality:

Suffering and fighting unsuccessfully: some people fight against life and try to find personal satisfaction by modifying the present reality in order to adjust it to suit their ideals. These are the most backward in spiritual terms, and they cannot stop suffering. They want to change external factors and fit them to their inner chaos, and the Law does not allow this.

Suffering and fighting successfully: people whose mission is to change the natural, social, economic, political, scientific, religious environment, etc. adopt this attitude. As it is their mission, they have the tools and ability to do it. Furthermore, this environment no longer corresponds with the people who live in it, it has been surpassed, and so must change. The price paid is high in suffering and in hostility. It is a process involving an external mission but it is not a spiritual success. It is not the path of a wise man.

Making the most of reality: some people accept reality as a great opportunity to overcome their inner limitations and find inner peace. They just try to modify their own interiors and know that this will lead them to experience new realities. If you have worked on yourself to reach a certain level of inner peace and harmony, you should no longer live in a troubled and tumultuous world. These individuals are the most advanced because they have transcended the lowest levels of evolution.

A wise man has already recognized the principles of the Universe and knows that external factors are only the result of his inner world, due to the Law of Correspondence. As such, he does not waste time trying to change what happens outside, as he knows that this will not bring peace. What he seeks is to facilitate evolution. In the world of relationships and in the outside world, the only thing that is needed is respect in order to achieve coexistence. The important thing is not to allow external situations to alter the peace.

The "science" of Acceptology can be summed up in two points:

• Maintaining inner peace, which generates a new reality.

• Acting within the realms of reality, the only place where you can act. This encourages firmness, peace and serenity. There is no need to suffer with reality, we must take advantage of it in order to achieve inner change.

The table below lists some of the symptoms which appear in cases of a lack of acceptance:

Table 1. Symptoms of lack of acceptance

ACKNOWLEDGEMENT	WHAT I AM NOT ACCEPTING
REJECTION OF LIFE	The learning opportunity offered by problems.
OVERPROTECTION	Everyone's mission and destiny experience.
PERFECTIONISM	The existence of different organization methods other than mine.
PREOCCUPATION	That I can lose something that I no longer need and that I cannot obtain something that I do not need.
FANATICISM	Different ways, paths, beliefs and options.
SHORT TEMPER	What other people do or say, or what is happening.
DISAPPROVAL	Behaviour and attitudes that are different to mine.
REBELLIOUSNESS	The need to adapt to my environment.
ANXIETY	That letting go of what I have, I can live another way.
SADNESS	Other people's experience and behaviour.
CRITICAL	Other people's customs, ideas and decisions.
RESENTMENT	That other people are not to blame for my own experiences.
JUDGMENT	That everyone does what they can, with what they know.
ATTACHMENT	That nothing and no one belongs to me and I always have what is necessary.
STRESS	That things can work out differently and not as I want them to do.
FEAR	The possibility of losing what I have, or not achieving what I want.
JEALOUSY	That I do not own anyone and only love can unite us.

ACKNOWLEDGEMENT	WHAT I AM NOT ACCEPTING
BLAME	That I am not to blame for other people's experiences, and they are not responsible for mine.

None of these symptoms of lack of acceptance modify external factors, they just complicate them. The problem with non-acceptance is exclusively internal to the human being, not external. Outside everything is designed with a specific purpose: that the human being understands the Law and his purpose in the Universe.

The lack of acceptance leads people to try and disorganize the educational models created by the Universe so that the human being can develop its permanent consciousness. For this reason, the need to learn acceptance as a fundamental part of the Laws of the Universe means that individuals face increasingly difficult situations, with a level of gravity proportional to the stubbornness, rebelliousness and disobedience displayed towards the Laws of life. As such, when individuals manage to accept in their minds the situations that seem hardest, these will cease to occur, since life no longer has anything to teach them.

If we look carefully at what has just been explained, something important becomes evident: the only thing that human beings really need to tackle is their own mind, own ego and own ignorance. The difficulties of life exist exclusively to transform ignorance into wisdom, and this takes place in the mind.

Nothing unpleasant, in the physical sense, can happen to someone who does a good job (the work of a wise man) and manages to accept everything that could cause them suffering in advance, except the extinction of their mortal body when they no longer need it; and that will not be a reason to suffer, but rather a reason for happiness (as shown by the examples of the Brother Francesc Castelló, Saint Paul, etc.).

Anyone who understands, accepts and obeys the will of the Father will be permanently free of all suffering because they no longer have anything to learn from it. As such, the best thing to do is to use free will to decide to be under the will of the Father. Making decisions is inevitable, but everyone can decide whether to follow the Father or their own will. When the individual's will falls in line with the Father's will, the Father's will is fulfilled; when the individual's will does not fall in line with the Father's will, the Father's will is also fulfilled. As such, decisions made using knowledge are based on recognition of the external reality and on the need to adapt and flow with this reality, not fight against it.

On the other hand, something is more readily accepted when we know the Law that governs it. Achieving deep acceptance entails having understood. The mind cannot accept something that it does not find logical. Firstly, one needs a deep understanding of the Laws which govern the Universe and the principles which organize human relationships; to know that everything that happens in the Universe is perfect and that it is managed and organized from divine wisdom; that everything that happens has a purpose of love, aimed specifically at the experience that every person needs to live.

Acceptance frees the human being from suffering, conflict and aggression; as well as from servitude, which is a mental situation that generates its equivalent in the exterior. Everyone has control over their mental processes; as such, if they do not liberate themselves, no one else can do it for them. Acceptance is the tool for achieving freedom. You cease to be a slave when you become an independent being, no matter what others say and do, free to make your own decisions and accept responsibility for the result, and free to respect what others say and do.

Acceptance also helps people to dispense with the bad habit of reproach. Reproach neither conveys wisdom nor offers any help, but rather expresses pride and anger and contributes towards others losing their peace after losing our own.

Life gives everyone the exact experience that they need; no more, no less. We have to make the most of this circumstance instead of looking for experiences that life does not offer because these are not necessary.

Situations of destiny are unavoidable; as such we must face them and transcend them. If we manage to avoid them it is because one of the following two alternatives is taking place:

• We no longer need them, because we have already accepted and are managing the situation with inner peace.

• Life enables us to postpone them until we are strong enough to tackle them.

If we have to experience a situation, we cannot step away from it even if we want to. As such, there is no other option but to accept it.

Acceptance is a very profound tool and it is based on a principle of elementary law: no one needs to sit an exam that they have already passed or do a test that they already know; nobody has to repeat an exercise that they know how to do, because it is a waste of time and the Universe is efficient

Acceptance is learning to set free, to let go. To let people go, to let life and possessions go and flow. Whatever does not need to happen, will not happen, and whatever needs to happen, will happen irrespective of what we do. Forecasting and planning are good, so long as we accept that these methods may fail or the results may vary. We have to practice letting go of our own agendas in order to accept the universal agenda. Decisions are essential, and we have to learn to decide and assume the consequences of our decisions, but handing over the control to Divinity.

On letting go of the fear of dying or losing what we have, the remaining symptoms of non-acceptance will fade away. A fear of loss is the basis of all anguish. We have to understand and accept the following:

I have nothing, and nothing belongs to me

I do not own anything or anyone

I administer what the Father gives me and

Everything I need will be with me.

By accepting this, we will free of all suffering, because fears, anguish, a quick temper and fights are no more than the fear of loss: of life, of others or material possessions. However, if we accept everything that happens, a quick temper will no longer have *a raison d'être*. If people knew how much life energy a quick temper uses up, everyone would think twice before getting angry, because it is a violent waste of energy. Meanwhile, if we could measure the value of life energy, most people would not needlessly waste it every day.

Anxiety comes from not accepting the possibility of something that has not happened, whilst suffering comes from not accepting something that has happened. In short, both are due to not accepting reality.

Throughout history, in all philosophical schools and in different religions, inner peace has always been considered to be a fundamental part of the development of spirituality. We constantly hear references to how to develop this quality internally so as to enable Love to manifest itself fully in all relationships between human beings. However, peace has another absolutely transcendental function, which is seldom spoken about, since it is only known by the Masters: its power to connect and awaken the higher faculties which lie dormant in the transcendental human consciousness. This consciousness is also called the *Cosmic or Mystical Consciousness*.

Inner peace is, then, a very powerful tool for awakening to the transcendence of the spirit.

4.2 Life energy and light zone

Inside every person there is an energy form with special characteristics, called "life energy", which is used in all human functions associated with thoughts, feelings and emotions. Life energy is produced in the body by refining glucose, especially during periods of mental rest, such as sleep or meditation. When life energy rises to the mental zone of light, it lets human beings connect with their higher faculties. Yet very few people manage to achieve this state, because they have permanent states of inner mental, sentimental or emotional conflict, which use up huge amounts of life energy. Furthermore, through fear, attachments and the tendency to become involved in unnecessary experiences, needlessly relinquish their life energy. So it is easy to conclude that the great hidden power of peace is precisely the ability to avoid pointlessly wasting this precious energy that turns humans into Wise men, Masters and Saints.

Life energy is extremely precious; it is the biggest treasure that exists within the human being. Often it is not valued properly because we do not even know how to use it, but it is too precious to waste on worrying about anything that we cannot change. Most people are not mentally healthy, since they act from twilight areas. However, they consider this to be "normal". Yet for someone who is in the light zone, these people are mentally ill. The symptoms of illness are as listed in the first column of the previous table. Suffering wastes life energy and causes the mind to enter darker areas; on the other hand, inner peace generates life energy and causes the mind to enter areas of light.

Properly managing the higher faculties entails great spiritual development, which is linked to extending understanding until a profound understanding is reached. Ignorance leads human beings to think that they only have five senses and that there are no further dimensions beyond the third.

The highest level of life energy is light, and this is an area of understanding or mental clarity; the medium area (twilight) is where we find people's systems of beliefs, also called ignorance; and in the lower area (darkness) it is depressing. Peace serves to boost life energy. Depending on how inner peace is handled, people can spend huge amounts of life energy, or keep it to a minimum. If they keep their peace at a constant level, they hardly spend any life energy. It is not the physical body, including the brain, that uses up most life energy, but the emotions and feelings.

As such, whilst someone remains at the mental level of feelings and at the instinctive level of emotion, they will spend huge amounts of energy and will oscillate within the "normal" twilight area. On the other hand, the normal area of the Masters is the light zone. When life energy permanently reaches this zone, what appears is what is known as "the halo", a golden projection around the head; it is golden because the energy of Love is golden in essence, and it is projected beyond the brain as an external emanation.

A Spiritual Master manages a very high level of life energy and succeeds in connecting his higher faculties. As such, Masters and Saints have outstanding abilities compared to other people. How do they reach this process? By means of the power of their inner peace. This is not the peace obtained from isolation, which is temporary peace. When something gets out of hand and we don't know how to manage it, a good solution is to isolate ourselves. Since we are human beings, it is normal for this to happen, and most of us find this exercise necessary and useful. Yet a Master does not need to do it, because he is unchanging, invulnerable and unoffendable.

One of the great secrets for starting to access the "awakening of the consciousness" is managing life energy. The Masters are such more as a result of the energy that they manage than for the wisdom that they possess. However, much wisdom a person may have, if they fail to manage their life energy, they will have no chance of using it.

4.3 Life energy, inner peace and understanding

Spirituality is the process and practice of personal transformation and is manifested in the ability to manage situations without losing inner peace. It is also known as *spiritual development* because both the personality archive or *temporary consciousness*, and the *permanent consciousness* or consciousness archive, form part of the spirit, not the physical matter. The personality archive develops as the capacity for conscious comprehension —which each individual uses here and now— increases, whilst the permanent consciousness archive assimilates all of the comprehension that a person has amassed in their temporary

264

consciousness following the death of the physical body. The temporary archive lives the experiences that are subsequently assimilated by the permanent archive. Both develop simultaneously.

Peace is the same as the absence of suffering or conflict. It is the result of acceptance. It is a neutral state inside a person; it is not even a state of happiness or euphoria, since these are characteristics of feelings or emotions. With inner peace one can voluntarily decide to experience any sentimental state, and this no longer happens automatically or subconsciously. Spiritual development begins when we refuse to get flustered by life events.

Irrespective of culture, social or economic condition and where they live, all human beings are performing the same exercise of developing inner peace. It is a universal exercise, although it is not carried out in the same circumstances, nor does it fulfill the same function for everyone.

Action is another of Love's tools, and is an external process, just like respect. Suffering does not make actions better, and wisdom is neither suffering nor satisfaction, but rather involves doing the right, appropriate thing in each situation, and doing it in peace.

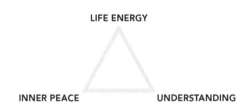

Figure 4. The magic of Love

The magic of Love is represented inside a simple triangle in which understanding generates inner peace, inner peace generates life energy, and life energy activates

265

greater understanding. It is a process of continual movement.

If any of the three elements is missing from this triad, the balance represented in the triangle no longer exists. If we lack understanding, we cannot have peace; if we lack inner peace, we cannot have great life energy; and if we lack energy, we can neither use nor increase our understanding, even if we have it. The three elements complement each other perfectly.

Looking for external peace serves no purpose. Until someone finds their inner peace, they have no chance of finding external peace. On the other hand, someone who has inner peace will find peace around them.

There is a story that illustrates this point:

Long ago, there was an oasis in the desert which was a routine port of call for caravans and travelers, and also where a wise old man lived. On one occasion, a traveler wanted to know what the people from the city on the other side of the desert were like, and the wise man asked him in turn: "What are the people in your city like?" The traveler answered that they were aggressive and unpleasant, and the wise man told him that the inhabitants of the city on the other side were just the same. A few days later, another traveler passed through the oasis and asked the wise man the same question, and he responded with the identical question, to which the traveler replied: "In my city, everyone is kind and calm". The wise man told him that in the city on the other side of the desert the people were also kind and calm. He knew that every traveler would find at his destination what he carried inside him.

There are two levels of peace that everyone may recognize inside themselves:

• **Temporary peace:** is what people recognize when they isolate themselves from situations that they cannot manage in order to prevent their life energy level from descending into areas of darkness.

• **Permanent peace:** is achieved when people are composed, invulnerable and unoffendable; when they have reached the level of mastery and do not need to isolate themselves because they are skilled and do not let any external situations disrupt their peace.

On the other hand, there are several pairs of concepts that must be analyzed:

Firstly, the difference between **faith** and **acceptance:** both manage the same archive, except that faith connects with it through absolute belief, whilst acceptance does so through recognition of the Law. In other respects, they act the same way.

Also,, the difference between **goodness** and **badness:** errors due to ignorance are known as badness, and good actions and decisions, as goodness; but both originate in ignorance.

Deep acceptance arises out of understanding the perfection of the organization of the Universe. The Father does not make mistakes; as such, if something is judged to be incorrect or inadequate it is because people are looking on from a standpoint of ignorance. "Everything that happens is perfect"; in other words, nothing happens that is not perfect. As such, when people have difficulties it is because they have failed to recognize this perfection and they are fighting it.

Throughout history, human beings have unsuccessfully tested many political, religious and social methods and systems; in addition to all kinds of prayers, exercises, practices and meditations, in order to try and achieve peace between nations and a harmonious coexistence between all of the people on Earth. However, to date we have not found the formula. Peace, like Love and all of the principles of the Universal Essence, calls for a deep internal understanding by every individual, born out of their own experience in the quest for truth. That is why peace is something that cannot be imposed; on the contrary, it is born inside each individual and projected outwards, to everything that surrounds them.

Peace is not achieved by fighting against evil, or by trying to impose good, but instead is the result of integrating conflicting extremes and not of eliminating any of them.

To say that "I am fighting for peace" is really incoherent. How are we going to fight for peace if fighting itself is not peace? The right thing to say would be that you are working for peace, and that this is internal work. Start to working for peace involves understanding that peace can only be achieved by those who spend time working on themselves and not on others. Achieving it entails establishing an education system for peace which begins at a very early age. So parents and everyone involved with education need to act and behave in a truly calm manner, underpinned by a deep understanding of Love and of the Laws that govern the Universe.

We frequently hear of certain people who have a special ability, both for managing different situations in life and for demonstrating a deep understanding of everything that happens around them. These people are usually referred to as Masters of Wisdom. People who know them say that these Masters are unoffendable, invulnerable, unflappable and unchanging, which is absolutely true. However, to reach a state of mastery, the person who has reached it had to deal with all of the necessary life experiences in order to develop a constant inner peace. This means that everyone can become a Master if they decide to make the most of the experiences that life offers them; because if the peace they possess is the result of not facing up to situations which involve conflict, it is not true peace.

Developing the ability to constantly maintain inner peace without allowing anything or anyone to disrupt it entails consciously training to make the most of all of the circumstances which life presents every day, but without searching for unnecessary circumstances. When we manage to understand that every situation that poses a certain level of difficulty, be it for the mind, feelings, emotions, or to control our instinctive reactions, is a marvelous opportunity to learn and practice cultivating inner peace, we will be ready to apply acceptance and renunciation, and free ourselves of mental conflict and inner suffering. As such, when faced with any situation involving mental confrontation, we have to accept that it is only a process of the Laws of Correspondence and Evolution, and refuse to try and change it and involve our own concepts, beliefs, feelings and emotions. Do what you have to do calmly and serenely and never react. Take action!

People who have inner peace, will never again experience situations which could be described as "hell" or within the lower triangle of the Laws of the Universe; because once a person has done the work required to take control of their own inner peace, they just have to experience situations described as "heaven" or within the upper triangle of the Laws of the Universe.

Love and peace are two elements which are absolutely connected. Anything that goes against peace is not a tool of Love, because the latter will always give rise to a peaceful result. The divine purpose is that people learn to build their inner peace.

As we have said before, everything that happens in the Universe is necessary; and if something is necessary, it is important that it happens; if it is important, it means that it has a value; and if it has a value, it is possible to see Love in that situation, and thus it will have been understood. The next task is training, which involves desensitizing our own feelings, neutralizing whatever we find unpleasant and seeing it through an understanding of Love. As such, to maintain inner peace, first we will need to prepare to resist the onslaught of ignorance, which will attack us with expressions such as indolent, resigned, indifferent, insensitive, bad, hard-hearted, lacking personality, conformist, subservient, etc.

Setting out on the path to understanding and acceptance is to get to the heart of the science that frees us from suffering, because suffering is absolutely pointless. However, everything that exists in the Universe fulfills an important function. What is, then, the function of suffering?

Suffering is a tool for the evolution of consciousness, and it fulfills three important functions:

• Preventing the evolution of the consciousness from slowing down.

• Measuring the level of individual ignorance.

• Facilitating the recognition of the truth.

"The truth will set you free" is a saying that makes a lot of sense; but, free from what? From everything, suffering too.

Another important question is: are we guilty of original ignorance? Are we condemned to death?

According to traditional teachings, human beings seem to be guilty of something, and to have a sentence to serve. Nevertheless, two things may be said: that nobody is guilty, and that, despite this, liberation and salvation do exist. This is true because both ignorance and suffering and death are necessary for the development of understanding and the assimilation of the truth by our consciousness. Yet when the truth is completed in the consciousness, suffering is no longer necessary; neither is being imprisoned in a physical body.

According to the Law of Nature, everything that is born dies; in other words, everybody who is born must die. Nevertheless, the matter from which bodies are composed is indestructible. Death only represents a permanent process of the Universe, in which matter is constantly organized and disorganized. What really gives life to matter is the spirit. Death only applies to the temporary part of the spirit. Truth and Love save us from death.

The Spirit of the human being is formed by two elements or archives: the **temporary consciousness** and the **permanent consciousness,** as we said above.

The **temporary consciousness,** also known as the mind, ego or personality, is composed of two parts: ignorance (such as everything that we inevitably learn) and understanding (such as everything that can be verified).

The **permanent consciousness,** also known as the Christic Being, is also composed of two parts: innocence (such as the space to be filled by the truth), and purity (such as the truth of Love and law accumulated through life).

Both consciousness, temporary and permanent, cannot be awake at the same time whilst the ego exists. When the permanent consciousness awakes, it does so to assimilate the information that is in the personality; whilst a certain level of contamination is present, the consciousness will need to sleep in order to avoid becoming contaminated. When the archives have been totally dissolved from the fifth dimension down, what remains in the mental realm is understanding, which is what the consciousness will assimilate. Whilst the personality does its job of verifying the ignorance and discovering the Laws, the consciousness sleeps calmly, rests peacefully; sleeps a timeless sleep, in a high spiritual dimension, where time means nothing.

Returning to a previous concept, acceptance frees people of any limitation associated with the contamination of the temporary part of the spirit, such as suffering, egoism, ignorance, wars, battles, anguish and fears. A personality that has been cleansed by understanding and acceptance will no longer die, because it has been reborn in life. This is called "the resurrection of the dead". Understanding the truth will save us from all processes associated with matter and nature.

The word sin, etymologically speaking, means "error", missing the mark, going against reason. The error does not imply a sense of guilt, but rather of learning. When we talk about guilt, in reality we are referring to ignorance. Innocence becomes ignorance with the information that it receives from culture; whilst ignorance becomes wisdom with verified understanding.

When someone does something that does not work well, really they are making a mistake. No human being or animal makes a mistake with the intention of being wrong. When we say: "He knew the damage he was going to do", it is just an assumption made by the observer, because it is not true. When someone causes damage, he really believes that this is appropriate and correct. Even somebody who kills someone else believes that it is the best option, although they are making a mistake.

An error is not merely a small mistake. It is an error committed with more or less interior freedom but with some degree of it. We might or might not learn from it, but if we don't, we will make it again. From the mystic consciousness, it is easy to see that responsibility exists but not guilt, because guilt is a low frequency energy and hampers spiritual growth. This is more a physical matter than a moral one. Furthermore, if I blame myself I will also blame others and we all know what happens in human relations when we do that, as will be explained in chapter 7.

Any error or act against the Law of the Universe must lead us to acknowledge it. In other words, a form of repentance without guilt or, to put it another way, repentance with positive guilt that transforms us but without negative guilt that self-destructs, because if we don't see it, we can't learn from it. We should also generate inside us an intense desire to learn from and transcend errors. Human beings are responsible for their errors because, apart from affecting themselves, they affect the whole universe through quantum entanglement.

In any case it is important to avoid errors because we cannot avoid the consequences. You can decide what to sow but not what to reap.

People make mistakes because they do not have enough information or what they do have is false. As such, they need to learn what they do not know. Badness does not exist, only ignorance, and ignorant people need to be taught, not punished. "Father forgive them, for they do not know what they are doing" were the words of Jesus on the cross. He could have said: "Forgive them, because they are bad, but even so we must forgive them", but he did not say that.

We are condemned to death, but to the death of our ego. Ideally, we would die from instant to instant, and that means being born from instant to instant, because every time a false belief dies, an immortal truth is born inside us. Day by day people are becoming immortal to the extent that "what they are not" is dying. This is the process of spiritual development.

The ego is the only thing that is concerned with what is not important. The extent to which each person uses the ego is what makes them dead, because it is focused on the mortal part of themselves. On the other hand, as the ego is cleansed, wisdom will manifest itself (or understanding), and this is when the dead are resurrected, when the awakening occurs.

In the **permanent consciousness** there is no ignorance, only innocence (absence of information) or wisdom. Ignorance dissolves through death. As such, whilst we display ignorance death is necessary; but in the absence of ignorance there is no death.

The only mortal component of a human being is the personality and the physical body, everything else is immortal. Yet even this mortal part, when it achieves truth and Love, also becomes immortal. The personality is immortalized as the ego is liberated. As such, when it is completely liberated, the light of consciousness appears: this is called "being reborn or illuminated". The exercise in which a person gradually places part of their ego in the comprehension archive (which verifies), and finally lets go of what brings them suffering (because it is revealed to be false), ends up completely cleansing the mental realm. That person frees themself without dying. From that moment onwards, the person is free of the need to be reborn and die again. Nothing is impossible, everything can be done. The only thing that cannot be done is that which goes against the Law of the Universe.

Understanding is immortal because the truths of the Universe will always be immortal. Understanding is part of the mental realm, but it is immortal because it is assimilated by the permanent consciousness.

4.4 The power of renunciation; learn to let go and relinquish our own agenda

Nowadays, renunciation is a technique that is applied in psychology to help people to overcome various mental conflicts, such as anguish, stress and a state of panic, or emotional and sentimental crises. Yet achieving this no longer involves seeking refuge in a monastery or escaping from the world.

Meanwhile, acceptance is a mental training technique rooted in philosophical knowledge and in an understanding of real life, and can be practiced as part of everyday life.

The power of renunciation, of letting go or of setting free, is far superior to that of psychotherapy. The latter aims to reset the ego so that it has greater balance, whilst the purpose of renunciation is the elimination of all emotional and mental limitations in order to achieve peace and access the higher faculties.

Integrating renunciation with acceptance results in absolute spiritual peace. Renunciation unblocks the mind and life flows; and if this is not the case it is because the individual has not renounced and has not accepted what life is and what it offers.

Ceasing to insist lets us see other options. What happens is similar to the moth that keeps on trying to fly through a window pane: it cannot see there is another way to get to the garden.

These are just some renunciations that boost spiritual growth:

RENOUNCE:
Forbidding others to do what they need to do to learn.
Imposing one's own beliefs, reasons or truths.
Condemning other people's attitudes or behaviours.
Protesting when things do not turn out as we want.
Answering back when faced with anything we do not agree with.
Performing duties which are no longer our responsibility.
Doing justice for what happens to us or to others. The Universe will take care of it.
Being offended by what others say or do.
Everything that could disrupt inner peace.
Forcing people to be with someone.
Trying to lay the blame for things that happen.
Objecting to the reality of life.
Suffering for things that cannot be changed.
Becoming anxious about things we cannot control.
Fighting to achieve things we do not need.
Suffering about things we cannot do.
Hurting anyone for any reason.
Defending what you believe to be right.
Worrying about what you don't know.
Suffering for what might happen.
Trying to find out who hurt you.

Allowing others to decide for you.
Worrying about loved ones.
Holding on to what you don't need.
Criticizing anyone or anything.
Ego and pride.

Renunciation must not be misinterpreted; there is no need to renounce whatever befalls you in life: one's duties and activities.

Everybody's peace is the result of renouncing everything that does not befall them. Until they do, they will not achieve peace. In conclusion, and very simply, the power of renunciation works as follows:

Renounce changing other people's reality.
Change your own reality by means of Accep-
tology.
Show others how to change their reality after
verifying that they are accordant with this in-
formation.

The differences between some concepts are outlined below:

Indifference/renunciation:

Indifference is a level of ignorance without feelings; **renunciation** through wisdom is a level of mastery of Love.

When we recognize that everyone is living their own experience, that there is no reason to live someone else's experience, and that this is a perfect process for developing Love in everyone, we are no longer indifferent but wise; and this wisdom leads us not to intervene inappropriately, but rather to simply offer to be of service.

Indifferent people do not care about other people's experience, whilst the wise person cares, but does not interfere, and instead supports it. How? By giving the information that people need to overcome their own difficulties. The wise do not give information to anyone who does not ask for it.

Resignation/Acceptance/Renunciation:

If **renunciation** is not combined with **acceptance,** in other words, with understanding, then it becomes **resignation** and peace is not found. Acceptance is a deep understanding and renunciation is giving up anything that is not yours. That way, you are free of suffering, guilt and resentment. If you are resigned, you continue to suffer in silence and maintain the level of ignorance inside you.

There is no way that understanding can be indifferent, neither can acceptance be resignation. Understanding can never contradict the Laws of the Universe that we already comprehend, nor will it ever descend into the resignation of he who believes himself to be powerless and incapable in life. Resignation leaves a constant frustration in the mind; it is the refuge of ignorance, the dark cave of the mind that is tired of fighting to no avail in order to adapt life to its own beliefs. Anyone who has descended into resignation feels a great powerlessness when faced with the circumstances of life and feels incapable of fighting any longer. However, when they stop fighting, even out of resignation, they get the chance to partly recover their life energy. This recovery could, eventually, lead them to understand that it matters more to have inner peace than to fight. Consequently, at some point the light of understanding will enter their mind and they will realize that the path to liberation from suffering does not involve fighting against life to try and change reality, but rather consists of changing the internal perception of life. Then they will have overcome the limitation of resignation and can set out on the path to acceptance, as the science that frees us from suffering.

4.5 Freedom, respect and desensitization

In order to develop understanding, these three words are fundamental. **Freedom** is inside the human being. **Respect** is an external tool: respect for others in their concepts, in their decisions, in the path they are on in their lives, and in what they wish to practice, do and not do.

Freedom and respect are related in the same way as understanding and peace: if someone is not internally free, they cannot respect anyone. People are not free when they depend on what others say or do in order to feel in peace. When this is the case, people try to change others in order to feel good, thereby acting outside the Law.

If we fail to understand that the experience of every person is neither good nor bad, but simply necessary; if we fail to understand that good and bad do not exist, rather that they are necessary elements and that, as such, people are neither good nor bad, but they can get things right or make mistakes; then we are not free, because we judge and condemn others. This judgment means that we are not respecting them, and that is true because we depend on them in order to achieve inner peace.

Hence the importance of distinguishing between **judging** and **discerning.** By judging we incorporate a specific emotional burden and generate aversion; by discerning or differentiating we observe what is happening, but without this emotional burden. Discernment avoids descending into relativism, without the need to judge. Furthermore, it increases the ability to serve, because it is difficult to help that which generates aversion.

Unless we "desensitize" feelings, the life energy spent is significant. **Desensitization** is not the same as insensitiveness, but the opposite. In order not to feel "bad" it is necessary to understand that Love is not a feeling, that it is superior to any feeling because it is a deep understanding. As such it is unchangeable, which would not be the case were it a feeling. Feelings are an obstacle to achieving Universal Love. It is important to understand this idea.

As such, a desensitized person, is not insensitive. The latter, the "bad guy", does not care about what happens to others and does not suffer. He is relying on instinct. The sensitive person, or "good guy", cares a lot about others and suffers for everything. The Master, the desensitized person, is someone who cares about others but does not suffer.

There is a mental duality that must be deconstructed, for there are several false ideas that are commonly accepted: that to be good we must suffer with the suffering of others, and that not suffering, or being in peace, means that you are bad. It is important to clarify the concepts and change these equivalents, assuming that not suffering is good and suffering is terrible. Saints, Masters, highly-evolved beings, never lose their peace, they are always in a state of equilibrium. Amongst other reasons because their function is to serve, and you cannot serve properly when you are suffering, because you lose mental clarity.

Goodness and badness are characteristics of the mind, which interprets what is happening around us, but they are not the reality of life; that is something else. As has already been said, everything that happens in the Universe is a necessary process and has a purpose of Love or learning. There is nothing good or bad, rather everything is necessary, which is an absolutely neutral term. The concept of good and bad serves no purpose, because what is necessary will always be important and will always have a purpose of Love. Bad only exists in the mind of the human being.

It is fundamental not to confuse pleasant and unpleasant sensations with good and bad. This distinction is important in order to deconstruct the mental program of suffering. Otherwise, it is impossible to do it.

In the evolution of spiritual development, firstly we use tools of instinct (the insensitive) and then those of feeling (the sensitive). Reaching the next state implies using tools of wisdom (the desensitized). Harmony and inner peace are tools of Love and enter the territory of neutrality, not duality. Everything that happens externally is a neutral event, since life events are neither good nor bad, they do not even have a positive or negative charge; they are simply necessary events. What has a positive or negative charge is the mind of the individual observing the event; this will classify it as good or bad depending on its sensations, and that is where the mistake lies. This is precisely what the Master does not do; he does not classify things in any way, he simply observes them, understands the reason why they happen, knows that they are necessary and respects them; that way he enters in a state of peace. In order to be able to do so, he needs to reach the third level of development of feelings, that is to say, to be a desensitized being.

The desensitized person has many more resources to serve others than the sensitive person. The latter has less means to serve because he exhausts his life energy suffering, just as he exhausts his external resources; as such, he loses the two tools for serving. The sensitive person escapes, suppresses or expresses his negative emotions, instead of observing them and transcending them.

When feelings are involuntary, that is spontaneous and automatic, they are totally subject to duality. There is a situation that seems pleasant or desirable and a very positive feeling develops. On the other hand, if an event takes place that is judged to be unfair or limiting, the feelings immediately become negative and aggressive. When feelings are "in automatic mode" they are a problem, because the mind is like a tennis ball: it goes from one side to the other and cannot be controlled.

When someone has managed to desensitize themselves and has taken control of their thoughts, they can voluntarily generate feelings; and no one would choose to voluntarily generate negative feelings, since they are inappropriate for action. Affection is the only feeling that does not have polarity, which is why it is what is closest to Love; but unlike Love, it still requires an object on which to project itself.

"Desensitize" means that our feelings cannot be hurt. The problem is not that others hurt us, but that human beings are susceptible to being hurt. As such, an insult should not be interpreted as an intention to cause hurt, but rather as an ignorant communication. When faced with an insult, the wise man thinks the following: "This person has the right to have an opinion about me; it is unfortunate that someone has an opinion that causes him bad feelings. I am no different to what I am in my divine essence, I am where I am in my evolutionary process; only the Universe knows that". Meanwhile, when given praise he might think: "Everyone has the right to have an opinion about me; it is wonderful that someone has an opinion that causes him good feelings. This has nothing to do with me but with him, I am no different to what I am in my divine essence and this does not change as a result of the opinions that others have of me". That is how freedom is achieved.

Training for imperturbability makes it possible to develop the maximum potential for Love, since it would be difficult to help someone unconditionally when you are not comfortable with them. If you are full of anger, hatred or resentment towards someone, will this feeling let you be of service to them? The answer is no. As such, this hatred works against us.

When the Master Jesus was asked: "What is Love?" he replied: "It is to love our enemies, bless those who persecute and slander us". That would be the true sense of Love. To help those that are unconditionally supportive is logical and easy, but this is not a virtue, it is normal.

Another important distinction that must be understood is the difference between Love and affection. Often both words are used as if they meant the same, which is another obstacle to reaching Universal Love. On hearing the Gospel teaching: "Love thy neighbor as thyself", many people soon give up before even trying it, because they think that it will be impossible to feel the same affection for everyone as they feel for their children, for example.

The difference between Love and affection is clear: affection needs an object on which to project itself, it is a variable sentiment and always starts with the word "my" or "mine" (I love my children, my country, my football team, my political party, etc.). Love is not a feeling, but rather an understanding that does not need an object on which to project itself and, as such, it is not variable. Affection can appear and disappear depending, amongst other things, on the behaviour of the person or people in which it is invested. The Gospel teaching was not referring to affection, but to Love.

If following an aggression by someone we understand that it is the aggressor who is making a mistake and we offer him our hand, that is Love. However, this cannot be done from a state of feeling, given that it has not been designed for that. The capacity to love and serve of he who desensitizes feeling is much higher than the capacity to serve of a sensitive person.

Once this training has been done, the true information is reinforced inside people; in other words, a self-transformation takes place: the truth is consolidated and it becomes normal behaviour. From this moment, the process called **spiritual awakening** or **spiritual ascension** begins, because an increase in the inner vibratory energy takes place; we cease to spend energy on suffering and pointless battles, and the deep process of "awakening" begins.

The objective is to reach a mental state that is known as "I am". I am the manager of my thoughts, I am the manager of my decisions, of my peace, of everything I do, and I am free to love and respect everyone else. I am spiritually free, my inner peace does not depend on the praise or criticism of others, or on their decisions, or on what is or is not happening.

If we ever notice someone rather aggressive near us, the first thing we should realize is that such people are meant for us, to foster our internal growth, so we can use them as an opportunity for spiritual training. Overcoming an internal difficulty entails facing up to someone who displays that same difficulty. As such, anyone around us who act in a way that makes others feel bad, also display their limitations and are perfect trainers for learning.

In order to face up to a situation we must first verify that it is destiny, and thereby not impose obligations in a masochistic way. The situations of destiny that everyone must face are easy to recognize because they cannot be avoided. There is no need to look for suffering; if it can be avoided, you avoid it. If not, it is part of learning and you must take advantage of it.

Chapter 5. Changing our thinking

Thought can be defined as a frequency waveform with a dimensional variable which we produce or perceive mentally and spiritually. Thought waves are a channel of dimensional transmission that carries information about the Universe, which is why thought joins all levels of manifestation in the Universe from the Absolute Unmanifest to the densest matter.

All the information in the Universe is deposited in what is termed the Absolute Unmanifest. Thought is the messenger of this information. Creation occurs when the information which emanates from the Absolute, through thought, comes into contact with the great cosmic ocean of elementary particles. This is what the Bible means when it says: "In the beginning was the Word, and the Word was with God, and the Word became flesh". In this context, the **Word** is the thought wave which emanates from the Absolute, and the **flesh** is the organized matter. It should be remembered that the great cosmic ocean of elementary particles is also an emanation of the Absolute.

Thought is one of the most powerful tools which the Father has provided for human beings. It is the instrument of Creation, the one used by the Father to make everything that exists. Human beings have also been granted the power to think; to direct their thought both outwards and inwards, sending and receiving. So, we can say that human beings possess the basic condition of creators: the ability to think, to perceive, to bring information and apply that information to matter.

Thought waves behave the same way as any other transmission wave but they have a characteristic which no other wave has: the dimensional variable. They can alter their speed of propagation and their vibrational frequency instantaneously to cover any dimension in the Universe.

The main transmission wave variables are **velocity of propagation** and **intensity of vibration. Thought waves** have a unique feature which differentiate them from any other type of wave –for instance, sound or light– and this is that their speed of propagation is infinite; i.e. they take the same amount of time to travel from here to the Andromeda galaxy and back as they take to travel from one side of a room to the other. More detailed information can be found on this in Chapter 3, here in Part II.

If someone decides to pay serious attention to their spiritual growth, once they grasp that this is the only reason why human beings are on Earth, they will realize the importance of thoughts in this process.

Changing our thought, or the "alchemy" of thought, is another spiritual science through which we can also change our attitude, character and behaviour by altering our thoughts. In addition, the results which we identify with also change. Again, as with everything which concerns the New Paradigm, this is a question of making an internal change in order for external changes to happen.

The first step in this **change in thinking** is to alter our own view of the structure and processes of the Universe. This issue was widely discussed in the first part of this book, so we will not dwell on it at this point. We should simply remember that it will be very helpful in this process to give up a materialistic and fragmented view of the Cosmos, which quite possibly almost everyone has been brought up on, to understand that the Universe has "intelligence" and "purpose". This purpose is creative evolution. It is also necessary to understand that human beings are spiritual beings who are living through a growing experience in the physical world, not physical beings going through a spiritual experience.

It is essential to be aware of the fact that resistance to change is common, even if that change is for the better; this is the case because change involves restructuring our minds, which in turn involves working through an internal process. Throughout its development, Mankind has undergone few changes in the structure of the mind. The history of human beings has always been full of conflict, due to the fact that information is transmitted from one mind to another from adult to innocent containig within it a code of ignorance and conflict. At some point these codes need to be broken.

All information is contained in the archives of the Universe, and this is where we have to go and look for it. The human mind can access it through lines of thought. The original source of the information is perfect, however, as it is passed on, it becomes corrupted. Therefore, it is essential to verify the truth of the information; this constitutes the exercise of **verifying results,** which is different from **transmitting information.**

All information produces a result. As is often quoted: "Ye shall know them by their fruits". By observing the result it is possible to assess what information has been used. If the results are unsatisfactory this means that the information used was false and not the "truth".

The lack of correct information can turn the mind into an obstacle for growth. This is borne out by any of the Gospel's teachings: "If you are offended or attacked, turn the other cheek". If we asked believers how they experience this teaching, many would answer along the lines of, 'Well, you know, it's a nice idea but in real life if you do that they can hurt you". Obviously, if you have a materialistic view of the Cosmos, that is a logical view. However, if someone has a spiritual view of life, and knows how the Laws work, they will quickly realize that "not turning the other cheek" has no practical use; it is just the opposite. If you do not want them to hurt you, you have to be willing to turn the other cheek, as suggested by the Gospel. Why? Because you have understood how the Universal Law of Correspondence works; and you will know, therefore, that the lesson does not appear if you have already understood what it can teach you. Consequently, the best way to avoid being attacked is to be willing to turn the other cheek; i.e. not respond aggressively but act calmly and with understanding, to prevent any more aggression. The same analysis could be made with many other teachings which most people have had difficulty in understanding because their mind did not understand the pragmatism and wisdom they contained.

The secret of changing our thinking lies in learning to sustain voluntary thoughts, focused and supported with sufficient intensity. We need to understand that we feel as we think and, therefore, if we want to feel better, we must learn to think better. For example:

> *You have arranged to have coffee with a friend to ask for advice, and he fails to turn up at the appointed time. Your thoughts can take two directions: if you think he's irresponsible, has no consideration for your time and doesn't care about your problem, you'll probably feel bad. Yet if, in the same circumstances, you think he's good and responsible, and that he's bound to have been held up by something unexpected, which he'll explain to you later, you'll most likely feel better. The fact is the same —your friend did not turn up— but your state of mind will be different, depending on how you think about it.*

Anyone can see how very often thoughts come into our mind which we have not put there voluntarily. The mind is like a recipient which continuously captures thoughts which are around us but are not our own. In fact, every mind tends to "receive" ideas which match the vibration of their level of consciousness. It would be easy to see what kind of thoughts enter the mind of a violent criminal, for example, and compare them with those which enter a more developed mind.

Thoughts are "things" –like a table, for instance– but they are things which affect other things. As they vibrate at a higher frequency than matter, we cannot see or touch them. However, they exist, only in dimensions which have a higher vibration.

When we allow thoughts at a low vibration (cumbersome, negative thoughts) to take root in our mind, we cannot escape from their by-product, which is an uneasy feeling inside. This occurs when thoughts of hatred, resentment, violence, revenge, separation, fear, etc. arise. However, when the mind turns to thoughts at a higher vibration (light, positive ones), the internal feeling is very satisfying. This happens when we produce thoughts of love, generosity, service, peace of mind, altruism, joy, etc.

Therefore, the wise have always said that "the quality of your life will be the quality of your thoughts".

Unlike what culture teaches us, the cause and effect relationship in the Universe is not an upward but a downward movement, i.e. it goes from the dimensions with the highest vibration down to the lowest. Thoughts vibrate at a higher level than the brain, so it is critical to understand that thoughts have the power to influence the physical structure of the brain itself.

As an example, consider what happens when someone gets a "depression". According to the old paradigm the explanation is simple: depression is a disease which damages the brain's chemistry, and this causes a series of negative, circular thoughts which the individual cannot escape from (upward causation). So the right approach is to use drugs that will get the brain's chemistry working again. This paradigm does not take into consideration the influence of thought upon this "chemistry".

In contrast, according to the New Paradigm, after discovering how causality works, one understands that thoughts change chemistry. This does not mean that if the chemistry is not working properly, it should not be treated; rather it means that, if possible, we should immediately replace the depressed person's thoughts with other, higher vibration thoughts: the chemistry would be restored of its own accord and we would not have to intervene in any other way. As we do not have a "machine" to carry out this process artificially, treatment is needed whereby "heavy" thoughts are replaced by "lighter" ones. Treatment of this type takes time. However, time can be cut down significantly when we work with the right information.

On the other hand, when we study how human experience is built up, we can see that the mind develops from innocence to wisdom, passing through different levels of ignorance. **Innocence,** as mentioned in previous chapters, is lack of information. The innocent do not suffer because when the mind has no information, there is no experience of conflict; for the innocent mind there is no right or wrong, guilt or punishment, justice or injustice which are the basis of human suffering.

We give up a state of innocence when the mind starts to load information and we begin to develop a system of beliefs. The problem is that these beliefs enter the mind without being verified, so sometimes the mind fills up with false information. We then reach a state of mental limitation which manifests itself as mental slavery and internal and external conflict. Much of Humanity finds itself in such a state at the present time.

The release from this state begins when, as individuals, we decide to replace false information with other, true information in our mind. Thus the process of wisdom begins. Such is the true process of spiritual development: it is the transformation of "beliefs" into "truths of understanding". Through this process we discover the Universal Laws, false beliefs are removed, and the Law continues to be verified.

At this point it is important not to fall into what integral philosophy calls the "pre-trans fallacy" (Wilber). Some romantics –with all due respect for some New Age thought– equates innocence with wisdom, since there is satisfaction in both. However, there is an important difference between the two: **innocence** is contaminable and **wisdom** is invulnerable; Innocence is an evolutionary step before ignorance, which is resolved at the next stage, which is wisdom; innocence does not reach wisdom without going through ignorance.

Knowledge of true information is totally liberating: "You shall know the truth, and the truth shall make you free"; free from suffering, anguish, sickness, pain, conflict and eventually from matter itself. If these results are not obtained, then truth is not understood.

As human beings, we reach personal and spiritual growth in the field of the mind. God has given us a neocortex for that purpose. If we were animals, angels or other beings, we would not use our mental field to grow. Even so, we must not forget that it is also necessary to develop intuition. Animals use instinct and angels use intuition; human beings, primarily use the mind.

Returning to thought, bear in mind that if thinking about a situation or event does not provide peace, then we are not thinking right. What does this mean? It does not matter that we have produced a perfect syllogism, or have taken all the right steps if, in the end, thinking about a situation or event gives us no peace. This is a sign that it *is not correct*. It is "as if you had many good reasons but were not right". This is because everything which comes from the high vibration; everything that has a large component of truth; everything that comes from God, produces peace of mind. This is not so, however, in the case of information which comes from human beings (from culture). This is a first criterion with which we must look at ourselves daily. Introspection must be continuous; we must ask ourselves how we can change that thought in order that it gives us peace of mind. A fairly illustrative example could be as follows:

> *A man once complained to me that he felt very frustrated because being divorced meant he couldn't travel abroad with his teenage son. He thought this restriction would be bad for his child, as it would prevent him from seeing more of the world, and his relatives who lived abroad. Up to that point, no-one could say that his argument lacked logic or that his thoughts were poorly constructed. But the truth is that it did not give him peace of mind. How could he change his train of thought without changing reality, in order to obtain peace of mind? A final postscript should be added: "It is true that ideally it would be better to travel with the child, but I know that everything that happens is perfect, otherwise it would not happen; and*

this situation is best for the souls involved in it, for reasons which my mind cannot comprehend at this time because I do not have all the information in the Universe. The will of God is what is happening, and I am flowing with it until the manifestation can be changed". The external situation has not changed but the internal one has, on altering the thinking. Once the internal situation has changed, the external one will do likewise.

Many might think this is a very clever trick, and that it is a shame it is not based on any reality to be able to use it and find peace of mind. However, as we have seen in Part I of this book, many scientists and modern thinkers, and many of the ever-wise, always say that this is the way the Universe works, and that everyone has the opportunity to try to verify this.

The problem which still needs to be overcome is the human mind's tendency to always label everything that happens: good or bad, pleasant or unpleasant, etc., instead of thinking of all events as neutral and necessary for learning processes. Peace is neutral; it has no polarity and will not be reached until thought is neutralized. The label depends on the point of view adopted. For example, is a serious illness good or bad? If as individuals we identify with our physical body and personality (ego), then a serious illness is very bad for both, as it threatens our existence. If we identify with the soul, however, the situation changes. From the point of view of the soul, a condition may be the best option if it leads us to growth as individuals, through the process of letting go of attachment and learning how to achieve peace of mind, regardless of what is external.

• Spiritual growth is a gradual loss of ego. The ego has two basic needs: that of control/security and that of being loved, respected, validated and accepted by others. Ridding oneself of those needs is essential in order to dissolve the ego.

• When someone has been trained in the expression of love in thought, word and deed, they are unlikely to suffer an internal drop in vital energy. That person definitely transcends and eliminates the chances of falling. The only way that consciousness –the part which remains asleep– can awaken, while the personality remains, is if the mind is already clean. This is called reaching the "state of the reborn" or "enlightened". In this state of enlightenment, the experiences of destiny, the need to confront concepts and beliefs, and the possibility of suffering all disappear because the mind can no longer be contaminated. All that remains is the mission of love and service.

5.1 Dematerialization: identifying with the soul or the ego

The human being is not a body and a mind which "has" a soul, but rather a soul which "has" a body and a mind. The soul vibrates at a higher level than the body and the mind, and therefore is more significant; i.e. it is a deeper holon (see Chapter 6 of Part I). This means that it contains more reality than the other bodies. If it were proven that the Universe is holographic –which is very likely– this would be even more evident.

It could be said that the main mistake made by human beings is that we turn an "illusion" into reality whereas we do not attribute reality to what is most real in the human being. We continue to be restricted by the major limitation of the physical senses and the ego, when knowledge and wisdom have already gone much further.

Achieving peace of mind entails "dematerializing" or spiritualizing our thinking. Dematerializing means ridding oneself of the attachment of the mind to matter and taking it to a more subtle area of higher vibration. Human beings are spiritual, not physical, beings but they possess physical components. The historical error lies in us not being able to grasp this truth clearly, so we have fallen into the trap of identifying ourselves incorrectly.

This has been a constant problem throughout history, and is logically so because, as we have seen, Mankind has been immersed in the consciousness of "self". Without waiting for Cosmic consciousness to arise, where this problem disappears completely, we can actually alter the information we handle from the consciousness of "self", and start thinking about things from the point of view of the soul. When human beings understand that they are not merely a mortal body but rather a spark of the infinite spirit wrapped in a cumulus of vital energy, they will be able to realize the internal Kingdom of God. They will understand that their body and the whole universe are not made of the "matter" that maintains the soul captive but rather they are made from energy and consciousness that are expansive and indestructible. Science seems to be discovering this truth and all of us can discover it on our own.

If we did this, i.e., thought from the standpoint of what we really are —the soul— any event would be seen as "neutral" and having the intention of love. The only possible attitude, then, would be lifelong gratitude for the opportunities for growth and learning which life offers. Moreover, if we are aware that nothing can happen unless it is meant to happen (according to the principles of the Law of Correspondence, outlined in Chapter 1 of Part II), human beings would free themselves of all kinds of fears; and we know that fear is the opposite of love. What can happen to a soul in the world of the third dimension? Can a soul have cancer or die in a car accident?

So far, it has only been possible for mystic sages to have this view because only they have the ability to develop a truly spiritual perception of reality

To better illustrate this point, we shall cite below the famous letter attributed to St. Augustine on his death. It says: "If you are fond of me, cry for me; but if you love me, do not cry. And he goes on: "If you knew what awaits ...". Few people throughout history could have expressed themselves this way at the loss of a loved one, if we take into account the excessively materialistic culture we have suffered up till now. However, the New Paradigm and the spiritual vision of man and the Cosmos are now within everyone's reach. Only the "crystallization" of the old concepts; or their stagnation, could prevent Mankind from beginning to think this way.

Identification with the soul, and not the body, will help to quickly resolve one of the great questions of theology today. John Polkinghorne, a physicist and christian priest, in his great book, *Quantum physics and Theology*, states that the problem of evil and apparent misfortunes that happen to innocent people is an issue still unresolved by theology. The author attempts to unravel the question of how God "allows" certain things to happen which are "bad" but this question cannot be resolved without a change of context: from a new, less materialistic viewpoint one can see that what is bad is only bad for mortal bodies but not for the soul; the soul cannot die in an earthquake, and a disease is not bad for the soul if it serves as a learning experience, even if it causes physical death.

So there is no need to complicate everything by thinking that God "allows evil" when we know that there is downward causation and therefore God "causes" everything and does not only "allow" it. The solution to the problem is not that God authorizes such situations, but that what the mind sees as evil is no such thing; rather, from the point of view of the soul, it is a learning opportunity and, therefore, good. Thus, a cancer is not bad and there is no problem in thinking that God causes this and not only allows it. Simply, there is no evil in the Universe; there is an absence of good, to a greater or lesser extent, but not evil as opposed to good.

> Some time ago I had lunch with a friend who had been in Intensive Care for a month, on the point of dying from a heart attack and other complications. During the meal he commented that it was the best thing that could have happened to him because he had grown a lot through that experience and had realized certain things which helped him to increase his peace of mind.

Is that something bad? If he had died, would that have been bad for the soul? When we come to understand that God's children are the souls, and bodies exist only to have learning experiences, these dilemmas will be done away with as belonging to the consciousness of "self".

We could cite here some evangelical teaching which confirms this last point:

> "Do not fear those who kill the body. They cannot kill the soul. Fear only what harms the soul" (Matthew 10, 30).

Dematerialization of thought can be used to experience more easily some of the spiritual lessons of the past, without the mind itself becoming an obstacle, as was the case before we had this information. If we manage to combine two basic ideas, downward causation and dematerialization (i.e. personal identification with the soul and not with the ego, as is usual) in our mind, we will find it easier to apply the teachings and obtain better practical results if we act in the same direction as the Universal Law. To illustrate this point and see what would happen if this mental change were achieved, here are some examples of teachings:

"If you are offended or attacked, turn the other cheek". This teaching has already been used in a previous chapter in another context, but it is worth going back over it, using similar words. We might wonder how to apply this teaching in real life. If the mind has not been dematerialized, most people would say something like it is a beautiful teaching but impracticable because, if we turn the other cheek against aggression, our mind thinks that we could be hurt. This is because if we have not understood downward causation: Consciousness collapses the electron. We are unaware of the existence of the Law of Correspondence, and we do not know that we are a soul. The mind will therefore not allow us to turn the other cheek. The subconscious' defense mechanisms will come into play, making it harder to put the teaching into practice. However, when we grasp that we cannot suffer any aggression which is not meant for the soul's growth, we grasp that, in practice, the only way to avoid being attacked is not to need the lesson. By the same token, the only way to not need this lesson is to be willing to turn the other cheek from the outset. So, now we have a new context of thinking which enables us to understand the validity —not only spiritual but also practical— of this teaching, which greatly facilitates experiencing it. In other words: "I turn the other cheek because I am not stupid and do not want to suffer aggression". Turning the other cheek is a lesson of non-reactivity. When we are able to maintain our peace of mind after an offense, we have learned that lesson and Consciousness will no longer collapse the electron in that direction.

"Seek the Kingdom of God within you, and all else shall be added unto you". Again, until the mind understands how that "addition" physically manifests itself, it will be hard to experience this teaching. Finding the inner kingdom can only be achieved through a change in perception which places the person in (Mystic) Cosmic consciousness. In other words, dematerialized consciousness. There is nothing odd about "this addition"; this is how the Universe normally works when we flow with the Law. As souls, human beings have come into the world to find that Kingdom. Such an encounter occurs when individuals move through the highest levels of consciousness, and from there understand how the Universe manifests everything which is needed by those who focus on the growth of consciousness and service. Again, this is a practical teaching, not just a spiritual one, which agrees with the laws of physics subordinated, in turn, to Universal Laws. It is no longer necessary to abandon "rationality" to understand and experience this education. This seems to contradict the sentence in Genesis which states: "Thou shalt earn thy bread by the sweat of thy brow". Really this is not the case because when Genesis speaks of "bread", it is referring to wisdom, which we do have to obtain with effort and dedication. Other evangelical teachings confirm this, such as one which advocates not amassing and being like the birds in the sky. There are many others.

We come to understand that if something is meant to happen, that something will happen to us without us having to be the "doer" of the action, as Consciousness will take care of that. Then we will understand that in effect we must advance as much possible to find the Inner Kingdom, in order to be worthy of something better, which will manifest itself "freely" to us.

"Whoever loses his life shall find it, and he who finds his life shall lose it". Once again, this teaching is best digested when it is understood that we are a soul and not a body; we came to do the Absolute's will for our own growth. This understanding helps us to lose our "own agenda", and make our life available to the divine plan without resisting it, rather accepting it. Human stress occurs when our own agenda and the Universe's for us do not match; the Universe's agenda will always come true; our own never will, unless they match. Everyone wants something: the sick want to be healed; penniless people want to get money; the ugly want to be beautiful, etc. We always seek specific things, rather than what is most effective for our soul's growth. As long as our own personal agenda fails to make the most of the growth experiences that the Universe has arranged for our soul, we will keep on resisting and suffering. And it is hard to reach that state without dematerializing thought, so hardly anyone achieves this in practice.

The teaching of the Bhagavad Gita:

"Just as a man removes an old garment and puts on a new one, the soul leaves its body to take another."

Again, this teaching invites us to identify with what we really are, the soul, and dematerialize our thinking.

We could continue to explain many other such teachings, both eastern and western, however, the examples given should already provide sufficient ways of understanding this idea.

5.2 The new understanding

Another aspect which leads to peace of mind is learning to solve "problems" correctly in our minds; problems are only resolved properly if the causes are identified clearly.

The primary cause of any problem is to be found at the level of the individual or collective consciousness and not in secondary causes which are merely manifestations of the primary cause. For example, when faced with an economic crisis, experts find many possible causes: excessive debt, unemployment, poor administration, lack of long-term investment, corruption, etc. None of this is a lie but it is not the primary cause. None of this would have happened if the level of individual –and therefore social– consciousness were higher. It is obvious that crises are more frequent, long-lasting and harder to solve in countries with a lower level of consciousness-population.

The problems which appear at one level of consciousness can only be resolved at the next level, and so on. Therefore, any solution which does not consider this will be ineffective.

A thorough knowledge of the levels of consciousness and its correlation with human behaviour implies a new understanding of the processes of human development. This knowledge, in itself, has the power to transform the mind. It will be a vital tool in the process of evolution and it will help distinguish much better between masters and the ignorant, although the ignorant may fulfill the roles of "master"; consequently, a great deal of confusion will be avoided in innocent or ignorant minds. This could accelerate evolution.

Our level of individual and collective consciousness is as discernible today as is our I.Q. By using this tool of knowledge, the mind can better evaluate the correlation between people and roles. Each level of consciousness has its corresponding roles. No good results are achieved if there is no good fit (suitability) between the individual and their particular role.

All human organizations, be they economic, political, religious or spiritual, etc., have their place within the spectrum of levels of consciousness. Their internal control systems should be appropriate to the level at which they operate. For example, democracy corresponds to the third level of consciousness because it does not clearly recognize wisdom and, therefore, it must be elected. However, this system would be obsolete for spiritual organizations at the fourth level; at that level, wisdom is "recognized", not voted on. At the fourth level, situations are handled through recognition of the Law; if this is not the case, one is not at that level. However, only people who have achieved it can undertake recognition. The leaders of religious and spiritual organizations should be agreed on the basis of consensus (not chosen) solely from among people at the fourth level, and by people at the fourth level. At this level the goal is to share and not to compete; to serve and not to control; to assume functions and not to have authority or privileges.

Science now knows that the most important role of service is to inspire rather than persuade or convince. It is more efficient to have a few individuals with a vibrational frequency which is "contagious" than many with less vibration. This is due to the exponential power of the highest vibrations, and the idea is best expressed by the theory of chaos, in mathematics, and more specifically in "critical point" analysis.

Each level of consciousness is divided into scales; the difference between scales is smaller than between levels. Human beings tend to interact with people from scales at the same level. Those of different levels find it harder to interact with each other because there are more differences in their respective behaviours.

The scales can be grouped together and are homogeneous. Homogeneous densities are fractional parts of the same level, whereas heterogeneous densities are at different levels. Heterogeneous densities group together but they do not integrate.

Society is full of heterogeneous groups which cannot integrate. We human beings are within a social network but we only integrate with homogeneous people. Even within homogeneous groups incompatibility exists, which prevents integration in some cases. So there are therefore incompatible homogeneous groups. In short, integration can occur only between homogeneous, compatible groups; in all the other cases it is impossible.

Social experiments which do not grasp this fact will not get satisfactory results. When they try to integrate heterogeneous people, the latter tend to destroy each other or become independent. This is because heterogeneous groups cannot reach agreements; and without agreement there is no coexistence. Without conciliation from the Law, (superior to agreement) there is no inner peace. Agreement is the best technique for compatible homogeneous groups to coexist in the consciousness of "self". At higher levels of consciousness, conciliation is used from the point of Law, which makes agreement unnecessary, since it is based on a common aim and focuses on the context.

This understanding delimits human responsibility and relieves many burdens. Not integrating within what is heterogeneous flows with the Law; not integrating with those who are incompatible homogeneous groups does also, since there is no fit.

Incompatibility between homogeneous individuals is termed **unconscious relationships;** these are characterized by conceptual and behavioral differences which cause permanent disagreement. This disagreement is manifested at lower levels of consciousness through aggression, poor communication and suffering. **Love relationships,** however, are characterized by the recognition of mutual values and those of the relationship. This recognition is manifested by accepting conceptual differences –seen as a great opportunity for learning– agreements accepted voluntarily, good communication, mutual unconditional support, and a high degree of satisfaction.

5.3 From entertainment "versus" introspection to entertainment "with" introspection

Entertainment is necessary to an appropriate degree. It is a great way to recover vital energy. Human beings are meant to learn through enjoyment not by suffering, however, suffering is necessary for growth because it is a consequence of ignorance but it is not the ultimate aim.

A mind that is not at peace cannot feel at ease with itself and needs always to be engaged in some external activity. In loneliness it will quickly become anxious, worrying about the past or the future, blaming itself or others, etc. And it will immediately return to its favorite activity. When it acts this way, the mind is kept busy but without introspection, almost unconsciously.

However, anyone who has understood the information of the New Paradigm knows that problems exist only in the mind; they have also come to understand that problems have their own external manifestation but can only be resolved in the mind. This understanding energizes the intention which makes the mind begin to observe itself "scientifically" because it observes not only processes but also their results.

An English proverb says that whatever we turn our attention to, expands. When human beings turn their attention to freeing their minds, the evolutionary process accelerates rapidly. The Wise say that seeing something is the beginning of its solution. In doing so, limitations are recognized, and this is half the battle.

Individuals committed to growth will have to slowly improve their willingness and capacity for introspection, and time will have to be spent on this. One can spend a lot of time meditating but if there is no introspection at the same time, difficulties will remain. Until we reach enlightenment, by definition there must be some resistance in the mind. It is important to "find" this resistance and transcend it. There can be no unity achieved if there is mental resistance to the world. Aversion has as much component of desire as has attraction.

The tool of introspection or self-observation enables us to begin taking over the helm of our lives and makes us more aware of our inner self, which is, as already said, the place where it is possible to solve "problems". It is a question of trying to find that part of human beings which is the very essence of the Universe. Through introspection we can discover what we are and understand what we are not. Being aware also helps us to "let go" of the strength of some of our own opinions on things, facilitating the relationship with ambiguity. This is very helpful as we progress, as the truth contains many paradoxes.

> "I am not what I think or what I feel, because both states are variable; nor am I what I do. I am the essence of Being which at this moment is asleep while consciousness is developing. I am not thinking and acting from what I am but this does not mean that I am not what I really am. When I understand and am at peace, that essence will be able to express itself."

When we become used to introspection and contemplation, a space opens up where we can enjoy conscious entertainment which is within the Law. We can convert entertainment into learning or teaching to flow with the universal purpose. "We are going to play at learning", could serve as the watchword for this idea.

As spiritual growth is reached and we ascend through the levels of consciousness, it becomes increasingly pleasant to be alone with one's mind. An exercise we can try is to spend an entire day sitting in a chair, alone with our own mind, without any distraction. What could we occupy our mind with? What would happen?

5.4 The depolarization of the mind

The mystic poet, Rumi, wrote:

"There is a place which is located beyond good and evil and we shall meet in that place."

We must accustom the mind to thinking not so much in terms of duality, of opposites. To do this, we must use the higher mind; because reason, which is the lower mind, tends to classify, and is also sequential and, therefore dualistic. With the lower mind we always think in terms of light/darkness, good/evil, guilty/innocent, reward/punishment, etc. As soon as something is created, the Law of Polarity creates the opposite in the mind.

In contrast, the New Paradigm does not consist of opposites but paradoxes; this is not so much "and/or" as "and/and". For example: God is impersonal "or" personal, or rather, God is impersonal "and" personal; East "and" West instead of East "versus" West; darkness is the absence of light; there is no such thing as darkness. Likewise, there is no evil as such, rather it is the absence of good. As already said, it is essential to accustom the mind to think less in dualistic terms and also give up any narrow-minded rationalism, and to admit paradox. There are no opposites, only relationships.

There are three elements of false information in culture and the human mind which create a major obstacle to achieving inner peace: this is the belief in the existence of evil, injustice and blame. Such beliefs are in the minds of most people on the planet and produce several consequences.

First, a **constant struggle against evil;** a useless struggle, since evil does not exist and therefore it can never be defeated. That struggle leads people to all kinds of internal disharmony, because every time we see something —a situation, behaviour, violence— which we consider to be bad, this immediately awakens emotion and an entirely negative feeling which lead to forms of self-destruction such as anger, resentment, revenge, hatred, etc. In turn, these results destroy the processes of internal and external balance in a person. The idea of goodness is associated with something false suffering; it is thought that good people suffer from the problems of others. Then the deterioration in vital energy is enormous: it is a question of avoiding the destiny of others; creating acts of interference, or trying to create them; or fleeing from the experiences which cause suffering; paralyzing the process of spiritual development.

Moreover, **the idea of injustice** leads to another process called "trying to do justice". This process results in war, class struggle and, ultimately, the great conflicts of Humanity. They all originate in the idea of injustice.

Finally, **the concept of guilt** lowers self-esteem and causes bitterness and resentment. Human beings even blame God, and from this comes the inability to accept the experiences of life because there is always someone to blame. "It is not me who made the mistake. Where is the culprit to punish him?" Hence the need for punishment and revenge arises.

However, these elements, which form part of ignorance, are needed in the primary processes of development: they make it possible for us to discover the existence of the Law, the order of the Universe, and the unsatisfactory results which come from not observing these laws.

These same elements are presented below and in the same order, but from a different perspective:

"There is no evil". So what is there? We can say that there are different levels of ignorance and confusion, not of evil; that is quite different. It is a state of ignorance, confusion, which is manifested in a simple way: mistakes are a reality. If someone makes a mistake, what do you think of them? That they need to learn. But if we think, "this person is bad", what would we think of them? That they deserve punishment. The process of relationship is very different depending on the idea used. The proposal of the New Paradigm is to understand that there is no evil but that human beings make mistakes and they are made for two reasons: lack of information or lack of training, or both.

This issue is explained very clearly in the Confessions of Saint Augustine (chapters 12-13), where he says:

> *"Everything which exists is good, and evil [...] is not a substance [...] because if it were, it would be a good. I clearly saw that everything you have done [God] is good and that there is no substance that you have not made yourself.*

This idea can also be found in Genesis: "Our God made all good things". (Genesis 1, 31).

Saint Augustine also said,

> *"There is no evil at all for Thee or for Creation as a whole. There is nothing beyond Creation*

which defiles the order which Thou didst impose. It happens that in some parts of your Creation there are things which we believe to be bad because they are not advisable [...]; but as these are consistent with others, they are good, as they are consistent with the lower part of Creation. In the light of a clearer view, I came to see that although the higher things are better than the lower, the sum of all creation was better than the higher parts alone. When I wondered what evil was, I saw it was not a substance but the perversion of the will when it distances itself from You."

In the words of another mystic, Rumi, of a different tradition:

"You need to understand that things which are opposite to each other work together, even though they are apparently opposed."

Instead of goodness, what we need to use is appropriate service. For that reason we said earlier that a service is misunderstood when it is associated with goodness rather than wisdom, which includes good intention, of course. Service is the way love expresses itself.

"There is no injustice, instead there is correspondence". Correspondence is exactly the experience which is consistent with the need to learn in a mathematically precise manner. Situations which human beings experience are not unfair; they are simply in keeping with the need to learn. For example: "I am capable of being offended, I am suspicious and easily hurt by what others do or fail to do. Where can I learn not to be all these things?". There is a corresponding exact location. The Law of Correspondence postulates: "There is a place for everything and a thing for every place".

Suppose I am learning not to get offended. What is the appropriate place to learn? It is not a place for Masters; there I could not learn because the masters are respectful. By contrast, I need to be faced with an ignorant person who attacks me, criticizes me or invalidates me, so that I realize I can be offended. The place where I belong is in the relationship with the ignorant because I have come to learn *not to be offended*.

"There are no guilty, rather there are ignorant people in a learning process". Realizing this facilitates the process of forgiveness. Not forgiving is like drinking poison oneself in order that another person dies. There are two levels of forgiveness: first, the "superficial", which could be expressed by the following example: "X has done me wrong, but I choose to forgive him; i.e. I decide not to react to his action". This forgiveness may be selective in the sense that this action is forgiven but maybe not another one. In any case, the mind of the person continues to see an offense, so an "effort" must be made to forgive. "Deep" forgiveness, in contrast, knows that "nobody does any harm to you". Offense does not exist; manifestations are created by their own learning needs. "X is an instrument of the Universe which becomes correspondent with making a mistake in order that both learn something". Seen this way, who do we blame? X is not to blame; getting angry with God is absurd. Young children get very angry when they are punished by their parents but when they are older they may tell their parents that maybe they should have been punished a little more in order to learn faster. Who do we get angry with then? Deep forgiveness, when things are seen this way, is no effort, it is natural. This brings inner peace.

5.5 Stand as a "witness", not as a "subject"

The ability to be a witness of the mind has to come from somewhere else, other than the mind itself, because nothing can be a witness for itself. To achieve this we must withdraw somewhat from that something. The other place, that witness, is the most real part of human beings. When a person makes himself a witness, they can quickly see that they are not the body and not the mind but the witness of both.

The field of consciousness is like a blank TV screen. The linear content is the program which we can see on the screen. All experience simultaneously needs the program –perceptions, thoughts, feelings, etc. and the lighting of the screen –the nonlinear field of context.

Nearly everyone has often seen how the emotional body can "hijack" the mind, especially when operating from the lower mind. Lower mind acts in polarity and has much more energetic contact with the emotional body than the higher mind. When someone is kidnapped by their emotional body, they lose clarity and creative capacity and increase their reactivity, which in no way contributes to resolving difficulties.

The problem of emotional hijacking is that it turns the person into a "subject" of their own thought or emotions. However, human beings have the ability to see everything as a witness. One can say to oneself … "Oh dear, you're getting angry again", rather than being the subject of the anger, so to speak. If we become the witness, our peace of mind will increase considerably because we will no longer be directly involved, but rather de-energized we no longer identify with the anger.

For example, an individual can go to the cinema in two ways: first, he can just go to see the film, pure and simply. He becomes emotionally involved in the film and the emotional body takes over. On the other hand, we can go to the cinema thinking: "What I am going to see is a film. I will enjoy it but I'm not going to become part of the film because I know this is not really happening; I know that these people are actors; there is a camera crew around them; they do not appear in the film but they are there".

The ability to stand as a witness is very helpful and can be practiced. There is a tale from the East on this point:

> A disciple and his Master were walking through the woods. Then the disciple said to the Master: "I have spent much of the day thinking about things I should not think about, wishing for things I should not wish for, and making plans I should not be making". The Master then showed the disciple a plant, and asked him if he knew what it was. "Belladonna", said the disciple: "it can be lethal to eat its leaves. But it cannot kill those who simply look at it," added the Master.

This example shows how feelings and negative emotions do not cause harm if we do not become the "subject" of them.

In many cases, the higher and lower mind operate simultaneously. As the Wise would say: "The mind has many voices". We must discern what comes from the higher mind and what from the lower. The work of human beings consists of gradually letting go: "de-energizing" the voices of the lower mind who give us no peace to focus more on the voices of the higher mind, which do provide inner peace.

When we understand all this we are ready to work on the famous three zeros and two hundreds of spiritual growth: zero suffering, zero resistance, zero reactivity. Then,

100% understanding of love and 100% of attitude or spirit of service.

5.6 Cleansing the unconscious mind

We need to cleanse out trauma to advance in spiritual development and have a peaceful and harmonious life. The mind is like an iceberg: most of it is underwater (the water of consciousness) but that hidden part is what controls life without us being aware of this (see Annie Marquier, *The Master of the Heart*).

In the past, psychoanalysis techniques have been widely used for this purpose. To explain it briefly, this consisted of accessing these hidden traumas in order to bring them to light and clean them out. This method has achieved some success, although it is slow and laborious because it faces a number of difficulties: for example, when we look for traumas they somehow still become energized. Moreover, sometimes it is hard to find all the causes of a problem, so we end up just working with partial causes. Since trauma and defense mechanisms acquire countless forms and reactions, it takes too long to clean them out one by one. It is better to simplify the procedure; this is similar to what happens with chess, where simply checkmating the king automatically ends the game.

It is easier to understand that the true origin of people's difficulties is to be found in their personal destiny; their conceptual limitations and unconscious traumas. We have already discussed the first two aspects in depth, so we shall now focus on cleansing the subconscious.

People who have worked on themselves can recognize that automatic reactions still occur within them that are hard to control, despite having reached a certain degree of understanding. These are primitive defense programs which have taken root in the unconscious mind and which we must get rid of to achieve total inner peace. This is the last stronghold of unconscious ignorance, where fear hides out.

Trauma should not be seen as an insurmountable problem but rather as a temporary process of defense which had its uses for preserving life in the primary stages of evolution. The best way to get rid of these programs is to understand why we no longer need to defend ourselves to survive, but rather to respect, let go and serve to be happy. Reaching this point lets us dismount the system of trauma in general, without searching for each trauma, one by one. It is as if, when connecting with the higher mind, with high vibration thoughts, the mind acts as a vacuum cleaner which "sucks" away all the traumas at once, thus accelerating the process. It is like dropping a bag of confetti and having to pick it all up, piece by piece, instead of vacuuming it all up at once.

To achieve release from all trauma or defense mechanisms it is essential that we renounce all physical, verbal or mental aggression. To do this, we must understand that only potential aggressors can be attacked themselves. This is because all defense programs trigger potential aggression in others, and our own defense programs react in response to the aggression of those who are unable to respect others. These individuals are automatically potential aggressors who become correspondent with other individuals' defense systems. This shows that there is a direct relationship between aggression and defense, and vice versa, i.e. any defense system becomes correspondent with being attacked, and any form of aggression is directly proportional to the systems of defense/aggression which we constantly come across. When we reject aggression and defense, we align ourselves with the universal order; we become peaceful individuals and will not come up against aggression of any kind. The Universe demonstrates its Laws.

This understanding will therefore enable us to break free of unconscious traumas, as we will understand that they are no longer needed, and that they are totally limiting as regards peace of mind, relationships, health, spiritual growth and success in life in general.

The frontal region of the telencephalon, where the analytical, rational and understanding mind develops, can inhibit and disconnect the defense systems which originate in the paleoencephalon –the reptilian brain–, where the fight or flight mechanisms reside, and which human beings share with all animal species. But in order for the rational mind to do this, we need to re-program it with understood and verified information on universal love. This exercise consists of visualizing and thinking about the principles of love and an understanding of the perfect working order of the Universe, and often repeating it until the mind accepts this and "installs" it. Thus we succeed in disconnecting the reptilian mechanisms. Reprogramming the mind is the only way to disconnect fear because the mind does not lodge information which does not seem logical. The old paradigm did not consider "turning the other cheek" to be logical, as it was unaware of the order of the Universe, the Laws which govern it, and downward causation.

Human beings have four basic fears: the **fear of loss;** the **fear of confronting;** the **fear of being abandoned,** and the **fear of dying.** We need to re-program the mind with the logical understanding of reality and the universal order in order to transcend these fears. The fear of losing connects up with anger; the fear of facing up to something connects with shyness; the fear of being abandoned, with jealousy; and the fear of dying, with uncertain-

315

ty because we assume that there are elements which endanger our physical safety.

It is the constant expression of love that ends up creating the habit of loving and being happy, and it is what will rid us of all sorts of fears which are the opposite of love. To achieve this we have to take two fundamental steps: one inwards —learning to be happy regardless of the external world— and then, and not before; another step towards the outside: loving our neighbor as ourselves because from the point of view of the soul and divinity, we are all one.

The ability not to react but only act in response to circumstances is not something we are born with; rather it is cultivated gradually through constant mental reprogramming. A little formula which produces very good results goes as follows: "Everyone always does the best they know how to, even if they are ignorant, and they do the best they are able to do. Everything that happens in the Universe is necessary for a purpose of Love, or it would not happen because the Universe is efficient and does not waste energy".

Chapter 6. Coming to terms with life

An important topic to reflect upon, once we have understood how the Universe is structured and works, is that of personal responsibility for and in growth. In what might be called "the old paradigm" and in today's culture, the *victim paradigm*, which is one of the biggest constraints to personal growth, is extremely widespread. All too often, humans blame themselves, or others, for life's hardships, but until they manage to fully come to terms with the experience of their own lives, they'll never achieve high levels of satisfaction, inner peace and conscious contact with higher dimensions.

The difference between Teachers and the ignorant is that Teachers fully come to terms with their life and mission there, while the ignorant want to change the world to suit themselves or their own beliefs, without changing anything in themselves. In other words, they are unable to come to terms with their own lives and feelings, and act from selfishness.

We need to completely rid ourselves of this habit of blaming, at its three fundamental levels, which are three ways of not coming to terms:

• Bitterness: individuals blame their problems on society, civilization, governments, etc.

• Resentment: they blame specific people for what happens to them.

• Personal guilt: they blame themselves for what they have not done, or for the mistakes they have made.

Ridding ourselves of guilt entails consciously deciding to fully come to terms with our own life because spiritual development is individual. If we do not come to terms with our own decisions, we learn nothing. No-one can develop spiritually on behalf of someone else, nor can they do so without others. It is a perfect interaction: every human being needs the other beings in the Universe to develop, however, they cannot develop on their behalf, nor can they for that individual.

Whether or not we know the source of life, it is easy to recognize its presence by using the five basic senses. The origin of life is not subject to any change, depending on different interpretations or speculations that human beings may come up with in this regard; rather, its presence is an incontrovertible fact which we need to take on board as part of the reality of our existence as human beings.

Following the biblical image of how God takes mud and blows on it, one could say that there are two clearly defined elements: **matter,** which, in this case, was simple clay, and the life that makes it animate, or **spirit.** Precisely, the Latin word *anima* or soul is used to refer to that which animates matter without being part of it. The spirit has also been termed the breath of life or divine breath for its relation with breathing, and *pneuma*, a term that comes from Greek.

In the perceptible universe there are three elements whose presence cannot be doubted: *matter*, studied by science; the *spirit*, which is dealt with by philosophy; and the origin of the previous two, which Humanity has called "*God*", and whose study is dealt with by theology.

So, everything that exists in the universe originates in "God's designs", regardless of what people may interpret, believe or feel about this; or the way one may want to refer to it; or the characteristics one wishes to attribute it with. We will always be able to recognize the presence of the Creator simply by observing what has been created.

Therefore, it is clear that humans need to come to terms with their relationship with science, philosophy and theology as a fact of life, regardless of the names or how they have been given, or whether or not one believes in the postulates that each of these proposes.

To truly come to terms with their relationship with life, people need to understand that death does not exist, and respect the experience of others because it is not life that must be respected but experience. This is because life is immortal and indestructible, i.e. eternal. When the state that is called "death" overcomes us, the spirit and life leave the physical body.

If you ask a materialist scientist: "What is life?", he will probably say it is "clay", i.e. matter. But as long as he thinks that way, it is impossible for him to understand the essence of God or life. The entire Universe, from the smallest insect, virus or bacteria, up to galaxies, is composed of three elements:

Life: is a divine particle present in humans and in everything that exists. Unlike the spirit, life is the essence of the Human Being; it is eternal information, of divine origin, that shapes and animates matter. It is therefore impossible to lose it. What is lost is the body or "clay", when current experience comes to an end.

Matter: it is an eternal emergence of particles which can be organized and disorganized. It consists of elementary particles; it is energy that becomes a little denser. When energy enters higher vibrational frequencies, it is no longer called matter, but simply energy. The energy bodies —the spirit— are not bodies made of matter, but they do have life. Matter contains life; energy transforms into matter and vice versa, since matter is merely dense energy. The matter and energy of the universe do not increase or decrease; they are an ever-present constant, which takes on all forms.

Form: this is the result of the action of the information from life on matter. Humans have a form called "design of God" and this is transmitted through genetics. The form has a purpose: to allow God's son (permanent consciousness) to have experience. Recognizing the form is the same as recognizing the designer.

Life is not matter or form, but manifests itself in two different ways: the information for the form, or genetics, and the information to make it animate, or the "divine spark".

Life constantly enters and leaves matter and its existence is independent of it. Often it is thought that being alive is being able to move around, but a stone or a table have life, although they do not move, because life is what keeps matter organized. Everything has life; only it can either be dynamic, active or animate, or static or inanimate. In the absence of life not even a rock can have a shape or form because, if it did, its molecules would become disorganized (see entropy, Second Law of Thermodynamics).

We could therefore talk of two types of life:

Inanimate life: that of inert bodies. They do not move as a structure but vibrate within.

Animate life: the capacity of beings to have experiences in this world. When there is experience it is because consciousness is involved because this is what animates the form; what enables it to move forwards i.e. enables it to have experiences.

Animals have a consciousness archive; they have an experience of life and a spiritual evolution, only this is "not conscious". Even humans are unaware of their own consciousness, only of their personality. Therefore animals, which do not have even personality, cannot possess consciousness. Even so, they are capable of assimilating information but do so slowly and automatically.

The origin of life lies in the dimension of the Absolute Unmanifested, which contains the complete information of the Universe and its manifestations and processes. It is eternal, perfect, immortal, unchanging. God, the Father, holds the information on the Absolute. That essence of Being is present in everything that exists in the Universe, a creation of the Father. It can be compared with the ocean: How many drops of water could be taken from it? Countless could. Every drop of water is the very essence of the ocean. So much so that if the drop were put back again, it would be lost among the others; it would merge perfectly with the ocean. Another drop could be taken out, but it could never be claimed to be the same drop. That is the essence of Being; the essence of life. The essence of Being is everywhere; there is nothing in what is not, and this is what is called "life".

6.1 Personal responsibility

God does not evolve. What evolves is consciousness, which has no human form. Actually it has no form whatsoever because it is neither human, animal nor plant. Sparks have neither experience nor evolution because they are the life that divinity grants to humans, and it is not the sparks that experience, but consciousness.

God is a real and constant presence but he possesses neither form nor shape. God's Laws are studied and his presence is recognized through forms; God encompasses all forms without being any of them.

We could say that the three elements of human experience, as was briefly discussed in the previous section, are:

Matter or body: consisting of genetic information. This is studied by science.

Mind or personality: this is studied by philosophy and psychology.

Spirit or consciousness: this is studied by theology and the science of spirituality.

Science is a critical component of the spiritual development of human beings because it studies the behaviour of matter: form and energy. To assume that matter is alien to the spirit is a mistake; it is the same as believing that philosophy and science are incompatible, or religion and theology with science and wisdom. All these elements make up the set of subjects we need to understand life. None can be set aside because all are equally important. Wisdom consists of exploiting to the full what each reveals, and putting together this information to reach full understanding.

Until recently, science went as far as studying the third dimension. However, it has now begun to explore others, and this will be vital to understand these. Science studies matter and this is also God's creation so, in this sense, studying science is also studying theology.

Philosophy investigates the behaviour of the mind in the face of experiences with the Law through matter. That is, it examines the experience of the mind through matter. The mind alone, without matter, could not have any experience because it would not have a recipient in which to keep it. The mind is not physical; it is not the third dimension, it exists in dimensions of a higher vibration. Therefore, an experience in the physical world has to take place through matter. In this way, philosophy and science are interdependent.

Philosophy is the study of wisdom; but what is wisdom? It is making use of the experiences that life offers. Philosophy studies the mind's structures and human behaviour, as opposed to their life experience, and consists of making optimal use of destiny. Its field of study is the mind, in which there is an aspect of divinity called **understanding,** which is the part of the essence of the divine that every human being has at the present moment, awake and consciously, and which they can use here and now.

Theology studies the behaviour of the Universe's Laws and its relationship with human beings. Therefore, God's relationship with men is studied, but really this should be understood as the relationship of Laws with individual persons, because they are how God expresses himself towards humans. It could be said that theology is the study of the Laws of the Universe and it researches into the spiritual realm, where the laws are codified.

Everybody needs to study the three main branches of human knowledge (science, philosophy and theology) in order to be able to come to terms with his or her own life. Without matter, there can be no mind, and without a mind, the spirit cannot develop. These three aspects constantly interact and form "the unity of the human experience".

The order of the Universe is perfect and all the elements that constitute experiences within it are equally important. So how do we accept this? This is a question of coming to terms with the relationship with matter, with one's own body and with everything that has to do with what constitutes matter in all its forms; of coming to terms with it wisely, that is, with respect for all organized forms of life, whatever they may be.

Human beings must also come to terms with their own internal changes at a mental level, i.e., applying philosophy to themselves and asking themselves how they can learn to live in harmony with the Universe; to make their own decisions and steer their own lives wisely.

People's relationship with theology develops through the questions: How can one awaken consciousness? And can we help these higher faculties to manifest themselves in each one of us?

This spiritual work unites all the constituent elements of the human being in relation to the Universe, so we cannot ignore it and need to come to terms with it as a reality; a release and a source of satisfaction, without becoming attached to anything material. There are aspects that are temporary, transitory —but that does not mean that they do not have significant value— only that it is not possible to take them to another dimension.

The work of developing consciousness also involves the disappearance of the idea of guilt, since no-one is guilty. Nobody can hurt anyone, beyond oneself. This may be difficult to understand if expressed this way. While the disappearance of the concept of "guilty" may be liberating, it has to be replaced by that of "responsible" with its corresponding natural and spiritual consequences.

"Salvation" requires that an individual makes mistakes, transcends and integrates. The term "salvation" is extended to include collective salvation.

In christian tradition the word "sin" has been used instead of "error", because sin is understood as an expression of evil. But the oft repeated sin/punishment dichotomy has gradually devalued this concept. Furthermore, as has been seen, there is no evil. But the fact is that within the same tradition there are different perspectives on the concept of sin, as in the work of *Teilhard de Chardin*:

> *"Sin, i.e. evil which is conscious and freely wished for; the rejection of God's love, comes from a cosmic structure, since it is evolutionary. Sin, like responsibility, has its degrees, and full responsibility requires full consciousness. Moreover, sin has a collective aspect. Man is orientated towards solidarity, not only that of the Cosmos, but also of men. It is true that individual faults are still individual but they do not harm only the individual; they hurt what is human; they harm all Mankind."*

There are two additional issues with which people have to come to terms:

• They need to make decisions, whether these are the wrong or the right ones.

• The consequences of their own decisions.

When someone recognizes their own mistakes without blaming anyone, they are coming to terms with them. If there is no guilty party, there is no punishment, only the consequences of the decisions made. Coming to terms with the consequences means that we learn without blaming anyone, let alone ourselves, because we need to make mistakes to be able to learn; this is one of the fundamental rights of human beings.

6.2 Destiny, mission and function

As explained above, human beings are made up of energy + information, like everything else in the Universe. Comparing humans with how a computer stores information, one could say that the information in humans is archived. The **consciousness archive,** or spiritual archive, could be called "permanent consciousness", since it is the one that encodes the Laws of the Universe in a stable manner. It is also called the "Christ Self", because it reaches crystalline purity and is the archive to which the teachings of, Jesus are sent: "Awake and strengthen the child within you". "Child", because it is a space that has not yet been completed; which has not finished developing.

There are other ways of identifying permanent consciousness in life experience. Every child, to learn, needs to go to school, and the school of the spirits is the planets. Planet Earth is a school for the spirits and is currently at the third primary stage. Technically, this is called the "evolutionary world of the third level of the development of conscience". As mentioned in the first part of the book, there is also a minority of spirits who are still at the second level, but others are at the fourth, and these are the ones who facilitate the development of all others, pulling them upwards. However, the vast majority are at the third level.

What do we learn at this school? The same as at any other: what we do not know. And how can we easily identify what we do not know? Anything that represents a difficulty and that robs us of our peace of mind; this is what is termed destiny.

Destiny is a purely pedagogical phenomenon, provided solely to let us learn the things that we do not know and to recognize the existence of the Laws or truths of the Universe. Conflicts in relationships; economic or health problems; situations of fundamental insecurity, and anything that causes unease and is difficult to deal with, are all precisely the presence of destiny. It is designed on an immortal plane, since designs are the work of the divine; but we live and experience at a mortal, time-constricted level, with a physical body and a mental archive.

Coming to terms means dealing with what happens within each one of us and observing what happens around us.

Coming to terms with what is internal means becoming aware of all internal, instinctive, emotional, affective, mental and spiritual levels; and learning how to handle them without blaming anyone or anything.

In this sense, it is important to see the differences that exist in feelings versus emotions. For the purposes of this book, we can say that feelings are produced from the movement of the mental body and emotions are produced from the movement of the instinctual body.

Negative emotions should be channeled and not repressed (they can be somatized) or expressed (it can lead to damaged relationships). We can heal negative emotions by observing them at their own level and also by maintaining our mind in the zone of light that will produce a general quietening of the emotional body by the contagion of higher vibrational energies.

Feelings can be healed more rapidly by changing the way we think since they are produced by mind movements. Higher vibrational thoughts will change feelings automatically since in a way they are byproducts of thought.

Coming to terms with what is external means becoming aware of the need to respect everything that happens around us, i.e., understanding that everything that exists and occurs is necessary for the processes of the Universe. Therefore, we must accept it completely and definitively renounce interfering with any process. To be able to come to terms, the first thing we must respect is the destiny of others. Every human being has come to life to perfect their spirit, learning and understanding through their own experiences what they have not yet completed in their consciousness. A wise person will never interfere with the experiences of destiny, however, difficult they may be, in order not to harm the person in the process of their own evolution.

In order for that destiny to come true, we need to face up to difficulties; and these too often arise in relationships with other people, who may act out of ignorance. In that case, you have to respect those people without attacking, criticizing, judging or invalidating them.

Destiny has a perfect design: no one will be set a test that they are not able to pass, and the most difficult tests will only be set when the individual is particularly stubborn and does not want to face the simple tests. Remember that transmuting destiny in mission is the fundamental purpose that has brought every human being to life, and there is only one way to do this: facing up to it, because transmuting it is changing it. It is the same as substituting ignorance for wisdom, or suffering for peace and harmony.

The Wise perform the function of setting an example of love and respect as a way of teaching, and also of providing information for the spiritual improvement of others, to transmute destiny more easily. When someone interferes with the destiny of others, this comes under the influence of the law of Cause and Effect. That is, if you try to take over the destiny of others, this complicates your own, because the law does not allow interference.

The **mission** is the accumulated understanding in consciousness, and is manifested in personality as the specific vocation or inclination that a person feels towards certain activities which they enjoy thoroughly, enabling their vital energy to increase in strength.

When the mission is not respected, this can produce frustration and rejection of life, and destiny is compounded through the drop in vital energy. Not respecting the mission is a common mistake made by parents, who sometimes do not accept the vocation of their children.

Our **function** is what people do to "earn a living". Every living being has a function that is independent of moral concepts or of what is generally seen as "good" and "evil". This function has a direct correspondence with the internal levels of ignorance or wisdom. That is why very often it may be associated with criminal activities or social diseases, as well as normal, technical or totally humanitarian activities, as a function always corresponds perfectly to the doer.

The function of confronting, disrespecting and attacking others in order that they recognize their own limitations is solely the responsibility of the ignorant, whose experiences bring on suffering. When a person is plunged into profound states of ignorance, their corresponding roles are usually associated with violence and death. At middling levels of ignorance, where feelings are heavily involved, this corresponds to roles of aggression, criticism, prohibition, imposition, bigotry, intransigence and interference with the roles of others, to thus create relationships with destiny where we learn through suffering.

The Wise never confront or attack anyone for any reason, since their function, and that of the spiritually developed, is to accept and respect others to be able to reach them through examples of harmony, messages of love and new information which makes change within them easier. The function of those with greater spiritual development is generally associated with teaching, examples of harmony, flexibility, adapting to the environment, the transmission of information for human improvement and the construction of new forms of peaceful coexistence, grounded in the development of inner peace.

So, respecting the function of all living beings is the universal principle of wisdom.

The proposal being made here, from the deepest respect, is that of putting down three weapons that humans possess:

Physical aggression, even only with gestures; **verbal aggression:** any hostile word; **mental aggression:** any violent thought

Teachers do not conflict with anyone, regardless of the levels of development that these people possess, because they respect them and handle them with wisdom; whereas those with little wisdom have many conflicts with others. The Wise are silent when they should be silent and speak when they should speak.

Everything in the Universe has a perfect purpose of love, whether we like it or not. If this is not understood, the tool of respect is lost. It is very hard to respect something that you think is wrong. When someone declares themselves to be in a state of total and absolute peace, in return they are completely and utterly respected by all other beings in the Universe. This result we can bear out as we progress through life.

6.3 Culture

Culture is the set of a people's principles, customs and traditions. Though it is true that imposing cultural principles limit the possibility of changing mindsets towards new experiences of evolution, as well as the development of civilizations of a higher level, the fact remains that these limiting experiences are necessary in order that we develop understanding and inner strength to release ourselves from the chains of "culture".

Respecting different cultures in the Universe means refraining from interfering in their traditional structures, which are suitable for the educational program that these individuals need. Individuals who reach the saturation point of a culture's limiting experience will seek information themselves in order to free themselves from it; providing that information is the job of the Teachers and Sages. Respecting different cultures and traditions is respecting the experiences of the evolution of different peoples.

Culture is a pattern that produces internal guidelines of behaviour in the individual. Unless we are able to come to terms with our own behaviour, guidelines and decisions, we will not be ourselves, rather we will be in a state of dependence upon something external. Teachers hope that everyone will reach a point of total freedom. However, freedom is not an external but an internal process.

The ability to voluntarily change one's beliefs, concepts and mental guidelines, as well as one's own structure of principles, leads to self-transformation. This does not mean disrespecting, bullying or interfering with the processes that exist around us because these are necessary. Changing cultural conditioning occurs within the individual, not outside.

This is not a question of changing what is external, as that would imply that it is not accepted, understood or valued. Rather it is about thinking: "This is no longer of any use to me; I do not need it".

The techniques of mastery have to be worked upon, and any behaviour that goes against the principle of maintaining harmony, growth and peace within, will prove unwise.

The purpose of human beings in any culture is to learn. People are not here to teach anything to culture, but to learn from it. Nobody has the function of instructing people who have not asked them anything, so only total respect for them and their ideas is admissible. No one should confront anyone who has not requested new information; in order to respect them, so that they do not feel bad, it may be necessary to use techniques of mastery, such as agreeing with them even though we do not actually ourselves agree, and waiting for them to look for the information to then offer it to them.

For example: a person is excited because they have just spent all day shopping and have bought lots of accessories. If someone says to that person, quite sincerely: "Look, I'd suggest you spent your time on something a bit more spiritual than that". How will that person feel? They won't understand, and they'll also feel attacked. It would be wiser to say: "I'm also happy that you're happy". That person, moreover, is not asking anything, only sharing their feelings.

Wisdom in relationships consists of learning to respect other people's customs and habits; of reaching agreements when needed; and narrowing down experiences or keeping out of the way of those you cannot agree with. Respecting others' behaviour is allowing everyone to get on with their lives and come to terms with their own experience. Behaviour shares a common characteristic with taste: they are totally individual, not universal.

To improve the relationship between two people it is better not to propose a change in behaviour, rather an agreement which leads to mutual respect to find a midpoint of harmony between the two.

If there is no agreement, then we need to accept that and adapt, or cordon off wherever possible, when there is incompatibility. In some cases, cordoning off only postpones the experience.

6. 4 Agreement and conciliation

The conciliation of Love is superior to agreement. Agreement is horizontal; for example, the agreement between two people in a business deal, or between two companies: they reach an agreement despite their differences, which are put aside. But you cannot reconcile horizontally. Love is finding a balance in which all differences disappear. That is, what can be called the "point of Law". Over the Law, there is no debate, and the only wise decision is to obey it. The point of Law assesses what happens without passing judgment.

For example, the statement: "This car can take me from A to B", lacks any emotional charge; it is not making any judgment. By contrast, the following statement: "This car is the best one for that journey" implies a rating, which could lead to the start of an argument. Disagreements are always conceptual; there are no disagreements over the Law. Beliefs or ignorance separate us; Love unites us. Love is like water, which adapts to fit all shapes, and like water, it can do so because it is not rigid.

Neutral managing in relationships follows a number of steps:

- Attitude of Love and service.

- Respect for the fact that every concept is true for the person who possesses it.

- Pre-design or visualization of a state of inner peace.

- Response from the point of Law and not from concepts.

- Putting oneself in another's place for better understanding.

- Use of a soft voice and gestures.

- Highlighting the qualities of the other and mutual benefit.

The common purpose is the point of Law where you will always agree. Finding the purpose that unites and not the concept that separates is within the Law. In the point of Law, agreement is not necessary; this is only needed until wisdom is found.

Human beings' feelings are very delicate. People are likely to be hurt and offended, as well as suspicious, if what happens externally does not agree with their system of beliefs. When feelings are deeply hurt, people can go as far as destroying themselves due to their mental confusion caused by suffering. Negative emotional states consume large amounts of vital energy and can cause severe depression.

Given the fragility of human feelings, it is very important to learn to respect them fully. For this reason, wise individuals are very careful not to hurt people's feelings. To this end, they make themselves the same as others by wisely using the technique of pairing. How can we relate harmoniously with people who are at a lower level of understanding than ourselves? By communicating with techniques of mastery, giving way and proposing agreements.

The **technique of mastery** is to go to the person with information that is logical for their way of thinking, and thus get in tune with it; respecting their experiences and supporting them with information based on wisdom that they are able to understand, without allowing them to feel bad in the interaction. If this happens, there has been a lack of communication technique and the information provided has not been understood. If you want to interact with people who have higher level of understanding than you do, you do not have to do anything because it is they who will use their techniques of mastery.

Bearing in mind that feelings are a tool for self-knowledge, destiny constantly places human beings face to face with situations or individuals who confront their feelings, to let them discover falsehood in themselves and come to know the truth which will free them definitively from suffering. However, the function of confronting the feelings of others will never be the responsibility of a Teacher, since they respect the feelings of everyone and establish harmonious relationships with all in order to serve them, i.e. to give them new information, full of wisdom, that they can accept.

Respecting others' feelings is the art of wisdom in relationships. Feelings are an emotional aspect of being human, since they originate in the mind, within the system of learned beliefs. They are necessary for evolution and are different from the emotions, which are produced on instinct.

The system of beliefs that we initially all develop in our child's mind, thus forming our personality, is not only inevitable, it is also necessary for the development of personal wisdom or understanding, formed in personality through the process of the transmutation of ignorance into wisdom. The Masters are well aware of the importance of the system of beliefs as a tool for the development of consciousness. For this reason, they fully respect the ideas, beliefs, concepts, religions and even bigotry of others, and come to terms with the need to become partners with them as a form of Love and respect for the experience that everyone has through their lives.

As there is no direct path from innocence to wisdom, it is inevitable that we go through the experience of ignorance, to then transmute it into wisdom. It is therefore necessary to respect the ignorance of others, coming to terms with it as a temporary state in the experience of the human personality.

When errors caused by ignorance become unbearable and are not part of the destiny of others who are in the same environment as the ignorant individual, then they have to cordon off and distance themselves from that person, or invite him/her to leave. When the relationship is part of destiny, and demarcation is not possible, this is neutralized with the tools of wisdom. Those who possess wisdom respect the ignorance of those who do not. The more wisdom, the more respect. To serve with Love, one needs to respect with wisdom.

Others should not be blamed for the decisions that each of us take. Even if a person feels threatened, it is that person who makes the decision about how to deal with that threat.

Thus, this chapter, which discusses how we come to terms with issues, can provide some useful tools:

Coming to terms with decisions is setting ourselves totally free from any dependence on what is external. So the Teachers say: "Spiritual independence is a state of expertise in your relationships with the world, where you are not dependent on the world but you relate to it".

Coming to terms with destiny's design means understanding and accepting that all events surrounding the life of a person were wisely chosen by that person before their physical experience begun, and are completely independent of the decisions of their parents, culture, location and situation within any civilization. What really happens is that the Permanent Consciousness decides to take advantage of all the elements which are located in a specific place to continue its own development from the point where this stopped in its last experience at a physical level.

Coming to terms with decisions on the choice of body: the physical body is a perfect design of God, wisely chosen by the immortal spirit that has borrowed it as an excellent vehicle for its own experience of development. Whatever the race and the specific characteristics of a person's body, this will always correspond perfectly with their own experience. It is a valuable tool that nature has given us and that we need to learn to appreciate, love and respect as part of the process of increasing the understanding of life.

Coming to terms with decisions on the choice of parents: when the immortal spirit chooses physical parents, it knows that they have the perfect conditions to be able to act as a channel through which a child can come into the world and have initial support to grow, while he can concern himself with his own support. Sometimes destiny is designed in such a way that the physical parents are not the people who should bring up the child. In that case, the biological parents only contribute the genetics; the true parents are those who are committed to the children so that they can grow and come to terms with their own life.

Coming to terms with decisions of the choice of place: the place the spirit chooses for a person's life experience may be temporary or permanent, but it will always be the best choice for the development of that person's evolutionary experience. When one fights against being in one's rightful place, one will come up against all sorts of difficulties that will prevent one from leaving it.

All situations which people find themselves in throughout their lives have been previously chosen, consciously or "spiritually" (i.e. in another dimension, when destiny planned it) by the person who experiences them. This means no one is to blame, let alone oneself, since the situation was perfectly designed for the purpose of spiritual development. The most appropriate course of action is to be deeply grateful for what we can learn from it, as part of the process that supports the growth of consciousness.

The real work of human beings is not to change the world but to reach the kingdom of God within ourselves. It is a state of total spiritual freedom: a person full of Love, peace, happiness who does not depend on anyone to maintain that status, reaches the kingdom of God within.

We never regress in evolution but we can lose energy. What is understood cannot fade away, or it would not have been understood. If a Teacher allows his energy levels to drop, he may behave like an ignorant person, but when his energy returns, he will once again be a Teacher. In contrast, if an ignorant person "loses" energy, on recovering it they will not become a Teacher.

Truth is not believed; it is known. Sometimes, people who believe they are in possession of truth defend it against all odds, but in reality they are defending their own beliefs. Truth does not need to be defended because there are no different truths, only partial truths. Any truth, however small, can be recognized in something simple: it works well.

In the face of aggression, ignorance leads man to blame others for his own fear. People can be manipulated in direct proportion to their emotional weakness, which originates in their own system of beliefs and in their deepest fears of losing what they are using, or who they are sharing with. In actual fact, we own nothing and no-one. People hurt or flee when they are afraid; they neutralize or delimit when they are at peace.

To reach a state of spiritual independence, where peace, harmony and your own decisions do not depend on anything or anyone but yourself, you must recognize that no-one can force another person to do something, or decide for them. While we blame others, we cannot free ourselves, nor advance spiritually because we are placing the problem in the other person's hands and not in our own, so it cannot be resolved.

When it comes to imposing something, others do not come to terms with it and become incapable. Rules are threats, so to better handle situations, agreements are reached, which are maintained thanks to commitment. Commitments are based on benefits, never threats. The threat of punishment, if the other does not do what one wants, is different from the benefit, where the other person decides to do something to obtain what they themselves want, without any obligation. For it not to be an imposition, it must be discussed it and agreements must be reached.

The exercise consists of not suffering or blaming, but acting.

Faced with a threat, one can take two decisions: negotiate to reach an agreement, or else cordon off or protect oneself by taking a number of precautions.

Moreover, from wisdom one can be grateful for what is learned from threat, which is always an opportunity to maintain one's peace of mind, serenity and acceptance, regardless of what happens externally.

To sum up, every human being can prepare himself/herself to use the tools of wisdom. To do this we can decide to:

- **Come to terms** with the results of our life and decisions; as well as our feelings and everything that happens around us —as this is produced by ourselves— and not blame anyone else for it.

• **Take action** in the face of the outside world and take different decisions about our way of behaving. We can decide to negotiate, define or protect ourselves according to how the situation arises. If we lose something, we understand that we cannot lose what we need, rather precisely what we do not need. We know that when something leaves our life it is because we do not need it, and when something appears it is because we need it. We decide not to attack in thought, word or action.

• **Be grateful** for everything learnt from every difficulty that life presents. Reject suffering in the face of difficulties, and ask oneself what can be learned from them. Learn to maintain inner peace, and not allow what happens externally to affect our mental state. It is difficulties that take us to the kingdom of God within ourselves because we become immune to them. This is why difficulties have such enormous value and we should be deeply grateful for them. So, how does one enter the kingdom of God? First of all, by facing up to difficulties without allowing them to perturb our inner peace. How does a master become "unable to be offended"? By facing up to all possible offenses, without allowing this to perturb him. The Teacher Jesus, did not lose his inner peace; he did not blame anyone but fully came to terms with his own divine process. Being grateful is the ability to be resurrected in love and spirit; it is to achieve immortality.

• **Appreciate** the fact that we always have what we really need. This is not measured in terms of quantity but in the internal result. If we are able to be happy with what we have, we have what we really need. The Wise do not complain about what they do not have, as they know that if someone is not able to be happy in want, they will be even less so in abundance.

  • **Respect** all living beings within the particular function they perform; their form; destiny; behaviour; decisions; attitudes i.e., choose never to criticize or judge anyone for any reason. This way, the individual becomes correspondent with being respected himself/herself.

  • **Adapt** to the environment in which we have to live and the result of our decisions. Reject fleeing from where we are and the situations we have to experience.

  • **Accept** the situations around us as necessary for ourselves and others. Decide to admit that the purpose of the Father is perfect.

Not coming to terms with one's own decisions is a widespread mental vice of Humanity: after taking a decision and experiencing its consequences, we blame others.

People are afraid that something unknown can harm them. However, this fear, although it is real and can have a powerful influence on each one of us, is proportional to our own personal level of ignorance. As we gain in wisdom, fear disappears. Throughout the history of Mankind, fear has been necessary as a defense, however, who needs defending? Only those who think they might be attacked; and who could be attacked? Only those who are not capable of respecting. So, those who know how to respect do not have to defend themselves.

We need to free ourselves from fear as, if decisions are taken through fear, we are also acting out of ignorance of the abundance and perfection of the Universe. Fear exists only while there is no wisdom, and it limits human experience terribly. When decisions are made through wisdom, one ceases to be liable to manipulation and has a respectful attitude toward others.

To manage external influences it is important to know that the only time that the human mind can be influenced or programmed externally is in the stages of innocence i.e. from the moment of conception until a child turns twelve, approximately. External influences are inevitable in the innocent mind, as they form part of designing one's own destiny.

The mind of the adolescent or adult accepts new information, suggestions and ideas, as long as the messages are consistent with their own system of beliefs. Otherwise, they will reject them and put up strong resistance to any change proposed to them.

To break the resistance to evolutionary changes that the system of beliefs opposes, divine wisdom uses the tool of feeling. In the face of external events which the false beliefs, accumulated in the mind, cannot accept, high levels of emotional distress occur. Then a mental phenomenon governed by the Law of Saturation comes into play. This consists of reaching a point where the mind no longer resists any more suffering. This is the point at which we exclaim: "I don't want to suffer any longer!". Then our mind is ready to accept new information that enables us to free ourselves from suffering and the limitations we initially learned. The saturation of suffering breaks the system of beliefs and leads to inner peace and spiritual development.

Hence the great importance of providing a true education in childhood, which produces a flexible mind in the early years, to prevent adolescents or adults developing a mental inflexibility which is so strong that it requires high levels of suffering to break through it. Inflexible people always opt for fight or flight; while those with mental flexibility make other decisions involving greater wisdom. Mental flexibility enables us to take decisions to give way, adapt to circumstances, and respect others. Proper education produces a flexible mind with low levels of suffering".

In the adult mind, the possibility of voluntary reprogramming is always there. Any kind of external influence will always be subject to a voluntary decision on the part of the individual to accept the idea suggested, or not. That is, the person needs to agree with the message for his mind to be able to accept it. Even in hypnotic states, if the message suggested goes against the beliefs of the individual, his mind will reject it. Any information or suggestion can only be accepted by the voluntary decision of the individual himself. If we come to understand that nothing can affect us which is not what we ourselves have decided, we become invulnerable.

6.5 Coming to terms

In a nutshell, what is **coming to terms?** It is being able to understand that each person is the only one who can solve their own problems. Everyone has the right to request information; lean on others; ask questions; investigate and, of course, make mistakes; but coming to terms with our mistakes and their results is called mental maturity. Blaming others is the vice of Humanity and involves evading responsibility. It does not help to think that the fault is the other person's. There are a number of different aspects to coming to terms:

• **Instinct:** one has to come to terms with the three fundamental characteristics of instinct, which are: producing, maintaining, and defending life. This means learning to manage wisely the messages which come from each. Some examples are:

Creating life: this produces states of infatuation, because instinctively genetic compatibility is recognized.

This means that falling in love can arise spontaneously with different people and with relative frequency. Wisely managing the states of infatuation means recognizing the function of instinct, without letting this affect the commitments already made to our partner, or the respect which others deserve.

Maintaining life: this is directly related to the needs and deficiencies of the physical body, expressed through desire. Coming to terms with all our desires and learning to satisfy them healthily ensures harmony and health for the physical body.

Defending life: this occurs when people feel threatened. Instinct then makes people react aggressively or run away from the situation to save themselves. Coming to terms with this characteristic means rejecting the option of attacking or fleeing, but instead opting for dialogue, agreement and commitments, or demarcation when it is not possible to reach an agreement.

"Instinct, managed wisely, enriches life."

• **Emotions:** coming to terms with emotions means that when states of sadness, anger, anxiety or fear accumulate internally as a result of external stimuli, they must be got rid of, without blaming or attacking anyone for what happens within us.

"Managing emotions is a sign of mental maturity."

• **Feelings:** if any level of emotional suffering originates internally, as a result of one's own mental limitations or false beliefs, we have to come to terms with it as our own internal experience, refraining from relating to others from the standpoint of these negative feelings, and even less so making the mistake of blaming or attacking others for what we are feeling.

"It is ignorance to blame others or ourselves for what we feel."

• **Ignorance:** inevitably, everyone initially accumulates certain levels of ignorance in their personality. Coming to terms with personal ignorance means understanding the importance it has as an element of contrast in order to discover inner truth. But we need to give up blaming or attacking others because of their own ignorance.

"Ignorance is necessary in order to find truth."

• **Destiny:** coming to terms with our own destiny means that we decide to make the most of the difficulties that life presents as a wonderful opportunity to develop physical skills, mental maturity, inner peace and the ability to constantly express love; all aimed at total and definitive liberation from suffering.

"Wisdom is seeing destiny as an opportunity."

• **Function:** coming to terms with the function that corresponds to each of us in life means understanding that all work or action directed at "earning a living" has a direct bearing on destiny and sometimes with the mission. Therefore, whether or not we like the work we do, it is best to do it with the greatest enthusiasm, joy and love, as this way destiny is transmuted and the mission is accomplished.

"Doing the job with love transforms destiny into mission".

• **Understanding:** coming to terms with one's level of mental understanding means beginning to love voluntarily in a universal way, rejecting tasks that fall exclusively to the ignorant and not interfering with the destiny of others. This also means performing the roles that correspond to each of us.

"Not interfering does not mean doing nothing."

• **Mission:** coming to terms with the mission means checking whether the mission is part of the function. If not, then we need to come to terms with the mission as something we occupy ourselves with only in our leisure time, as it will not be possible to make a living with it. When the mission itself is part of the function, then it is important to come to terms with it as a commitment to life and prepare to enjoy it intensely, understanding the deeper meaning of service.

"Serving with Love is coming to terms with our function as a mission."

• **Thoughts:** coming to terms with thoughts means first observing them carefully, and as soon as they come into our minds, discarding everything that causes suffering or is likely to disturb our inner peace and the perfect balance of the mind; being ready to voluntarily select thoughts of love, peace, harmony, joy and, in general, always directing our thoughts towards anything that could produce an improvement personally or in our environment.

"Selecting our thoughts is tuning into Love."

• **Perceptions:** coming to terms with perceptions involves understanding, accepting and verifying that besides the five senses humans have other "senses" and powers which are not yet very clearly defined but are obviously real.

• **Parapsychology,** or "super senses" are normal faculties in humans, who are able to perceive information from other dimensions. These powers are still not very well developed in most people, so sometimes we have doubts about their existence. Its manifestations are spontaneous, without us actually knowing exactly how they occur; however, they are completely real. Therefore, we need to come to terms with these as other forms of communication; other ways of receiving information.

6.6 What is death?

At this point we should resolve a number of questions about the state which is called **death.**

First, what is genetics all about? It organizes form. Genetics is not separate from the body: it dissolves but is not lost. It is like the original of a recording which we can make copies of.

For example: when wood burns, it turns into very basic, elementary particles. The genetic information that was printed disappears but it is not deleted from the original archive where the copy came from. The same happens to the body when the higher level archives are separated: matter returns to matter, the form disappears and the genetic information dissolves; but it was only a copy.

Another example: if two people are talking on the phone and someone cuts the cable, the call ends; but nothing happens to them; they are still where they were. And pure consciousness cannot be destroyed; it can only be expressed differently. Thus, with physical death, nothing happens to humans; only some forms of communication are altered, but they continue to exist without anything happening to the soul. The transformation after physical death does not consist of a movement to another time or place, but a qualitative change in the focus of consciousness.

It is a misconception to think that the human soul resides in the physical body. Not so; it is outside space and time, although it is projected through a body and a mind. Only what is physical occupies a place in space and time, therefore only the mind and body occupy a place in space.

It is not correct to ask "where" the soul is, because the word "where" implies a place in space and time, and the soul is everywhere and nowhere at the same time because it is non-local. The soul vibrates, and through that vibration it creates the body and the mind in order that it can express itself in the physical world.

Archives are separated in reverse order to their vibrational frequency, i.e. first the physical body separates itself i.e. matter, from the other archives; next in vibrational frequency is the personality archive. Personality, now outside matter, remains in the vibration of the fourth dimension. Then the ego, the system of beliefs and misinformation, begins to dissolve, as these cannot be sustained without the energy provided by matter through suffering.

The personality enters a state of dissolving ignorance, a state that lasts some time. Little by little it distances itself and gradually changes dimension. When it reaches the seventh dimension, the ego has completely dissolved. The understanding that is stored safely at that point in the personality is assimilated by consciousness, and the mind completely disappears, leaving only the transcendent spirit.

Consciousness is timeless, and does not have any experiences, rather it assimilates the understanding gained by the personality. Once our consciousness has freed itself from the physical body and personality, it is assessed: our accumulated understanding is examined. If we "pass an exam", our teachers prepare more teaching material for the next exam. But if we fail the exam, they redesign the same material so we can take the exam again.

Consciousness is the sum of understanding of many different people. We have to get 100% in the "exams"; passing with only 50% does not work, as in the case of the schools of Earth. Every human being has all the time they need and they will keep up the pace which is appropriate to their dedication, focus and intensity.

What happens when the Being (the life that animates the form) is separated from the body? After the assessment has been completed and destiny has been designed, the spark of divine essence returns to its cosmic ocean in the centre of the Universe. It has never lost its essence, nor is it subject to changes of any kind. When it is no longer necessary to maintain life, this spark returns to its place; to its own origin. When consciousness once again takes over a body to enter a new experience, the spark returns to restore life.

The definitive destiny of each one of us is the automatic and impersonal consequence of energy patterns established in the aura of our spiritual body or soul. There is no reward or punishment arbitrarily handed out by any power or divinity. The "self" gravitates towards its destiny because of its essence. This is "divine justice" which guarantees complete impartiality. "Heaven has many abodes".

The soul is like a small particle within an electromagnetic field. Its attractions and repulsions depend on its charge and polarity within a larger field that has scales of energy and power frequency. All eventualities are therefore a reflection of the level of development within the whole.

6.7 What is the difference between life and death?

Life is eternal; and death is only the dissolving of ignorance. The only thing that really dies in the Universe is ignorance. It is not correct to say "he/she lost his/her life" but rather "he lost his physical form and ignorance or ego".

Life and death are the same as the dawn and dusk of a day. One is happy to see the sun come out and springs into action, but also when dusk arrives and one can rest. We do not lose anything valuable —this is never lost— but only what is no longer needed: physical form or ignorance.

Human beings do not need to suffer before death, since this is a wonderful event, like a change of course or school. This would be equivalent to suffering because a son had finished secondary school and was going on to university; there is no cause for suffering, but happiness. Death is not the end of life but the beginning of a new experience. Coming to terms with death means understanding that death is not the end of life but the end of this experience in the material world. It is important to prepare for death while we are alive. Good preparation can be summarized in the following steps:

- Acquiring sufficient spiritual information.

- Accepting death as natural.

- Sorting out the affairs of the world of physical form.

- Releasing all feeling and attachment.

- Making the appropriate decisions about what will happen with one's body.

Death is as beautiful as life itself; man is always being born: he is either born into matter to experience learning, or born to the spirit to assess what it has already learned.

Death, in turn, is necessary. When the ego crystallizes, it is no longer useful for consciousness' evolution because it does not obtain any more understanding. At that point the development process stops and some time may pass during which that person is used as a "trainer" for others: those who do not change, who do not move, are trainers for others. Mental flexibility consists of always being willing to change, adapt and learn new things. When someone thinks: "I am the way I am and nobody is going to change me", they have just pronounced their death sentence. If a person does his/her inner work efficiently, he/she may reach far beyond the expected time because renewal becomes unnecessary when there is a constant process of change.

Death serves to break the crystallized ego and renew all the processes of evolution. It renews our body, mind, our destiny and our mission. So it makes no sense to see it as an enemy, rather as a wonderful process when the right moment comes.

Chapter 7. Human relationships according to the New Vision

Throughout the history of Mankind, human beings have found it enormously difficult to establish harmonious relationships. One need only to look at the armed conflicts with which each group fruitlessly tries to impose their ideas, in the false belief that they are right or that they hold the solution to human problems. However, the sad truth is that with each attempt to arrange social structures to suit their own ideas, new difficulties, disagreements, struggles and wars arise that are increasingly destructive and distressing. This clearly shows that the path of imposition and of subjugation to any idea –however good it may seem to those who defend it– is not the path that leads to peace.

The inability to achieve harmony in relationships is what leads to the existence of borders, properties and individual boundaries, which make it impossible to properly harness the resources that are available. This gives rise to a society that is unbalanced and chaotic, where everyone strives desperately to achieve a relatively secure position that will enable them to satisfy their individual needs. However, obsessed with that effort, people do not understand that the real problem is inside them, since not knowing how to get on with others makes it impossible for them to share existing wealth, or to find full satisfaction of all their physical, social and spiritual needs, and thereby achieve a state of peace, harmony and happiness.

The different types of relationships that human beings establish with each other are what determine the social structure. But in addition, if we analyze it throughout life, the way of relating makes it possible to measure fairly accurately the nature of the limitations acquired by the human personality. In this measure, learning to engage in harmonious relationships becomes an important tool for evolution, since as well as being what builds civilization, it helps people to transcend their own conceptual and traumatic limitations. Thus, at the end of their constant striving to find satisfaction in relationships, an individual can ultimately discover the principles of Love beyond their learned concepts and limitations; and, as a result, they can recognize it as the only authentic inner guide to reach personal happiness. In this way we can aspire to building a new civilization in which personal conflicts and wars among our fellow men no longer exist.

The origin of human behaviours

The behaviours of human beings originate in three different inner archives. Although the conduct of some people may at times seem incomprehensible, it can be said that all behaviour has a well-defined origin, which we can learn to recognize and manage consciously in a simple way. It is possible to classify such behaviour into three categories:

Natural behaviour

This has to do with survival and selection. It is "innocent" because it is based on the functions of instinct, which are expressed by selecting a mate with the best qualities and their genetic compatibility for procreation. It also has to do with seeking all the necessary elements to stay alive in the best possible way and as comfortably as possible; its main purpose is to stay alive. Natural behaviour, in the field of relationships, is basically "insensitive" to the needs of others, since the individual is concerned only with themselves, and their conduct can be interpreted as "selfish". This is purely impulsive behaviour that has to do with the instinct for survival and is unconscious, automatic and lacking in feelings.

Learned behaviour

This behaviour refers to the cultural and intellective nature. It can be considered "ignorant", because it is based on limiting traumas acquired in experiences that were not understood, and on all kinds of learned knowledge that has not yet been verified. The intellect experiences this type of knowledge through the process of analyzing, investigating, drawing conclusions and experiencing the consequences of the person's own conduct, which are verifiable. Its main purpose is to "experience life". Learned behaviour makes relationships difficult because it leads people to interpret the behaviour of others based on suppositions and conceptual beliefs. This, in turn, leads an individual to develop sensitivity associated with feelings.

Correspondent behaviour

This behaviour comes from a certain level of consciousness. It can be considered "conscious", because it is based on the understanding of the different aspects of life, their levels of evolution and the recognition of the Laws that govern the Universe and life. Its main function is the expression of Love, through which the limitations that originate in the other two archives that manage behaviour are transcended; its main purpose is to "understand life". Relationships supported by congruent behaviour always flow without difficulty and achieve marvelous levels of human and social satisfaction, because this behaviour makes it possible to fully develop "acceptance".

If an individual does not progressively transcend the temporary characteristics of instinct and personality, they will find it difficult to establish Love relationships.

Instinctive behaviour (an animal characteristic) is what dominates a person when they have not yet developed another archive or higher centre that can guide new behaviour. As soon as the personality archive or learning centre starts operating, instinct should be reduced to its life-long basic function, i.e. that of generating life and staying alive; but that is not what happens. Instead, it also introduces concepts about how to stay alive into the personality archive, which of itself cannot understand the basic law of nature.

When the lower centers (instinct and personality) run behaviour, life is a permanent inner conflict which manifests as constant disharmony in relationships with others; this then leads to aggression, defensive behaviour and conceptualization. Learned, or conceptual, behaviour inevitably involves dissatisfaction and suffering, until the archive of the higher centre of understanding, or consciousness, comes into operation, even if only partially. When this happens, the learning centre is reduced to its basic function: "to experience life and obtain verified results to nourish the development of consciousness".

Behaviour that is congruent with the Law and with harmony is governed by the archive of understanding or consciousness, which is not unaware of the importance of the other two centers in their complementary basic functions for the development of understanding. The problem with human behaviour is that it originates from other centers that do not have the necessary information or characteristics for the expression of Love. For this reason, until we achieve behaviour that is supported by the centre of understanding, we will not be able to find happiness in our relationships, or satisfaction in life; for in the same way as it is not possible to express feelings through instinct, it is not possible to express Love through concepts and interpretations originating from ignorance.

In order not to confuse what happens in instinct with what happens in the personality, we need to distinguish the "pain" that the physical body experiences when it is hurt, injured or ill, from the "suffering" that is experienced in the mental field when we do not accept something. It can be said that it is possible for there to be pain without suffering, and also suffering without pain; in the same way, there can be pain with suffering and suffering with pain. Suffering is typically mental, and that is why it is called sentimental suffering; it is associated with feelings and with the mind's beliefs, whereas pain has nothing to do with beliefs or concepts, it is purely physical; it is one of nature's defense mechanisms, because if there were no pain, the body could disintegrate without us realizing. Suffering is also a defense mechanism, but it is of the ego, which does not want to disappear and defends itself by suffering.

7.1 The purpose and function of relationships

The purpose of relationships is for human beings to learn to live in harmonious coexistence with all the other beings that inhabit the Universe; their function is to maintain balance, enabling individual satisfaction through integration with others. That is why we cannot find personal satisfaction in isolation, since on our own we cannot adequately develop our human function of linking up the different levels of evolution in order to integrate all of the components in balance. This is necessary not only for personal satisfaction but also to facilitate understanding of the importance of universal cooperation.

When someone turns once again towards the centre of balance after verifying that they are and form part of the universal whole, they find themselves with a series of learned limitations that hinder their intentions. These obstacles present them with the opportunity of recognizing them and overcoming them through the necessary understanding and training in the field of relationships because integration with others cannot be achieved without first having broken down the external barriers. But this cannot be done without first having eliminated our internal limits. The best way of overcoming these limits is to consistently practice the principles of Love in all our relationships, because it is our relationships that enable us to become acquainted with our inner selves.

The fact that relationships are a measure of our level of inner harmony means they enable us to accurately recognize our personal limitations, and they facilitate conscious work to overcome them. The objective is to achieve harmonious integration with full satisfaction in all areas of relationships.

Relationships are an ongoing learning process through which, ultimately, we are able to move from fear relationships –based on instinct– and suffering –full of egoism– to Love relationships –founded on understanding–, in which there is always mutual satisfaction. The degree of ignorance or understanding can be measured by the result of selfish behaviours –those coming from ego, from limitations– or loving behaviours. This is so because the outer result speaks clearly of the inner methods used; this result shows whether someone used a false belief or a true belief that they turned into wisdom. This is summarized in the following table:

Table 2. The selfish person

BEHAVIOUR OF A SELFISH PERSON	RESULT OBTAINED IN OTHERS
INCONSIDERATE	ABANDONMENT - LONELINESS
COMPLAINING	ESTRANGEMENT - ANNOYANCE - WEARINESS
BAD-TEMPERED	ESTRANGEMENT
IMPATIENT	DISTRESS - BAD TEMPER
RESENTFUL	ISOLATION

BEHAVIOUR OF A SELFISH PERSON	RESULT OBTAINED IN OTHERS
DOMINEERING	REJECTION - ABANDONMENT
OVERBEARING	REBELLIOUSNESS - RESENTMENT
HYPERCRITICAL	ARGUMENT - ESTRANGEMENT - LONELINESS
AGGRESSIVE	DEFENSIVENESS
POSSESSIVE	IRRITATION - SEPARATION
SHOUTING	DISCORD - DISPLEASURE
MEAN	UPSET - ESTRANGEMENT - IRRITATION

Table 3. The loving person

BEHAVIOUR OF A LOVING PERSON	RESULT OBTAINED IN OTHERS
UNDERSTANDING	CLOSENESS
RESPECTFUL	FRIENDSHIP
CONSIDERATE	ADMIRATION
ADAPTABLE	HARMONIOUS COEXISTENCE
THOUGHTFUL	DIALOGUE - COMMUNICATION
HELPFUL	SUPPORT - INTEGRATION
AFFECTIONATE	TENDERNESS
CALM	PEACE - HARMONY
PATIENT	COMPANY
FLEXIBLE	WISH TO SHARE
NEUTRAL	TRUST
CHEERFUL	ENTHUSIASM

Another important function of relationships is to manage the levels of inner **vital energy.** Thus, relationships that stem from selfishness and ignorance produce different sentiments from those founded on Love and harmony. Consequently, how we handle our relationships determines our inner levels of energy.

Vital energy is being produced constantly within each of us, and is consumed normally in the different activities in which we engage. When our state is one of inner peace, we use less vital energy than we produce, which means our energy increases and manifests as a state of peace, understanding, satisfaction and inner well-being that makes it easier to express Love. In contrast, when our inner state is one of permanent conflict, the consumption of vital energy is very high, which means our energy decreases and manifests as states of apathy, sadness, depression, anxiety, confusion, fear, despair, etc. That is why it is so important always to manage relationships lovingly, from understanding and harmony.

Another thing to bear in mind is that we obtain nothing by leaving a difficult relationship if we make no inner change, because otherwise the next relationship will be equally difficult. The reason is very simple: we cannot run away from ourselves; wherever we go, there we are, so if we have inner conflict, this will manifest anywhere and in any relationship.

Therefore, there is only one way to go, and that is to change inside. This is the way that does bring an end to the problem, our problem, because other people's problems must be resolved by them.

7.2 Zones of the mental field

We will comment again on this topic that was introduced in a previous chapter:

There are three zones in the mental field:

1. The zone of light: this is the upper zone that the Masters use; that is why they are called enlightened. Light is energy, and when vital energy that activates the zones fluctuates considerably in this zone, there is a deep inner sensation of love, peace, understanding, acceptance, freedom, completeness and optimum mental capacity, and vital energy is at very high levels. Masters do not allow their energy to fall; that is why you are unlikely to see a Master who is depressed, sad or suffering; in general, they will always be in a state of peace that is invulnerable to any external element; they do not connect emotionally or sentimentally with external situations, they just understand them from Love as something that is necessary. That is why, because they do not suffer, they do not consume energy.

Sentiment possesses duality, but Love does not. In the zone of light, sentiment is disengaged, and the result is directed voluntarily thanks to understanding; it does not arise spontaneously or automatically.

2. The zone of half-light: this is the zone which normally most people are in; here there is a mixture of light and darkness. In the upper part of half-light we may feel satisfaction and enthusiasm, but disappointments and suffering use up a large amount of vital energy. In the upper zone of half-light results are more or less automatic, with positive emotions arising spontaneously in response to favorable external situations, and negative emotions arising in response to unfavorable external situations. This is because they are not voluntary.

The zone of half-light is the duality between light and darkness, and whether energy rises or falls will depend on how feelings or emotions are managed.

3. The zone of darkness: this is the lower zone of the mental field. Darkness is the absence of light, and in the presence of light it cannot exist. If our energy drops we enter into a state of irritability and touchiness, and ill humor and aggression towards others begin. We may even fall into profound states of confusion, suffering, apathy, anxiety panic, deep fears, and finally, despair about life. All this may lead to suicide: the energy was extinguished.

People find themselves in these zones more or less continuously, but what is not continuous is the energy that activates or deactivates them. In general, in most people only up to the zone of half-light is active, but it would be possible to activate the zone of light, which would increase the vital energy, with a greater process of understanding.

It is wise to pay attention to the first signs of depression and not wait until the depression leads the person to a deep zone of darkness; because in that zone the mind is so confused, so subdued, that it sees no option whatsoever and believes that life is not worth living. The options are always there, they never disappeared, but without light they cannot be seen. At the first symptom of depression, pay immediate attention to your vital energy!

In general everyone produces sufficient vital energy each day, but emotional or sentimental conflicts use up so much that the resulting imbalance can be enormous. For example, energy is consumed by work, a poor diet, worries, stress, etc. Someone who is stressed can recover their energy by going on holiday for a few days, but someone who has had an emotional conflict may take two years to recover their level of balance, unless they have a good mental training and understanding to enable them to recover it in less time. The biggest consumers of energy are, as we have said, sentimental and emotional conflicts.

7.3 What is needed to build highly satisfactory relationships?

Two points associated with the zone of light have to be reached in order to be able to build highly satisfactory relationships:

1. Happiness = Zero suffering.

If we are suffering it is because we are not accepting something. If we are unable to be happy by ourselves –if our happiness depends on others because we do not manage our own inner energy– we are a danger to others. If someone believes that there is a person who can make them happy, when they face the reality that that person does not exist, they may react by blaming the other for their own unhappiness, and then by wanting to "punish them" with indifference, resentment or even physical aggression, which means that at this point the person may become quite dangerous. This kind of reaction is based on ignorance.

2. Loving = Zero resistance to others.

To build a Love relationship it is first necessary to understand that happiness can only arise from within us, and that is expressed as a total acceptance of others, as complete respect, without offering resistance to what they are or suffering because of what they are or are not. That is the beginning of Love.

To be able to reach these two zeros we need to have sufficient comprehension to be able to understand several things:

- No one can be harmed by or harm another. If this is so, then there is no one to blame, and everyone accepts their own responsibility for managing their energy. If we feel bad and we understand that that feeling is the expression of our limitations, we can decide to stop feeling bad, but that has nothing to do with anyone else. When we feel good, then we can begin to love.

•   Making mistakes and hurting ourselves always result from interpreting what others are doing or not doing.

•   Other people are not good or bad, they are just doing the best they can. We can agree or disagree with what others do, but if we offer resistance to them then we are not loving them, because instead of accepting them what we want is to change them. How can we resolve a sentimental conflict? By understanding that other people are not to blame for what happens to us, by accepting that everyone has the right to behave as they wish and as they can, and by ceasing to blame others and suffering over them.

Love is the result of a verification of the Law that is achieved through experience and training. When we suffer, the first thing to do is to find out where the error is; experience enables us to establish that it is inside us. Having done this, we need training to dismantle it, which will be followed by a great process of inexhaustible energy, the source of which is Love.

7.4 Giving value to the Love result

Because Love is a characteristic of understanding and consciousness, not of sentiment, it is not actually possible to "feel" Universal Love. However, most people are so used to operating from sentiment, that they put Love in second place, and nearly everyone finds it difficult to think that it can be expressed without the sentiment. This is the biggest mistake in relationships and it comes from placing too much value on sentiment. The other concepts learned by the personality are also a source of problems. Because they are changeable, they become double-edged swords in relationships. Thus, in most cases we end up acting from egoism, which leads to hurts that damage or break up many relationships.

Giving value to Love means always acting from understanding, beyond what we feel or believe, in order to achieve a mutually satisfactory result in relationships, in which the most valuable thing is to share Love.

Certain cultures teach us that we should always express exactly what we feel; this is called sincerity and honesty. When we take these principles as values —which in fact they are not–, we end up expressing our own ignorance and acting from egoism, because everything that we feel has its origin in learned concepts, not in truth. What is actually being expressed in that way is the imposition of our own beliefs on others to make us feel good, in the belief that in this way we are acting in accordance with a set of values. What a huge mistake! In fact, a value is everything that makes it possible to live together in harmony, sharing Love. That is why, when we express ourselves from the true values we will always obtain a mutually satisfactory result that enriches any relationship.

Wrong is the one who always says what they think. Wise is the one who always expresses the best. It does not matter why we express Love; the result of doing so will always bring satisfaction. Because the one who expresses the best, expresses truth. By doing so they are recognizing the qualities of Love in everyone. The Wise one directly recognizes people's worth and expresses it, whereas the ignorant one goes directly to the limitations and spells them out.

The following is a helpful example for illustrating this:

At a company rife with industrial disputes, it occurred to the manager to hire a psychologist to try and find a solution. The psychologist spent a fortnight saying nothing, just taking note of all that he observed. He assessed what he observed, gathered everyone together and told them: "The cause of your problems is this, you are doing this wrong, and this, and this, and this..". And he gave them a very long list of the mistakes the employees were making and he told them that the solution was to stop making those mistakes. The company was very appreciative of the psychologist's work and they all began to operate on that basis. In a short while they realized that instead of getting better, things had got worse. What had happened?

It occurred to the manager to hire another psychologist. This one spent another fortnight saying nothing, taking notes. Then he gathered everyone together and said to them: "I would like to congratulate you, because just see how many wonderful things you are doing well. The only thing you need to do now is to reinforce what you are already doing right". In a short while there began to be extraordinary results.

The second psychologist minimized the mistakes and highlighted the virtues, whereas the other one had done the opposite.

The false belief that the most valuable thing we have is authenticity, shaped by tastes, concepts and beliefs, and the right to have satisfaction in life, leads us to fight to defend this. Then it is a question of imposing our own beliefs and personal tastes, we "wish" to have many things and to "hold on to" people because we need them for our own satisfaction. However, these attitudes produce the opposite effect to the one we want.

The "result" of wrongly valuing things in this way is suffering. By defending our authenticity we do not allow integration, as a result of which relationships end, people become estranged, things are no longer satisfying, and complaint becomes our constant work tool.

True valuing, however, consists in understanding that there is only one way of finding total satisfaction, and that is by "integrating" all opposites in a single Love result. To achieve this all we need do is value relationships above any individuality, and transform them into Love relationships, which we can recognize because they result in "mutual satisfaction". But to reach that mutual satisfaction we need to admit that everyone is right, since in understanding we are all equal, because understanding always leads us to the same place, to the recognition of truth. Therefore, no one is authentic in their true values, and there is nothing to defend; relationships happen by integration, in a context in which for each person what is most important is the other's happiness and decisions are something that is totally secondary.

7.5 Love relationships

The commitment and ability to be in a relationship with others by reaching agreements is the way to establish conscious or Love relationships, instead of unconscious (or destiny) relationships.

- **Commitment** and the ability to reach agreements.

There is a special characteristic in human relationships that clearly distinguishes them from those established by other species. This characteristic is easily recognizable in the ability to make a commitment. In fact it is impossible for someone to engage in any activity without there being a commitment, whether it be with children, studies, clients, work, neighbors, etc. When someone has not yet developed the ability to make commitments, they are unlikely to be loyal to any relationship, and those they establish will be founded basically on the animal characteristic of the instinct for survival, that is to say, in satisfying their own needs without taking into account those of others. Based on this we can say, without fear of making a mistake, that:

The ability to make commitments is proportional to the level of loyalty and the skill in building Love relationships.

What decisions generate commitment? All of them.

What commitments require agreements? Also all of them.

What agreements create relationships? Once again, all of them.

People who have commitment "phobia" and say things like "I don't want to lose my freedom"; "committing takes my freedom away"; "why make an agreement when everyone knows what they want", I'd recommend that they live in isolation, on their own; because all those beliefs are what prevent them from striking up harmonious relationships. Yet if someone aspires to building satisfactory, stable relationships then they must be ready to assume their decisions and commit to them, and to give fluidity to their commitments by reaching agreements which they abide by.

Where there is no ability to commit, there can be no relationships either. A commitment is a complement to life that does not take away freedom but generates it, because it makes it possible to do other things.

For agreements to be founded on Love it is necessary to carefully observe the following recommendations:

- To value relationships above individual tastes.

- To be always ready to offer support.

- On all occasions to establish Loving communication.

- To depersonalize situations; to speak only about what is positive.

- To stay in the present.

"Agreement frees you, whereas rules and beliefs enslave you."

7.6 Unconscious relationships and conscious relationships

There are two types of relationships depending on the circumstances that arise in life and they are related to the needs for individual experience for the development of consciousness. Unconscious relationships are characterized by egoism, whereas conscious relationships are characterized by the expression of Love.

Unconscious relationships are recognized by the presence of aggression and dissatisfaction, as well as the lack of appropriate options to be able to get away from the relationship or avoid the situation. These relationships generally begin because there is strong point of attraction (fatal attraction), which may be physical, financial or social, or based on any other personal convenience. However, despite this, from the start certain difficulties can be observed that are characteristics of unconsciousness, such as fear, doubt, mistrust, uncertainty, lack of shared objectives, and disagreements.

In this type of relationship those involved generally apply the "method of resistance", precisely the one in which the Law of destiny is fulfilled (the greater the resistance, the greater the pressure). This method takes different, well-known forms, which always generate suffering and discontent in the field of relationships; some of them are: criticism, rejection, aggression, indifference, annoyance, rebelliousness, heated argument, contradiction, sulking, not talking, not valuing, bad temper, scolding, nagging, threats and physical, verbal and psychological violence. They finally end in a relationship of endurance, with continual attempts to escape that are never successful.

In contrast, **conscious or Love relationships** are characterized by the "understanding" that every situation that we experience is a marvelous opportunity for learning and mutual growth; the use of excellent communication; and the manifesting of a permanent willingness to serve, and to create options for managing differences and giving mutual support in order to develop adaptability, flexibility and the awareness of true sharing. All this makes it possible to achieve a high level of satisfaction in relationships.

These relationships generally arise when there is mutual admiration or recognition of the other's values. The first manifestations of admiration are observed with the appearance of shared interests, wanting to know more about the other, wanting to share, sense of trust, feeling of loyalty, sensation of peace and certainty of finding support, and the perception is one of an atmosphere of integration with the other person. In this type of relationship, those involved apply the "method of acceptance", in which the Law of Love is always respected the integration of extremes in a single purpose of Love and peace. The method of acceptance cancels out all possibility of suffering in relationships, and this is only achieved by using the tools of consciousness, which are: valuing, acceptance, commitment, calm, understanding, appreciation, cheerfulness, service, respect, communication, recognition, enthusiasm, kindness, reflection, information, congratulation, availability, owning, action, dialogue, support, tenderness and gentleness. Conscious relationships lead to a process of steady growth in Love, and they bring great satisfaction to the people involved in them, which makes them very stable and long-lasting.

To summarize, we can say that to achieve truly conscious relationships, founded on the principles of Love, it is necessary to have learned enough about unconscious relationships so that we no longer need to have that type of experience. We must also be capable of distinguishing clearly between the behavioral characteristics that stem from egoism and ignorance, and the principles of conscious relationships that are supported by Love.

In addition, we must continually train ourselves in applying conscious behaviour, until those principles become our habitual conduct. Then it will be possible to experience a genuine renewal of life and to enjoy the marvelous complement that relationships provide.

7.7 The way to Love

There are three pre-requisites without which it is impossible to set out on the way to Love. The first is to avoid the impulse to make conceptual interpretations about other's behaviour; the second is to recognize the truth; and the third is to learn to manage our expectations of others.

1. Avoiding conceptual interpretation

One of the biggest obstacles that human beings at the third level of development of consciousness have in establishing and maintaining Love relationships —and thereby succeeding in finding true contentment, harmony and mutual growth in sharing with others– is due to the conceptual interpretation that each of us makes about the intentions, feelings, attitudes and behaviours of others. This interpretation generally leads us to blame, judge and condemn others, and naturally to damage the majority of our relationships because we do not realize that our beliefs may be a long way from the truth.

The elements that the mind uses to interpret the different situations of life and relationships do not contain real principles of Love –such as understanding, acceptance, valuing, appreciation and respect–, which means that the interpretation the mind makes based on those elements is not real, does not bring satisfaction and generally damages most relationships. There is only one belief that is true: the one that fills us with peace and makes us happy. Any concept that is not of Love is false, it is a learned limitation, it is part of ignorance. That is why it always brings dissatisfaction, separation, pain and suffering. Nothing else can be expected from ignorance.

All results we obtain in life are by Law; therefore, the consequences of the behaviour of each of us cannot be changed or interpreted. However, it is possible to modify the causes that generate results, and they are subject to interpretation. If the causes are changed, that is to say, the methods used, different results can be obtained, but those already obtained cannot be modified. Learning from them is what enables us to recognize the Law.

So rather than interpreting the results, it is in the results that we verify the Law. The following statement serves as an example: "Two cars were involved in the accident and there were two casualties". This result is subject to verification not interpretation: someone made a mistake and as a result two cars were in an accident and two people were injured. However, what is the usual interpretation?: Who was to blame? Whose fault was it? What will be the punishment?. Someone who is wise makes no interpretation whatsoever but concludes: "There is a result that shows us a Law, and there is simply the need for learning". From wisdom one asks: "What do we need to learn?" And this is how we succeed in establishing Love relationships. The origin of something undesirable will always be an error, and that error is an opportunity to learn something so that it is not repeated. What we must look for is a learning experience, not a guilty party or an accusation. In every clash there is a learning experience for both sides, in which each one learns what they need to learn. For example, the person attacked is learning not to blame their attacker, not to judge, and to let go of some things that they do not need through acceptance. For their part, the attacker is learning to respect, not to attack, and is going to verify the Law of Cause and Effect.

The result that each one receives shows what they have inside them. The Law of Correspondence says that everything is in its place, because each event and each location has its place in the Universe. Therefore, each person is in congruence with the location where they live and with the experiences they have each day. Everything that happens in the life of a human being has been generated by them, which means they have no reason to blame anybody for it, or themselves either. If they have generated events, they have done so for the purpose of learning and discovering the laws that govern the Universe. Therefore, they will have done it from a "pedagogical need" and there is no one to blame or to punish for any reason.

For as long as we fail to understand this we will have conflict-prone relationships, which arise from conceptual interpretation; this is nothing other than modifying what we do not understand to reconcile it with how we want to understand it; a widespread skill among human beings.

2. Learning to recognize truth

In order to have Love relationships we first need to have recognized the difference between a belief and a truth, and to know how to recognize them within ourselves in a result.

In order to achieve a physical, real and scientific recognition of the truth, to liberate ourselves and to be able to establish Love relationships, we need to observe the results of our behaviour:

• Inner results –in the mental field–: either happiness, peace and contentment, or suffering. Happiness is present in the absence of suffering, and Love arises only when there is no resistance. If someone resists something or someone, they will generate a conflict through lack of Love.

• Outer results –in the physical field–: regarding relationships with others, health, material resources, and adaptation to one's surroundings. All of us can make a personal evaluation in these four spheres to determine what percentage of satisfaction we have in each one of them. These percentages present a direct relationship with the mental field, and it is there that the process of spiritual development is recognized.

The quickest to verify are the inner results; they can be changed in seconds simply by changing our thoughts. As for the outer results, we can verify those of the present moment, and they will also change when internal change is made, though not always as fast as the inner results.

Any external problem is in fact showing us our mental limitations. If someone has problems in their relationships with others, it is because they are unable to accept them as they are, because they wrongly interpret them as "bad".

The truth has no charge, because it is like Love; that is to say, there is not a positive truth and a negative truth, there is only a neutral truth. What is neutral puts up no resistance, in neutrality there is no suffering, no anxiety, and there is no problem. Truth, because it is neutral, does not interpret, judge or condemn, it does not blame anyone, and it is therefore totally freeing from all conflict.

When we observe any event whatsoever from truth, we understand that it is necessary, regardless of whether it is classified by some people as dramatic or whether it is classified as satisfactory or pleasant. Independently of that, **every event is necessary;** if it were not, it could not exist.

Our first exercise of inner "neutrality" must be to understand that external events, because they are neutral, have no possibility of causing harm. However, people inflict much harm on themselves when they interpret external events or the behaviours of other people from ignorance, and blame others for what is happening to them. While there is blame there will be no peace or good relationships.

If, in contrast, events are understood from truth, then they can be utilized. If an event hurts our feelings, we can always see it as an opportunity to learn something new. At that moment, since a value has now been found for it, it begins to stop being painful or challenging and becomes satisfactory, because of what can be learned from it.

3. Managing expectations

People often deceive themselves by believing that they can make others happy, or that others can make them happy. However, the only way to be happy is to find happiness within ourselves and to learn to share it with others.

Expectations do not pertain to wisdom, but to ignorance. That is why it is better not to have expectations, but to enjoy each moment of life. That is all we need to do.

"Have an expectation and you will find disappointment."

7.8 The keys to Love in relationships

The seven keys to Love are found beyond concepts, beliefs, interpretations, culture, traditions and learned limitations, and they can be recognized very simply:

1. Love always brings as a result **inner peace, happiness and satisfaction** in relationships and in all that we do. If this is not the result we find in our own lives, the answer is simple: we are not acting from our centre of understanding, nor are we giving of our best.

2. Love is a Law that is always verified with **results that produce satisfaction.** Anything that does not leave us with inner peace and harmony is the result of acting from learned concepts and beliefs, and that is what leads us directly to unhappiness in relationships.

3. Happiness in relationships **is the result of loving and supporting the happiness of those with whom we are in relationship.** Those who love work, life, the Earth, plants or people, and are always looking after them and valuing them without expecting anything, that same thing —work, life, the Earth, plants and people— will give them back abundance and satisfaction. All that we give is given back to us, because this is the natural result of Love.

4. What we decide to sow in life is voluntary, but **the harvest is obligatory.** If we constantly sow cheerfulness, enthusiasm, cooperation, service, support, optimism, understanding, appreciation and respect, we will gather

abundant harvests of Love, happiness, well-being and satisfaction in all our relationships. Egoism is a characteristic of the opportunist who, without having sown anything, expects to reap a harvest and calls it justice. But the fact is that those who sow nothing, will reap nothing; and, as the Spanish saying goes: "He who sows the wind will reap the whirlwind". The basis here is an elementary principal called "the harvest of life": everyone reaps what they sowed. When someone reaps harvests of suffering, conflicts, aggression or hate, it is clear that the seed they sowed was one of hate and violence. There is only one way of reaping abundant harvests of satisfaction: by sowing seeds of Love; otherwise, we can expect a pretty poor harvest.

See what results you obtain in life in the four aspects mentioned: health, relationships, resources and adaptation to surroundings; and consider that to aspire to obtain a different result requires a different seed. If someone begins to sow a different seed, right now –even before having finished reaping the previous harvest– a new harvest will begin to thrive that may possibly cancel out the previous one. This is the Law of cause and effect.

5. Love is a **deep understanding** that is expressed with an **attitude of service, appreciation, valuing, acceptance and respect** for people, things and life. Constantly valuing and appreciating everything that life gives us will ultimately generate inside us the ability to enjoy all things and situations, and to establish excellent relationships that are characterized by a high level of satisfaction.

6. Love is the feeling inside that we can always express ourselves with **kindness, gentleness, tact, prudence, simplicity, absolute trust, total dedication, complete freedom and unconditional support.** When you feel Love calling at your door, you must always express kindness itself; then you will find that life is delicious and re-

lations are exquisite; because then you will know that there are always many things and beautiful moments to share and enjoy.

7. Acting with Love consists **in always doing what is necessary for others to feel happy** to share with us.

7.9 Conclusions

The main conclusions that may be drawn from the ideas presented in this chapter are as follows:

• We cannot build relationships without accepting commitments. We have to be willing to commit ourselves to achieve success in any area of life.

• We have to agree on our commitments before-hand. That is to say, in order to commit to something, first we have to reach an agreement, and to do that we have to sit down and talk.

• We have to base agreements on Love commitments, since some agreements are instead disguised impositions that never work. Agreements must be free, spontaneous, reached with others by mutual agreement, if you will forgive the repetition. Sometimes it is said that we reach agreements with children when we say to them: "You must tidy your room, do your homework and do these chores, is that okay?" But this is not an agreement, it is an imposition. Instead, reaching an agreement involves sitting down with a child, or with the other person, and saying to them: "How would it seem to you, how do you like it, how do you feel best, what do you think…" Giving orders and then asking if someone agrees is easy to do, but it is no way to reach an agreement.

• Love commitments are made using the following tools: acceptance, respect, trust, freedom, service, support, tenderness, loyalty and firmness.

• There is a commitment that comes before the ones we enter into with others, and that is our personal commitment. This is an individual decision, in which we decide to commit to managing our inner energy as a human being. When someone behaves indecisively because they have difficulty or they are afraid of taking decisions, energy accumulates inside them, stagnates and does not flow. As may be supposed, the sole fact of taking a decision, even though at times it may not be easy, releases the energy and there is immediately a psychological rest. The Masters say this: "Always take a decision; even if it is not the best one, it will release blockages and let the energy flow". Afterwards, if you see that it was not the best decision, you can make a different one.

Chapter 8. Unconditionality and abundance

There is a mathematical equation that appropriately defines **abundance:**

Right information + Action = Abundance.

Abundance is the natural state of the Universe. It is as natural as the fact that the sun is always "up there". There are times when it cannot be seen because it is covered by clouds. When the sky is cloudy, and we want to see the sun, the clouds have to be moved out of the way; once this has been achieved, the sun reappears, because it was always there.

There are a number of values that the soul must learn in order to generate abundance naturally, without effort. As always, it is an inner state that determines the outer manifestation.

Those values lead to the idea of **unconditionality.** To be unconditional means to be ready for service in any circumstance with joy and enthusiasm. It is the ability to transmit and share the best values with no restriction or condition whatsoever. Nobody who imposes conditions can open the door to abundance. The concept can be likened to the process of sowing and reaping, in which the sower does not know exactly where their seed will fall.

Abundance is an inner state, and is not measured only by the resources one possesses or obtains. Once again, the importance of one's inner attitude comes to the fore. What one achieves by imposing conditions on one's service due to outer circumstances is to block the Law. Abundance, however, is a consequence of inner unconditionality, and if we have problems with abundance, then that is where we must look for the causes.

In contrast to what culture teaches us, there is another condition that restricts abundance: it is called "setting goals". Doing this causes a diversion of the flow of energy. One never knows whether such goals will be reached or not, whether the person will be in correspondence with them being met, and that will generate anxiety, which, in turn will diminish the capacity for action. We should not impose restrictions on life, it is useless to attempt to quantify the Universe; it is better to open up to receiving whatever comes. An "abundant" person has learned to give and to receive. Goals are always of the ego while a purpose is always spiritual.

Many people are on the lookout to see what they will receive from others, and yet they have nothing to give. Others have things to offer, but their ego and their pride make it hard for them to receive, because it interprets this as a weakness. It is difficult to find people who are in balance here. The lack of inner balance also blocks abundance. Life does not give much or little, it gives whatever matches each individual's capacity for service.

Some of the main inner values that generate abundance are:

- **Trustworthiness.**

- **Enthusiasm.**

- **Commitment.**

- **Respect.**

- **Loyalty.**

- **Service.**

- **Openness to constant learning.**

It is relatively easy to verify the effectiveness of these values because the Universe always shows the results. Since we know that abundance is a natural state that can be accessed, the question would be: what blockages are in the way of achieving it?

If the inner functioning of a person based on the values mentioned above is good, then there will be no problems with abundance. And if a person does not have those values in them, then however, hard they try in the outside world, things will not happen.

It has traditionally been said: "By the sweat of your brow you will eat your bread", and then: "Seek ye first the kingdom within, and all else shall be added unto you". These two maxims seem to be contradictory. Which one is right? The thing is that both of them would be right if we understand that in the first, when "bread" is mentioned, the reference is actually being made to wisdom, and not to food; it is wisdom that is achieved with sweat, with suffering, by making mistakes in order to learn. Misinterpreting this maxim has led culture to turn subsistence into a struggle, when it should be based on enjoyment.

We human beings have our subsistence assured as a result of our function. Those who are happy and enjoy what they do will always have an abundance of resources at their disposal. It is essential to learn how to humanize work, since it is human beings who act out that experience. Our work or job fulfills an essential role in the development of consciousness, and we should not forget that that is its principal meaning and its reason for being.

To quote Kabir:

"Work has no other aim than the getting of knowledge [of truth]: when that comes, then work is put away. The flower blooms for the fruit: when the fruit comes, the flower withers."

We will now go on to discuss briefly each of the values that generate abundance.

Trustworthiness is a value that opens all doors and every heart. It has two legs: confidence in oneself, or **self-worth,** and being trustworthy to others. Achieving the latter has entailed learning not to feel resistance to anything or anyone, and to behave normally. It is also necessary to be able to serve others without suffering with them, and not to be offended by their attitudes "If I am offended and I say so, they will cease to trust me because I attack, criticize or judge". To be trustworthy it is necessary to have learned how to give others the right to make a mistake.

Temperaments that are shy, irascible, oversensitive, overemotional, excitable and sloppy, are not trustworthy. Temperaments that are active, calm and peaceful are. Mental rigidity is not trustworthy either, because a person with that trait may at any time run away, attack or misinterpret a situation. People open up when they recognize another's capacity for respect.

Enthusiasm means living from an energy level that is inspired and purposeful, always looking for situations for service. To give and to give oneself to others will generate an amount of joy that will be converted into vital energy. Any intention to take action attracts the information, the resources and the conditions for the action. Enthusiasm is the "gasoline" of the action. However, a reluctance to act blocks all resources. Poverty and misfortune are the result of inertia.

Enthusiasm generates loyalty in others, and the ability to focus.

Commitment. Trustworthiness opens the door to abundance, and commitment makes what is behind the door flow. This value implies the ability to share without restriction. There is no obligation, since commitment is a decision taken freely; it must be for it to be valid.

A false concept about freedom can cancel out the capacity for commitment. For example, the belief that if we commit ourselves to something or to somebody, we will lose the freedom to act and be independent within the world of matter. However, freedom is an inner quality, and in the world of matter there is no independence, only processes of giving and receiving governed by the Law. Nothing is independent and alien to the principle of sharing. Freedom is the right to take decisions and also to make mistakes in order to grow, and it is ruled by free will up to the boundary of the rights of others. Independence is being able to be happy without depending on anything or anybody. Commitment, therefore, can never diminish either freedom or independence when these concepts are properly understood.

Those who are committed to what they do are successful, because they flow with the Law. Love, to give just one example, is committed. Entitlement, is the result of commitment + action. Rights do not exist in and of themselves, they are acquired through commitment. "The more I give, the more I receive. The more I do, the more I need, and the more I need, the more I receive". If someone complains about what they have, they are not committed to it, they do not value it.

If we were to ask people who own a business what they expect to obtain from it, and they answered that what they expect is money to be able to travel round the world, that would mean that they are not committed. The appropriate answer from a standpoint of commitment would be to strengthen the business and give excellent customer service.

Respect means allowing others the right to their own destiny, to their own learning experiences. Not going in "like a bull in a china shop", not trying to change everybody, particularly if one is not invited to do so.

Loyalty. There is a saying: "The difference between an exam grade of 'very good' and one of 'outstanding' is 5%, but the difference between loyalty and disloyalty is … infinite". There can only be loyalty when there are clear agreements; it is a spiritual state of understanding that occurs whenever commitments have been established.

Rules are dictated unilaterally and generate obligations that must be fulfilled; breaking a rule involves disobedience, but not necessarily disloyalty. However, agreements are established bilaterally, which involves negotiation, and they are fulfilled through understanding. To be able to negotiate requires mental flexibility and the ability to give way. Loyalty therefore does not arise from rules, but from agreements that one has decided to respect.

Being loyal means not breaking commitments unilaterally; they can be changed, but not broken. Change is bilateral; it can cancel an agreement and generate another one, which will also require loyalty. Compatibility implies being able to make agreements and change them with ease when appropriate, involving both parties. There is no disloyal competition, because in competition there is no agreement; what there is, is unequal competition. The difference between Love and loyalty is that Love does not need agreements; Love is unconditional and only requires a commitment to oneself.

Service. The capacity for service is fundamental for abundance. Those with limited abundance tend to have a limited capacity for service. Service is given when one does not think in terms of: "I'm not paid to do this" or "this is not my job" but, on the contrary, serving wherever an opportunity is found to do so, offering service selflessly and without a specific expectation of reward. Compensation may come in an unexpected way or from an unexpected source.

Prosperity and personal satisfaction are always there for those who do not limit their own potential. Action as a mission involves giving the best of oneself in all circumstances. Service consists of speaking one's own truth with the truth that another can accept. Any task carried out in the spirit of service is a door that opens to success in life.

Service consists in wanting for and giving others the same as one hopes to receive. The greatest individuals always do what they have to do for their service and trust that the resources will appear later.

It is necessary to engage all four bodies in the function of each individual: the physical body, adequately energized; the emotional body, calm and connected; the linear mind, focused on the purpose; and the spiritual body, aligned with the Law.

To be open to learning. There is a saying in the United States that says: "There are only three things certain in life: death, taxes and change". Everything changes, and it is fundamental to learn with the changes. Many people close themselves up against change, because they think: "Well ... I'm already comfortable here in my comfort zone". In fact, learning occurs outside our comfort zone. All learning is, in some way, a "death" to the previous information and a "birth" to the new. Imbalance disappears when those who do not know decide to learn from those who do. When the one who knows teaches the one who does not, both gain in wisdom.

On the basis of these fundamental inner principles or values, we will move on now to some points about abundance that it is important to consider:

First of all, **respecting the relationship between compensation and the generation of value:** to receive compensation without generating value is against the Law of Compensation. Although one may achieve this on occasions, the Law will always show the results later on.

Always "fuel" the Universe. What does this mean? As the Master Jesus said: "Leave the tithe on the table". We should not want to keep everything for ourselves, we must give the Universe the sign that we wish to grow, but that we wish others to grow as well. We have to be magnanimous in this. When something is being negotiated, we should not aim to come away with every penny, because although we might manage it on that occasion, the Universe will have us pay the price next time, and we will not know why other matters have been blocked.

Fueling the Universe also means leaving others with a reasonable margin to be able to continue with their activity. Life consists of abundance or lack of abundance. The Gospel teaching of "one hundred fold" is not just spiritual, but also practical; it is now easier to understand through which mechanisms this teaching is manifested. The "small" mind blocks abundance, even though the individual may have resources.

Letting money be a "consequence" of work, not the goal: one does not work to earn money, but to achieve inner growth by serving others and oneself, and to contribute to society. Money is a consequence of activity. This involves a change of mentality, another way of seeing life. It is very common in job interviews for the interviewee's first question to be about the pay. However, it is advisable to first find out about the function and then talk about the pay.

Finding or "inventing" work: some people think in terms of "I have to find a job", but we can think in terms of "I can invent a job". This is undoubtedly more creative. A good example may be the problem of unemployment. Someone without a job goes to see a businessman and says: "Right now I don't have a job, but I'm loyal, helpful, committed, trustworthy and respectful. I'd like you to let me show you, so I'm willing to work for you for free for a month. All I ask of you is that when you have seen for yourself what I am worth, you might recommend me to some of your contacts to see if they can offer me a job". What would be the response to this? Would such an attitude contribute to solving the problems of unemployment?

Taking suitability into account: this is a concept that must be borne in mind when choosing a function. Everyone has different talents, which is legitimate and very appropriate to ensure that all human beings are complementary. For example, if someone with no artistic talent decides to be a ballet dancer, it is obvious that they are not suitable. Each individual must judge what talents God has given them; not just talent in terms of technical ability, but also as regards the tendency of personality. We cannot go through life always fighting against the current, because that expends a great deal of energy.

Working on efficiency: a recent best-seller in the United States is a book called *"Don't sweat the small stuff"*. When we get into the habit of focusing our attention much of the time on "the small stuff", among other things that happen, creative capacity diminishes, inspiration disappears and then the doors to something greater close. Experts in efficiency and productivity always speak of the 80/20 rule; what they mean by this is that only 20% of the activities that are performed as part of "the job" are really important for its success. The rest of the time and attention –and, therefore, energy– is occupied in what is superfluous.

Win-Win: the desire for success has to be "two-way", i.e. it must be shared, in a win-win situation, meaning that we win and so does the other person. The following example will help to illustrate something that is very important about this issue: "Someone drops a $100 note and someone else sees them and says nothing, with the intention of picking the note up without being seen. That person's mind will tell them that there are no consequences, because there were no cameras and no one saw them. One might think that that person has got away with it. But the fact is that they have picked up a banknote that does not belong to them. Although no one saw this person, the Universe did, and absolutely no one escapes the natural consequences of mistakes made (Law of Karma or Law of Correspondence). What the mind does not "see" is that the capacity for future abundance will be reduced by the Universe.

Concentrating on the process: this aspect is paramount when performing a function; we must leave the results in the hands of the Universe. If we do this, we will have abundance. The problem with human beings is that we want to "control" the result. People attach little importance to the process. However, stress is caused by trying to govern the result and seeking the approval or admiration of others.

Business enterprises seen as an iceberg: business models work with strategies, production processes, communication systems, organizational models, etc. All these aspects contribute to the success of businesses. The error lies in thinking that that is the only thing that assures success. These aspects belong to the world of "doing", and when businessmen believe themselves to be the "doers" of things, it means that they have not yet understood the workings of the Universal Laws. Because of this belief, the main discussions at company board meetings are centered on these aspects. Yet a company is like an iceberg. The part that is visible is the smallest, and it is the part that is above water. It is hard to accept that the true cause of all that happens in the visible part of the iceberg is the part that cannot be seen: the level of consciousness of the company's employees.

The New Paradigm invites us to make that large part, the biggest part of the iceberg that is not visible, the focus for the main discussion, on the understanding that if that part is optimized, what is above water will function without difficulty. Every company should have a manager whose function is to raise the level of consciousness of all the staff. When businessmen and managers begin to have a better understanding of the visions of this New Paradigm, they will invite individuals with a high level of consciousness to join company boards, even if they are not highly knowledgeable about the business itself. A person with a high level of consciousness will assist in taking decisions with greater common sense, in making procedures and interactions at meetings more enriching, and will contribute to the company's long-term success.

Poverty is a state of consciousness, not a financial condition. Those who do not know how to generate abundance will not know how to use it, and will not be able to hold on to what they receive. Abundance can only be used by those who know how to generate it. It is outside the Law of Correspondence to simply give to someone who does not have without also providing the information they need to learn how to keep it. If those who do not have anything cannot use the tool, both of them, the giver and the receiver, will end up poor. To those who do more, more will be given. To those who do nothing, even what little they have will be taken from them.

Thinking about solutions not about problems: thinking about solutions attracts solutions; thinking about problems attracts problems; thinking about the problem does not stimulate creativity.

Using intuition more than the mind: to do this we must trust our own intuition; and to do so we have to identify it. The difficulty lies in distinguishing intuition from instinct; intuition is easily distinguished from reason, because reason is sequential and consumes energy; after all, it is tiring to think. Conversely, intuition is direct and non-sequential, much more accurate and it consumes less energy than the decision trees that are taught at business schools. Reason, if it is highly developed, tends towards paralysis through analysis.

Intuition is post-rational and consists of a direct and accurate grasping of information that already exists (and always existed) in the Universe; it can be distinguished from (pre-rational) instinct because it brings with it as a by-product an inner feeling of peace and certainly that instinct does not. But the education we receive teaches us to pass instinct through reason to redirect it; if we do the same thing with intuition its potential is destroyed.

We are the biggest enemy of our own success. How many times has the reader gone to work without being in the appropriate inner conditions for it? For example, after an argument with the family the previous night, without having slept well, worried by a thousand things that have nothing to do with the function itself, etc. This is how we destroy creativity and we prevent ourselves from giving our best.

This new information may revolutionize personnel selection procedures in the future. The level of consciousness of candidates will begin to be one of the selection criteria, and not just, as until now, their IQ or their *resumé*. The level of consciousness is key to achieving peace in organizations. As occurs with people, in companies, collective peace is the portal to higher faculties and creativity.

Chapter 9. Service

In this chapter we will focus in greater detail on the theme of service that was touched on in the previous chapter.

The capacity for service from the perspective of wisdom has two strands: service as information and service as action.

9.1 Service as information

We must give information from a place of knowing, from a place of wisdom. But how do we know this? Because we can verify it from our own results; we "know" that the information produces a result, we don't just "believe" it does. So, when someone has a problem, we know that they lack two things: better information and training in how to use it. This is knowledge in action.

We can say: "Look, the information that can help you to solve your problems is this, and it is installed by means of this training". If the other person follows this advice, their problems will soon begin to turn around and they will overcome their difficulties. Yet it also might be that they do not want the information. In that case, we need to use another tool of wisdom: to respect their experience because it is not yet their time, they have not yet reached the saturation point. This strand of service involves offering sufficient, effective and timely information to someone who is open to receiving it; it also involves teaching that the perfect world that everyone is looking for already exists —since everything already exists in the Universe–, and that all that is required is to come into correspondence or alignment with it. Recalling the holonic nature of reality, what we are trying to do is to take the greatest depth possible to the greatest extension feasible, while practicing respect.

9.2 Service as action

This strand of service is a powerful tool of abundance. What it means is that whatever needs to be done in a person's life –whatever that may be, from the simplest basic task to the most complex and scientific–, must be done wholeheartedly: with all energy, quality and enthusiasm; without attaching any importance to where it is done, for whom, when, or the benefit that may be obtained from it (unconditionality). Pure service is free from expectations. Another option within service as action, if we are not able to serve directly, is to help those who serve.

When someone's aim in doing something is to be rewarded with recognition, it is the ego that is engaged. However, when the result of the action taken is abundance, it is evident that it comes from a purpose of inner commitment. Purpose is prior to all creation and all activity; it is an inner disposition toward something; and the purpose of the Universe is evolution in consciousness.

When the purpose has its origins in false beliefs it leads to a subsequent design that is chaotic. All designs are implicit in the purpose; it is not possible to harmoniously administrate a design arisen from ignorance.

When human beings come to understand the purpose of the Universe, we become the architects of Love. For service to be excellent it needs a wise purpose, a commitment to that purpose and the use of wise information to put it into effect.

For someone to be able to serve someone else, they first need to have obtained a result. It is also important to think of ourselves: if we have no tools, then we have nothing to offer someone else; and it is not possible to have tools if we have not thought about ourselves and how to acquire them. Some people say: "Thinking about myself is self-centered, and thinking about others is kindness". Those two postulates stem from ignorance. In fact, thinking about oneself is called self-worth; and if someone does not value themselves, then they have very little to offer anybody else.

Everyone knows that to **help** is to do something for someone else that they cannot do for themselves. Helping is an important form of service.

The definition of **service** is to give someone else the information they require to solve their problems and acquire the training that they do not possess.

Helping has a certain relationship with the Laws. We have to check that we are the ones who are in correspondence with that help, so that we do not interfere, or in that way prevent someone from assuming a responsibility that is in fact theirs. e.g.: "If my father is ill, it's up to me or my brothers and sisters to help, not my next-door neighbor's children". Another example: "If I'm driving along and I come to the scene of an accident, it's up to me to help, not someone who's not there".

In their service, Masters furnish all the information, but they do not move a finger to do anything for someone else who is able to do it for themselves, since that would be a sign of scant wisdom. If someone does not have the opportunity to develop their potentialities, they will not achieve success. In such a case, helping inhibits the process of developing such potentialities; so helping can be harmful instead of beneficial in certain situations, and harming someone else shows a lack of wisdom.

9.3 The rules of service

Service has certain rules that we need to learn. The first is to **do no harm,** even if it is with the best of intentions, and the second is **respect.** Sometimes it is better not to give information about "truth" if the person who receives it cannot handle it. How can we tell? It is very simple: if the information that is offered does not give the recipient peace, then it is not appropriate even if it is true; we should not say anything to anyone if it means they are not left in a state of peace; nor can we go in like a bull in a china shop and offer information we have not been asked for, because that would be showing a lack of respect for that person.

Teachings are inseparable from the consciousness that expresses them. They are then interpreted by those who receive them, and in that process they may lose their purity.

Learning how to give service from wisdom is one of the final teachings in the evolution of consciousness in the human kingdom. This is because spiritual beings at this stage are only devoted to service, and to become one of them we must learn to do it without making mistakes. Also because, until the final stages of the development of consciousness, minds are occupied with other tasks, such as those of "getting".

Many people ask themselves how they can find the right balance in service. Once more we can find the answer in teaching: Love others as yourself. We are also the others. Therefore, the idea is to give ourselves to service until we see our vital energy descending. That is the time to stop and rest. We cannot be of service to everybody all the time. The internal energy will stay high for a longer period of time when service is given without expectation and without clinging to results. If we seek a result (being understood or respected) we will be operating from a "getting" energy and that will block in many ways our capacity for service and consume more of our internal energy. Service cannot be a doing as if it was a business activity. The absence of expectation will greatly increase the joy in service.

We also have to keep in mind that the best service we can offer to the Universe is our own growth, because our increased vibration will be available for use in all the Universe and not only for the individuals with whom we may come into contact, as they will be more limited in numbers for obvious reasons. Every time that we transcend a limitation, we make it easier for others to transcend that limitation as Rupert Sheldrake has demonstrated through the functioning of the morphogenetic fields.

9.4 Living service: The Masters

It is essential to understand also that in service, energy transmission is more important than intellectual transmission. That is to say, the service is more effective of someone who lives the ideas —meaning, someone who has become what they teach— than someone who has the ideas in their intellect but does not practice them in their own life. After all, teaching is by example. It is important for a Teacher to be able to see god in the others because this will "awaken" divinity in them.

A Teacher of God is someone who decides to be one and has the necessary tools for it. Teachers come from anywhere in the world and from all religions; they are the ones who answer the universal call. It is a matter of time, all human beings will answer at some time; for the call, time has no meaning. Moreover, it does not matter what the Teacher may have been before answering the call: when they answer it they become a co-savior.

It takes great learning to be able to understand, and beyond that, to be able to teach that all circumstances are helpful for growth, since it is only to that extent that they can be accorded a degree of reality.

Service must be directed at those who are compatible and are ready to learn; otherwise it will be ineffective and conflicts will be generated. Ineffectiveness does not flow with the Law. Compatibility has nothing to do with blood relationships or falling in love; people fall in love with others who are incompatible and later on the problems appear. For example, the members of a criminal organization are homogeneous and compatible with each other, as may be the peaceful members of a spiritual organization; but criminals are compatible at one level and the members of a spiritual organization are compatible at another level.

No social problem is solved while the mental confusion that generates it continues. Solutions are individual, not collective. To find new solutions the previous method has to be changed.

In fact, the way the world thinks reverses the roles between disciple and Teacher; it appears that the two of them are separate, and as though the Teacher is giving something to the disciple, instead of to themselves. The true beneficiary of service is the one who gives it, not the one who receives it; the recipient has become correspondent with receiving it, and the Universe always has a plan B, it does not depend on the willingness of a particular instrument. When we teach joy and hope, our own learning finally comes to an end.

Teachers have realized that the world is not governed by the laws that the world invented, but by a "power" that is it within them but not of them. Once this power has been experienced, it seems meaningless to go back to trusting in one's own strengths. What is it that leads Teachers to make this change in their perception? The following are some of the steps in the evolution of Teachers:

First, Teachers must go through a period of **undoing:** they have not reached the point where the inner shift has been completed, and it seems that only the external circumstances are changing.

Then, Teachers must go through a period of **sorting out.** In this stage they will discover that many of the things that they valued before are merely obstacles to growth and to transferring what has been learned.

The third phase is a period of **relinquishing** their own interests for the sake of truth. In this stage, Teachers learn that where they anticipated grief, what they actually find is a happy "lightheartedness".

After that comes the period of **settling down,** in which Teachers rest in peace for a time, consolidate their learning and experiment with it. The potential of what they have learned seems astonishing. They need this period of respite because they have not yet come as far as they think.

The next stage may involve some **disturbance.** Teachers must recognize that they have not yet distinguished completely between what has value and what does not, although they have learned by now that they do not want what is valueless. Their own idea of sacrifice made it impossible to reach this perfect discernment before. They must learn from now on to lay all judgment aside.

Finally, Teachers reach a period of **achievement.** This is the stage of real peace that reflects the heavenly state. From that peace now all is possible.

The real changes required take place in the mind of the Teacher, and they may or may not involve changes in external conditions. There is no rule in this respect, because the training is always very personal and individualized.

9.5 Truth for spiritual teaching

Following is a list of characteristics concerning truth that are appropriate and helpful for persons or institutions devoted to spiritual teaching, from the point of view of the New Paradigm:

Universality: truth is true everywhere and at all times, regardless of cultures, personalities or circumstances.

Inclusivity: truth is not sectarian, secret or exclusive.

Availability: there is nothing to sell or to hide; there are no magic formulas. Truth is open to all.

Purity of intention: there is nothing whatsoever to gain except growth.

Truth is **free of linear positioning:** it is not "anti-" anything; ignorance is not its enemy, it merely shows that it is absent.

Absence of force or intimidation: there is no brainwashing, or adulation of leaders, just respect.

Freedom of movement: participants may come and go without being pressured and without consequences.

Simplicity: everyone must be seen according to their development, not the letters after their name, or adjectives that describe them.

Inspiration: truth is not consistent with "play-acting" or seduction.

Austerity: truth does not need prestige, pomp or wealth.

Benignness: truth has no enemies to oppose or punish.

Non-dualism: everything is manifested because of and through the field of consciousness, instead of through cause and effect in the world of form.

Tranquility: there are no conflicts or taking of sides; there is no intention of imposing anything on anyone. The transference of high vibration is innate and does not depend on the effort of propagation.

Equality: there is delimitation instead of opposition, and all levels of manifestation are respected.

Neutrality: truth is complete in itself and there is no need to gain adepts, followers or members; those who must come will come.

Mysticism: truth is experienced as a realization of enlightenment that takes the place of the illusion of the separate ego and its mentalization.

Ineffability: truth cannot be defined; radical subjectivity is experiential; context replaces content; truth is above all conceptualization.

By invitation: truth is not imposed or promoted.

Compassion: this is the by-product of truth.

Self-sufficiency: truth is not mercenary or materialistic.

Naturalness: truth is free of altered states of consciousness, the manipulation of energy through artificial exercises, drugs, etc.

9.6 Suitability in service

Each individual has specific gifts for their mission, that they have received for some reason, and they would be outside the Law if they did not use them in their service. In addition, each individual is where they are supposed to be in their evolutionary process, and that situation does not depend on the opinions of others.

The Universe uses different instruments and skills to fulfill its purpose; none of them is more important than another, they are all complementary.

It is not a good idea to consider an activity of service until we are ready for it; that is to say, until it corresponds to our own level of consciousness. Here, many mistakes have been made throughout history, and they continue to be made. Such errors hinder the evolution as much for the person who serves without being ready as for the recipient of the service. It is important for religious or spiritual institutions to understand this aspect.

All religious confessions aspire to "be of service" in accordance with their specific concepts. The temptation lies in becoming preoccupied with administrative and pastoral needs and entrusting that service to persons who are not able to do it wisely. For example, in the Catholic Church there are approximately 400,000 priests. However, it is very difficult to find, at this time in human evolution, 400,000 persons who are at the fourth level of consciousness and also wish to be priests.

What happens then? Well, persons are ordained who are at lower levels. The result is not satisfactory —although it may be perfect and necessary— and this can be verified by observing how a variety of problems appear as a result: explaining spiritual teachings from mythical or merely rational cognitive levels that perpetuate ignorance among the faithful; power struggles; financial scandals, and even sexual problems pedophilia and the like. When the latter type of problem arises, the causes tend to be mistaken, and sexual orientation is blamed instead of the level of consciousness. A person who is at the fourth level will never be a pedophile, whether they are homosexual or not. These problems have been more or less common in all religious organizations throughout history.

Why has this happened? The fundamental reason is that until now there was not sufficient information available to discern the levels of consciousness of different individuals, and willingness has been mistaken for suitability. But it is essential to realize that this has also been perfect and necessary for human beings to be able to understand the Law, which says that no one can give what they do not possess, but also that everyone has a function. A solution to this issue could be to differentiate more between functions: to assign administrative functions within religious institutions to individuals who are in correspondence with them, and pastoral functions only to individuals who are at the fourth level. This would work well, because both types of individuals would become more effective in their evolution, and the time and efforts of the more advanced individuals would be freed to be invested in the more valuable aspects of their mission.

For example, celibacy is a great treasure, and it releases whoever practices it from responsibilities that are more in accord with the third level, to be able to devote themselves to universal service. But it cannot be lived in peace if a person is not at the fourth level. If the intention is to respect the first rule of service, to do no harm, it is essential to reserve the activity of spiritual teaching to persons who have reached the fourth level of consciousness and, within it, to those who have at least achieved vision logic in the cognitive line.

We can remember here how Jesus explained to Nicodemus that the mere fact that he held a position as expert in scripture did not mean that he could understand the mysteries of life. Sometimes people are put in positions of spiritual responsibility because they have an intellectual understanding of scripture, without understanding that we can only acquire a correct understanding of truth through spiritual intuition. When Jesus answered Nicodemus: "We speak about what we know" he was referring to a deeper knowledge that the one we can obtain from our reasoning that is dependent on our senses. Because our senses are limited, so is our reasoning.

Spiritual and/or religious education has traditionally been taught by different religions, and it has been based on faith, logic and intellectual understanding. Through study, someone can receive the title of Doctor in theology, philosophy, or the like. Such studies reinforce faith and lead to intellectual mastery of complex data, but they do not of themselves produce great progress in the level of consciousness; they can lead to progressively higher levels of erudition, but not necessarily to the equivalent in enlightenment. In these cases, the difficulty usually lies in paradigm limitation, rather than in personal disposition. Such a limitation may be due to the fact that Theology and Philosophy, while elevated disciplines, are located just below the 500 line on the Hawkins scale. That is to say, they have a high rational and linear component in their elaboration.

According to Schmedling:

"Life is the university of the higher sciences of existence, and the degree obtained is that of human master in Wisdom."

Another aspect that needs to be understood is that the effectiveness of Grace and, therefore, of the sacraments and other religious rites, also depends on the level of consciousness of the ministers and of those receiving them. This includes the sacrament of marriage, in which the ministers are the marrying couple. It is much more likely that a civil union between a high third level couple will work than a sacramental union between a low third level couple, to give an example to check this out we would only need to look at the statistics. This does not mean that a sacramental union does not offer a high third level couple Grace or special assistance that they would not obtain from a civil union. Therefore, present-day religions should change their approach to one of assisting in the raising of the level of consciousness of their congregations.

Chapter 10. Integral practice in the New Paradigm. The three pillars of growth

The New Paradigm is integral. We human beings know we have four bodies; we know that, in essence, we are a soul; and we know the Laws of the Universe. With that information, how can we promote growth?

The first point would be to begin handling the right information in the mind. It is not effective in any activity to work hard but in the wrong direction. Without the right information, efforts lead to failure and frustration, increasing the likelihood of abandoning the path. In the same way, without the right information, our efforts will only serve to fill ourselves with false beliefs, which will subsequently have to be dismantled; meaning that we will face double the work.

The second point would be the training in applying the right information. In personal evolution, it is not much use having the information if the individual does not "become" that information. Knowing about something is not the same as becoming that something. In the first case, the person concerned could even teach that subject at university, but they will not reach freedom. Intellectual information is recorded in the mental or personality archive, which disappears with physical death. From an evolutionary viewpoint, the only information that is utilized is what is recorded in the archive of consciousness; and for it to be saved there the information must be experienced and verified in our own lives. Knowledge acquired makes it possible to advance, while knowledge applied makes it possible to evolve.

These first two points have already been addressed extensively in this book, which is why this chapter will deal with the third pillar of growth in a little more detail.

10.1 Spiritual practice or the management of energy. Prayer increases vital energy

The third point relates to spiritual practice or the handling of energy. Vital energy is key to spiritual development; really, it is the most important factor. When our vital energy is high, its inevitable effects are understanding and peace. If it were possible to raise vital energy artificially, the whole process could be avoided St Paul would bear good witness to this.

Yet vital energy cannot be raised artificially. So, how can it be raised? The answer is simpler than the process: look after our body, think from our soul, expand our heart and practice prayer which is the form of personal relationship with those "above".

Human beings have a **physical body,** so how should we look after it? First of all, by respecting the appropriate times of sleep and rest; also by respecting the appropriate diet, and the necessary spaces for physical exercise. All these issues have already been fully addressed in other books that deal specifically with them, so there is no need to spend more time on them here. All that remains to be said is that human beings were created by God to feed themselves with fruits and seeds, and mental clarity is clouded by consuming dead animals, alcohol and other toxic substances that do not fit with the original human genetic design.

Human beings also have an **emotional body,** so how should we look after it? Fundamentally, by learning to calm it through a better mental understanding of the processes of the Universe; also by increasing our contact with nature and engaging in appropriate practices for releasing the emotional energy charge.

Human beings also have a **mental body,** so how should we look after it? In this case, by learning to hold thoughts in the mind that are voluntary and directed at high vibration, and by rapidly letting go of low vibration thoughts when they appear. The mental body is also cared for by making an effort to acquire right information about the functioning of the Universe and of the individual.

Lastly, human beings have a **supramental body,** so what should we do to look after it? This body vibrates at a higher frequency, and to some extent looks after itself. We look after ourselves by learning to use our supramental body more often and by placing ourselves in it more quickly. To do this we can use breathing (*pranayama)* as a technique and also mature prayer. It is curious to see how through a short period of concentration on the breath it is possible to easily resolve the problem of a runaway mind. Conscious connection with the higher dimensions through prayer and meditation also raises vital energy substantially. This can be verified by anyone and it is not a belief, but a reality.

Another practice that helps us with our vital energy is to foster our personal contact with people who are highly spiritually developed, because energy is very infectious. Moreover, there is a saying that says: "We tend to become what we admire". So we all need to ask ourselves whom we admire. If we do not admire, above all, individuals with a high level of consciousness, then we have not yet understood the order of the Universe. To admire a great professional or a great sportsperson or artist (who undoubtedly do deserve admiration) more than a Gandhi or a Dalai Lama or a Teresa of Calcutta (for example), is not going to help us in our process of spiritual development.

One of the difficulties that a person who has decided to grow spiritually may face is how to actualize, in their subjective reality, the spiritual information that they have understood intellectually. The right path for this is that of meditation and contemplation, the effectiveness of which increases with intention and devotion.

Calm reflection and introspection make it possible to integrate information and re-contextualize it. They enable us to achieve a more open and intuitive state than the mental state focused on reaching goals. On the one hand, contemplation facilitates the discernment of "essence" over linear discernment; it gives a better understanding of meaning and value. In addition, it facilitates surrender of attractions, aversions and desires, and invites us to reach progressively greater levels of abstraction. Meditation reverses the mind's tendency to alight on any external element instead of paying attention to its own inner processes.

In the same way as the intellect "wants to know" about something, contemplation facilitates direct apprehension of that something. It is like a new way of being in the world, through which life becomes prayer. When we practice contemplation, one part of the mind can relate to the matters of the world, but another will always be focused on transcendence. As Swami Purna says:

> "Think about what's highest and take care of what's immediate."

We can see how another contemporary mystic expressed these ideas. Paramahansa Yoganada said:

> "Internal concentration is the way to become aware of the Heaven that exists beyond the dense Universe. Those who are willing to use some of their time to move their attention from the manifested world to the search of divini-

ty within will learn to appreciate the wonder-ful factory of creation from which all things are made. All souls incarnated in material bodies have descended from the causal and astral planes and all can ascend again through the practice of meditation and the conscious effort to elevate the vital energy. We need to shift our identification from the material body to the soul and the union with God."

Many mystics have insisted through time that in order to be able to love God with all our soul we need absolute stillness. We cannot find that union so efficiently if we pray verbally or we move our hands here and there or if we sing and dance. We cannot find that union if we are engaged in corporal activity that keeps stimulating our senses and our muscles. Only the mind that has withdrawn from sensory experience can begin to achieve the connection with our true Self.

In any event, it is important to remember that it is not good to become obsessed with the methods we use, because it could lead us to focus so much on them that we forget the objective. To quote Krishnamurti:

"Meditation is not a means to an end. It is both the means and the end."

Seeking is the end itself; to reach the truth, we must follow the path.

Spiritual progress is an exploration that offers greater rewards than other more worldly objectives. Daily life continues to be pleasant, but that pleasure is more aligned with the development of our potentials than with passing sensations.

Time, place and space are merely projections of consciousness, and have no reality in themselves. (see, for example, Haropokos, *"Power as a cause for Motion"* and Stapp, *"Mindful Universe"*). This paradigm expansion dissolves the differences between faith and reason. For example, in the christian tradition the sacraments are a source of elevation of the levels of energy of those who receive them. Even if nothing that we suppose and assume to be correct were behind the sacraments, even if their effect were illusory, two thousand years of being repeated gives them an important value. Rupert Sheldrake's *theory of morphic resonance* –which refers to morphogenetic fields– as applied to the sacraments, suggests that those who in the past have turned to them seeking Grace resonate with all others when they partake of them. Since many people have found peace and rest in the sacraments, that peace benefits others in an atemporal and non-local way. A broader vision and understanding of the sacraments makes it possible to make use of tools that are within reach of everyone in the christian culture.

When conceptual thinking, with its tendency to classify and categories, disappears, a space opens up for direct realization of the truth. With the dissolution of complexity, the simplicity of the revelation of the essence appears.

There are two types of prayer: mental and non-mental, or meditation. Both are essential to spiritual growth, and both serve to increase vital energy. There are many ways of practicing **mental prayer:** verbal repetition of prayers or mantras, mental dialogue with the higher dimensions, contemplation of wisdom texts, etc. However, we must remember that nobody can reach salvation only by repeating the name of God or by singing many alleluias. We cannot reach enlightenment only by praising Christ or by adoring his personality. Rather we have to be able to experience

Christ directly in the temple without walls of our expanded consciousness.

Non-mental prayer or meditation has a different objective: halting mental activity to open the way to something more profound. Through meditation we attempt to access spiritual knowledge through direct, subjective revelation. Research in this area shows an increase of *theta* waves, which replace the faster *beta* waves in the brain's activity.

There are many different meditation techniques, and much has already been written about them. They all attempt to facilitate the flow of spiritual energy (*kundalini*) through the *chakras*. This practice can bring many benefits, but they must be accompanied by an equivalent understanding for them to be interpreted and utilized.

One of the greatest benefits of meditation is the ability to discover that the mental field is intrinsically empty of thoughts, images and feelings, and that these activities occupy a very small percentage of it. Like the ocean under the waves, most of the mind is still, silent and empty of content. The undisciplined mind is attracted by content, since the ego is addicted to mentalization and needs constant entertainment and stimulation, even when that includes a part of negativity. The ego always prefers to be right rather than to understand the truth.

As progress is made in mastering meditation, fear of disappearing into nothingness may arise. This represents the ego's resistance and fight to maintain its sovereignty. That fear is an illusion, as are all fears, and we can let it go with the appropriate understanding. Real power lies in wisdom beyond mentalization or, what is the same thing, in intuition, as we said earlier. We must fall in love with the process of transformation in order to energize it.

As the level of consciousness increases, non-mental prayer becomes more frequent. Practicing meditation enables us to place ourselves in the mental space of a "witness", a space in which the last thought has gone and the next has not yet arisen. It is the space of the deep mind. When the mind is concentrated on this space, there are greater possibilities of receiving information of a higher vibration.

The prayer of a wise person possesses characteristics of appreciation, offering, or the petition of wisdom, not the petition of elements of the world of form. Now it is easy to understand why.

The Universe is ruled by mathematically exact Laws. Nothing ever happens that is outside those Laws —in other words—, creation does not slip through God's fingers. When we ask God for something in the world of form, there are two possibilities: that the request matches the will of the Father —what is called "the order of the Universe"—, or that it does not. In the first case it will be given, even if it is not asked for, because it forms part of the order of the Universe; however, if it does not it will not be given, the will of the Father will be done. The order of the Universe cannot be changed with a prayer or a petition; we human beings will always have what is necessary for evolution, which is not the same as having everything that the ego desires.

In any event, even if this type of prayer does not serve the mind's apparent purposes, it does help to take the mind to a state of peace and recovery of energy. A person who prays asking for something material that they do not possess is neither accepting their own reality nor utilizing it; but that prayer will bring them something that is beneficial within their state of ignorance: a momentary peace, because they think that what they are asking for is going to happen and some time will pass until they become disillusioned. Until that happens, they will enjoy greater energy.

This is how the eastern Spiritual Master Swami Purna expresses this idea:

> "Most people, regardless of the religion to which they belong, pray. Everybody prays. But what is prayer? Normally people ask for favors: "God, give me this or give me that; oh, God, give me a Mercedes Benz". That is what they do, and they call it "prayer". Prayer is something different."

Mahatma Gandhi prayed to his beloved God every night; he asked Him for wisdom and that He be the only master of his heart. Nothing else.

In the Gita, Krishna says to Arjuna:

> "I promise, when you die in my consciousness, you will be with me forever."

And Swami Purna

> "That is real prayer: Lord, give me the wisdom, the fire so that I can follow your teachings in my life; so that my life becomes purposeful, so that every act of mine is divine and all my talents and resources may be used in the service of Divinity. Lord, give me the power and the energy so that I may know you and serve you, and that I may contemplate you. Clear my mind and fill my heart."

The following clarification can serve to avoid confusion. Some of us ask God, or some intercessor, for something, but what we ask for is not in accordance with our own correspondence, i.e. with the Law of the Universe. Consequently, it is not going to happen even if we have asked for it with much faith. When we see that what we have asked for does not happen, we might come to the wrong conclusion: "God does not listen, God does not exist, God is capricious, God does not love me ..." Someone who thinks like that does not know that what they asked for was outside the Law. Precisely so that no one draws the wrong conclusions it is essential to realize that if what one is asking for is not within the Law, it will not be received.

Since we do not really know whether what we are asking for is within the Law or not, instead of running that risk and wasting energy, it is better to pray, study or meditate and then let go; "what is meant for me will come to me, and what is not, I do not need". We need to think: "Thy will be done", and then we will benefit from the exercise.

Apart from that, the value of humor should be mentioned as an important support for increasing vital energy. Humor accepts the existence of ambiguity and re-contextualizes everything; it is different from ridicule or malice, and accepts human limitations; it helps us to wear the world "as a loose garment", and to bend with the wind instead of breaking through rigidity. The ability to laugh at oneself threatens the ego and helps to maintain self-esteem. Reacting to everything as though it were important is the result of the narcissistic vanity of the ego. In contrast, humor evolves in acceptance and has a great healing effect. Humor enables us to rise above circumstances and keep our personal dignity. Humor also facilitates wisdom, because it enables us to see mistakes as belonging to human experience in general, rather than as personal failings. Humor, in short, is an expression of freedom and joy, besides which laughter has very positive biological effects.

A good exercise to verify the power of humor and laughter in growth would be as follows: choose a specific time each day in advance and for a month, when it is that time, stand in front of a mirror and spend a few minutes laughing out loud. It is important that you do so at the time you decided in advance, and not at the easiest time to do so. Inevitably there will be days when, at the chosen time, you do not feel at your best emotionally. You can anticipate that the ego is not going to feel comfortable doing this every day, besides which it will say, particularly at the beginning, that you are doing something artificial. But anyone who tries it will be able to see the results of this exercise.

Chapter 11. The concept of God versus personal realization of God

Humanity has in the past conceptualized a God who is "out there", in heaven, remote from human beings. God was represented as a large bearded being (for example, in the Sistine Chapel), suspended in space, who sometimes approaches human beings.

The idea of God as Creator rather than as permanent presence has given rise to conceptual limitations in the past. He has been attributed many anthropomorphic features and it has come to be believed that he is an emotional being, who feels happy or upset; who is liable to be offended and has almost a human ego, which can make Him vengeful, punishing, jealous, or judgmental. It has been thought that He is a capricious being who creates human beings who are unequal in their knowledge but equal in their responsibility, and that he has favorite peoples.

All of this has given rise to images that portray God as both a benign being and one that is also able to condemn His children to eternal suffering. These and other similar beliefs have led many thinkers to reject such ideas, and make the mistake of denying the existence of God. However, the fact that the anthropomorphic ideas about God are wrong does not necessarily lead to ruling out the existence of Divinity.

The ancient vision of a judgmental God and the existence of a poorly defined hell, purgatory and heaven, is certainly not what most contributes to spiritual growth, because it does not make clear the map to follow, nor does it provide sufficient motivation for radical transformation –it leads to the understanding that "it is enough to pass the exam"–, nor, lastly, does it offer a clear understanding of what is really going on.

The Old Testament separates Creation from the figure of the Creator by using dualistic language (subject, object and transitive verbs). Beyond the mind, it is understood that Creation or emergence is located beyond the limits of the arrow of time. The Universe is the content, and God the source and the context where everything takes place. The Grace of God makes it possible for potentiality to be manifested in the observable Universe.

The world is in constant creation; this means that the Creator is acting as an inner animating principle; the Absolute acts as an "evolver" *"interior intimo meo et superior summo meo"*, as Saint Augustine said.

A completely made, finished, i.e. static, world detaches from its Creator. In contrast, a world that is being made, that is to say, that is in the process of unification, could not become detached from its Creator, from that "evolving" and unifying principle that is responsible for its development.

Independently of this, some human beings have succeeded in becoming aware of the constant presence of God as a contextual power beyond the mind. Beyond certain levels of development, spiritual concepts cease to be something intangible and become an actual everyday experience. Sharing these experiences with others at a similar stage of development gives us experiential corroboration. As a result, belief is replaced by direct knowing, by experience.

Some monotheistic religions have contributed to creating a concept about God that gives God superhuman characteristics and converts Him into a definable entity. However, God, as the ultimate reality, is revealed through the search for the substrate or the source of one's own consciousness, and appears as the ultimate non-linear context, beyond all possible definition. With enlightenment comes the understanding that there is no separate relationship between God and human beings.

This revelation (*Unio Mystica*) is the basis of the christian mystical traditions, Sufism, Buddhism and Hinduism through yoga. The "revealed presence" is beyond concept, definition, intellectual discourse or dispute. The resolution of any intellectual doubt is always experiential.

On another level, the **state of no mind** is the awakening to a new sphere which, initially, can appear a little overwhelming. What is left of the old "I" is somewhat bewildered at the astonishment of realization; everything is alive and shining, everything is divine and one; there is a palpable peace and the sensation of "having finally returned home"; there is no possibility of fear. These realities are evident and replace all previous thoughts, concepts and images. Serenity pervades everything.

In this situation, one realizes that the "I" is everywhere, not localized, and there are no desires for anything. All is known and is present, so there is nothing to be known and nothing to know about. All questions are answered, so there is nothing to ask questions about either. Feelings disappear and are replaced with an absolute peace from which positive feelings can be generated at will.

At first there is an agony of the "I" (ego), and personal will is dissolved into divine will. Everything appears to be as it is as a consequence of the continuous evolutionary course of Creation. Everything happens by itself, as an expression of its essence and the prevailing conditions. As a witness, one is present to potentialities as they emerge as actualities. The essence of the Universe is revealed as a great spectacle, as a gift of Love and trust.

On reaching the state of no mind, identification with the body is lost and initially it takes some effort to pay attention to matters of the material world. As the process advances this becomes easier, until perfect integration of the two worlds is achieved. The initial difficulty lies in the fact that, upon discovering peace, what is left of the ego is reluctant to jeopardize it, and sees worldly matters as untranscendental, like a movie in which one is no longer taking part.

The presence of the Holy Spirit appears as a translator, and there is a slight delay between what people say and the understanding of it. Ordinary thinking is no longer habitual; in its place silence and rest appear, and a small effort must be made to use it. When the ordinary mind reactivates, it does so against a backdrop of serenity and silence, which is not replaced. It takes time and energy to change the approach from essence to form. The world seems to be preoccupied with details instead of with essence.

In that state, one uses the old personality to communicate with the world, and humor to re-contextualize people's distorted points of view. The "I" attempts to have a healing contact with the "I" of the person who is suffering; it opens up to having contact with the other "I"'s by means of writings, talks, or conveying information that may be helpful.

Put simply, **enlightenment** is the state in which the sense of the "I" changes from being material, linear, limited to being infinite, non-linear and formless; from the perception of form as objective and real to the realization of the purely subjective as ultimate reality.

Moreover, spiritual growth speeds up when it becomes the dominant intent. Also worth noting is that, in the past, spirituality sometimes has been confused with devotion, without highlighting the importance of proper psychological development to integrate and accurately interpret spiritual experiences. As the master Swami Purna says: "There is no peace without wisdom, but there is no joy without love". It therefore seems clear that devotion should be combined with perfection of the ego in order to transcend it; it is far harder to try to transcend the non-perfected ego, however, devoted one might be.

There have traditionally been two different paths to enlightenment: **the path of knowledge** (*Jnana*) and **the path of devotion** (*Bhakti*). The first is less juicy but more stable; the second is the opposite. Eventually they both join, because understanding opens the heart and devotion clears the mind. Wisdom is like firewood and devotion like fire; knowledge keeps devotion constant. Wisdom is equal to knowledge + surrender. As Lao Tzu said:

> "On the path to acquiring knowledge, every day something is added. On the path of spiritual development, every day something is let go of."

An important question here would be: why do more people not reach the state of enlightenment? Basically for two reasons:

First of all, culture and context do not help, because they are very "materialized". People are taught to try and change things "out there", and that attitude prevents enlightenment.

Secondly, there is a lack of intention and intensity of focus. If we do not seek enlightenment more than anything else, the gravitational attraction of the world will be sufficiently strong to prevent us transcending it. The problem of understanding lies in giving priority to other things over enlightenment.

The fundamental question that we should all ask ourselves was already asked in the Gospel: Are you willing to let go of –not necessarily "give up"– everything to find everything? Most people are attracted by their own lives in linearity, with little creativity and joy. But it is possible to change the paradigm in the mind, which in turn will open the heart through a hierarchical entanglement.

In the words of Paramahansa Yoganada:

"Purity of the intellect gives one the power of correct reasoning, but purity of the heart gives one the contact of God. Intellectuality is a quality of the power of reason, and wisdom is the liberating quality of the soul. When reason is purified by calm discrimination it metamorphoses into wisdom ... The pure-eyed vision of wisdom must be combined with the untainted feeling of the heart. Wisdom reveals the righteous path, and the cleansed heart desires and loves to follow that path. All wisdom-revealed soul qualities must be followed wholeheartedly (not merely intellectually or theoretically)."

Chapter 12. Do we need a Teacher?

The answer to this question, as is often the case in this new vision, is not *yes or no* but *yes and no.*

Strictly speaking, we do not need a Teacher for our development because human beings have the aid of Grace and the Law of Saturation, according to which there comes a time when we can stand no more suffering and decide to try new ways of understanding life. The Law of Correspondence or Karma is an impersonal teacher which helps us with the need for personal growth and accountability. When we are ready to learn, we will come across a large number of books, movies and other people's testimonials who can guide us towards the truth in a more "impersonal" way than a Teacher. The truth has already been extensively explained throughout history, in the Gospel, the Gita, and the Tao, etc. In addition, there is a great deal of literature devoted to the interpretation or explanation of that truth, and although some works are better than others, each of us can use our own judgment to steer our way through them.

On doing so, we can follow two different paths: firstly, using the intellect to see what seems most advisable in an abstract sense, or secondly, using our inner being to see what gives us greatest peace. If, in order to assess different interpretations, we use the criterion of an inner sense of peace, we will be making use of a superior power (intuition), which will be more efficient than using the criterion of the mind. As explained above, everything that comes "from above" brings peace as a natural consequence. "By their fruits ye shall know them" refers not only to trees or prophets but also to ideas and interpretations.

If we want to have access to the best versions of the truth, it might be better to go to the interpretation of the teachings of the mystics (Cosmic consciousness), and leave aside a little the interpretations which come from the consciousness of "self"; this is because, no matter how intellectually brilliant rational constructions may be, they do not escape duality and linearity. The truth, however, is Love, and that is not linear or dual. This, so far has only been understood by the mystics, not by theologians or philosophers. The whole truth cannot be constricted by rational dogmas, but is expressed through love, peace and compassion.

Let's see some phrases from the mystics: for instance, by St. Augustine: "Love and do what you want"; or St. Paul: "If man could reach the inner kingdom only through obeying the law, Christ died for nothing" (Galatians 2, 21). Another example is from St. Paul to the Galatians: "Do not be slaves of the law". These phrases are not dogmatic, although they may be confusing to a lower level of consciousness, which might interpret them as an invitation to relaxation and chaos. Nothing could be further from the intention of those who spoke them. The Law of Love is much more demanding than moral law; law and morality are necessary in this world of form, but God's kingdom is not of this world. So, having discovered the inner kingdom, what belongs to the world is respected, but not necessary. Love is the unity of being and not some partial aspects of it which are sometimes taken as absolute.

We cannot internally achieve a higher level of consciousness by just listening to the words that are pronounced from there; we need to actually enter that level, hence the difficulty of correctly interpreting the words of the Wise. Many people who serve as teachers today have not yet discovered the kingdom within themselves, and that limits their work. Every good interpretation of truth leads to decentralizing and dematerializing of thought and, above all, it brings peace.

That said, in addition to listening to and confiding in the inner Teacher, it may be very advisable to have one in order to accelerate the discovery of the inner kingdom, or enlightenment. Nobody can do the growing for us, but a good Teacher serves two important purposes: to help people tell the wheat from the chaff, and to transmit his own vibration. But who is a true Teacher?

It is not easy for the mind to discern the essence of things, rather it is an instrument used to classify and analyze. However, just as the mind can be used to play chess, the higher mind (intuition) is the right tool to discover the essence. There is a danger of being influenced by false teachers or false gurus who, despite having a lot of charisma and numerous followers, if they themselves have not discovered the kingdom within them, will not be the right Teachers. Do not be impressed by qualifications, extravagant clothing or paranormal powers. The question should be rather: do they transmit peace? The signs of identity of the true Teacher is humility, simplicity, compassion, wisdom and peace.

For the true Teachers it is irrelevant how many followers there are, and no interest in money or material things can be found in them. They also avoid the cult of personality.

Many religious leaders and groups, including many New Age ones, place the emphasis on strange costumes, all kinds of symbols, card reading, channeling, mediums, chanting, etc. They have even come to adopt a sort of festive atmosphere, and often sell their spiritual integrity in exchange for power over others, mired as they are in their delusions of grandeur.

By contrast, the gift offered by the true Teachers is not limited to the information or wisdom they convey but has to do directly with the level of consciousness which they emanate from. Their power is based on the purity of the context; the value of many teachings has been undermined by the error of the context from which they were transmitted, thus distorting their meaning. Thus, one can excuse and rationalize any crime through distorted statements proclaimed as true by the mere fact of having been taken from the Scriptures by those seeking power and control over others. This is how sometimes entire civilizations have been dragged piously but arrogantly to an inevitable death. The good news is that all these empires come to grief sooner or later because they are not aligned with the truth.

All the alleged differences between the teachings of truth are misunderstandings and limitations of context. There may be differences between religions but not in true spirituality. The truth is indivisible, all-inclusive and everlasting. The state of "Self" is self-evident and covers everything that it is, since totality cannot be divided.

Because of the blocks that the ego puts up when awakening from Cosmic consciousness —which is within every human being as potential— people need to reconnect with the truth through their inner Teacher, or through an external teacher. The Teacher, due to his own evolution, is better connected with the "Self" which allows him to teach and be a guide, thereby shortening the process of the disciple. Merely listening to a great teaching is, in itself, a consequence of spiritual correspondence.

True Teachers are already enlightened beings and, as such, are total and complete. They do not need to meet with disciples, nor do they obtain anything by having followers. For them, the body is only relevant as a vehicle for communication with other people who want to learn but, for the rest, the world and its contents holds no attraction for them, nor do they feel aversion.

A true Teacher has gone beyond having had the good fortune –in some way incapacitating– of experiencing the appearance of Cosmic consciousness, and exists in a state of unemotional joy, which consists of an omniscience and certainty as to the totality of the Absolute. It is his job to translate the ineffable into the understandable, and attempt to anticipate the misunderstandings that may arise in the process which the disciples go through.

The Teacher also serves his followers nonverbally, where the enlightened consciousness transmits that vibrational frequency to the field of human thought. This teaching is a decision and the result of an agreement. There are religious pastors who have studied philosophy and theology or comparative religion, so they know a lot about the subject; but if they have not themselves entered into Cosmic consciousness, they cannot transmit a vibration they lack themselves.

For the consciousness of "self", the intellectual teachings about all this will be very useful, and it is a process through which many souls will have to pass. But for a disciple who has already completed this process and who is seriously committed to attaining enlightenment, only the true Teachers will be of help to him/her.

As mentioned above, everything in the Universe consists of energy plus information, and the greater the energy vibration, the more the information it can contain. As also discussed in previous chapters, if we could invent a machine that increased the vibration of people artificially, they would not need to go through the process of spiritual growth –which really consists of increasing one's own vibration– because they would acquire the information automatically from that vibration. Unfortunately, technology cannot achieve this because, if it did, it would destroy the universal processes. A true Teacher is the closest thing to that hypothetical machine, and *infecting* his disciples with his own vibration can accelerate their growth process.

In the West there is little tradition of energy transmission between Teacher and disciple, although there has been in practice in the past, because no one can escape from the processes of physics. There has also been a great tradition in the West of having an advanced spiritual director in the process who helps the disciple in his growth by sharing his teachings with the disciple. However, in the East the Master-disciple tradition *has* existed since ancient times. The relationship between disciple and Teacher in Eastern cultures dates back to Vedic times, and is equivalent to the relationship between divinity and the individual soul. "The search for –and recognition of– a true Teacher is considered one of the most important steps in the development of any committed disciple" (Swami Purna).

We shall now briefly describe how this process would be understood in terms of Eastern spirituality. In the East, the relationship between the Teacher, or guru, and disciple is strictly spiritual, not worldly or material; and it is different from the relationship we have with family or friends. Before coming to have a personal relationship with a true Teacher or "*Satguru*", very often disciples have previously been involved with less qualified teachers. The fully enlightened Teacher appears in the disciple's life when he is ready to face the final steps before release. If the Teacher appeared before that, the disciple would not be able to recognize him or benefit from the full potential the Teacher can offer him.

In the Vedic tradition, one of the most important services that the Teacher performs with his disciple is the transmission of *shakti* (spiritual energy) through what is called *Shaktipat*. According to this tradition, spiritual energy, *Shakti* or *kundalini*, remains "screwed into" the *mulad-*

hara chakra at the base of the spine. The word *mula* means root and *adhara* means support. *Shaktipat* is the mechanism through which the Teacher transmits his own spiritual energy to the disciple, thus awakening it in the disciple. *Kundalini* can awaken by itself through spiritual devotion and karmic merit, but the most effective way to awaken *Shaktipat* is through the *Satguru*. When it is the *Satguru* who activates this energy, he also manages its appearance, avoiding unpleasant or incomprehensible physical effects in the disciple which sometimes occur if awakening is spontaneous and unguided.

Once *kundalini* energy has been awakened, the path towards enlightenment is a sure thing. *Kundalini* has physical, psychological and spiritual effects. Upon awakening, *kundalini* rises more or less rapidly from the *muladhara chakra* to the *Sahasrara chakra*, purifying everything that it finds blocked on its path. The Teacher cannot give *Shaktipat* to everyone, as doing so prematurely, without the disciple having already reached a certain level of vibration, could be dangerous. This is up to the Teacher's own judgment. Generally the disciple has had to develop some prior understanding; and be trained in the application of spiritual truths in his own life, at least to some degree. He must also have previously calmed his emotional body to a certain degree; and have developed an intention to serve.

The awakening of *kundalini* can take different forms in each person. Sometimes it appears as a sudden very strong boom, and others, more smoothly and gradually. But in all cases it is a transformative and exquisite experience. The rise of *kundalini* purifies everything in its path; it clears and calms the mind and produces a feeling of inner peace, which is experienced as a thick, almost tangible peace. The awakening of *kundalini* is the beginning of the process of enlightenment. It is a great gift from the Teacher to the disciple, as this way the traumas of the subconscious are cleansed away very effectively without having to go through the usual tedious process. It is as if everything happened for the first time; as if there were no acquired emotional patterns conditioning the response to any situation. One becomes a child in the sense that there are no unconscious emotions to distort the responses, and every moment appears as fresh or new. However, this child, unlike the real one, always knows what should be done without the need for a reflective process.

It is possible that many mystics, through their own ignorance, have not been aware of awakening this energy in themselves but that does not mean that they have not experienced it, just that they have not been able to identify this as the cause of their transformation.

Some effects of awakening *kundalini* are as follows: we begin to have lots of energy, so that numerous acts of a spiritual nature or of service can be performed without fatigue appearing; the mind calms down when attention is not specifically fixed on something concrete; intuitive capacity is considerably increased and reason is used much less to take decisions at specific moments; compulsions are lost and we are much more sure of ourselves; we begin to feel a great unity internally with everything that exists, and compassion is awakened. A great deal of spontaneous realization and understanding of the truth takes place, and sometimes it seems as if there were a sort of "infused science". For example, complicated answers to difficult questions may spontaneously come to mind without us knowing how the information appeared at that moment.

We also begin to gradually abandon mental prayer to replace it with a more contemplative form, where the rational mind is stilled. The feeling is as if a spiritual black hole had engulfed us more and more deeply; the emotional body is greatly calmed, so it is impossible to suffer emotional damage, which increases inner peace. As we no longer have any emotional suffering, the ego gradually fades away; we lose our emotional memory, so our own personal past is cleansed and we live in the present with no anxiety. Physical health greatly improves, as if this energy, of its own accord, cleansed all the body tissues automatically; the personal relationship with the Absolute becomes less dualistic and God is no longer seen as an object separate from ourselves because we see that we exist "in God" and not outside him. In short, when *kundalini* is awakened and moves forward through the various different energy centers, a new person appears and little of the old "self" remains. Finally, it is common for some kind of psychic, paranormal abilities to be awakened.

Thus, the conclusion drawn is that all souls will evolve, with or without a Teacher, because they are made in the "image and likeness" of the Absolute. That being true, so too is it that souls who that have managed to become correspondent with receiving the help of an enlightened Teacher will evolve much faster; not only on account of his teaching but, above all, through the contagion of vibration and Grace. It is always the disciple, and not the Teacher, who puts limits to the contagion effect.

Conclusion

As seen throughout this book, the Universe is now defined as an interactive wholeness of thousands of energy fields of infinite frequencies, awaiting the influence of intention to produce a formal manifestation. Thus, today there are sufficient means with which to describe and understand the easily identifiable principle that creation and evolution are one and the same process (emergence).

Perceived "reality" seems to be separated into different categories or realms, such as physical vs. non-physical. But what was thought to be distinct categories of existence, are just different categories of perception. In "reality" there are no separations. Consciousness alone has the capacity with which to compare and unite seemingly disparate realities and realms into a comprehensive unity with stratified expression.

The understanding of consciousness reveals that all that exists, with no exception, physical or non-physical, does so along an identifiable and discernible "continuum". There is no discontinuity because there is only energy that is expressed in the characteristics of its different frequency ranges. The physical Universe is a vibrational frequency spectrum.

Throughout time, spiritually inspired individuals who have engaged in the inner quest for truth have reported that beyond the ordinary mind lies a potential experiential capacity that lets the existence of the energy field be realized as the source of all existence.

The phenomenon traditionally called "enlightenment" has been rare because few people are willing to surrender their favorite illusion, identification with materiality, or their personalities.

Major advances in understanding the essential nature of the Universe and the evolution of consciousness profoundly facilitate the comprehension of physical and spiritual evolution. It is no longer necessary to forsake reason to grasp nonlinear realities and the invisible influences that let us move towards personal realization of the ultimate reality.

The dichotomy between faith and reason might be better explained today as the difference between focusing on non-linear dimensions or focusing on the linear and verifiable through logic and the senses. That primary focus depends on the individual's level of consciousness. Wisdom brings together both focuses. The Universe has "hardware" and "software", and software is more significant than hardware, which only exists in order for software to be developed. Reductionists will keep on studying the hardware, and that's fine, but there's no longer any denying the software. The fact is that the Universe has intelligence and intention. One could say that software is where one has to look for the causes, and hardware is for studying the effects. Hardware limits itself to the "how", without managing to find the "why"; therefore, it is in software where you have to look for the "what" things are or "why" they happen.

In this regard, the commitment to the intention of growth alters the energy field according to Heisenberg's uncertainty principle, which in turn collapses the wave function into manifestation.

For any human being interested in evolving, these findings are fascinating and their implications are profound. This new thinking invites us to see things in a different light, which will show that conflict is on the decline and peace of mind is on the rise. The world is not what it seems, nor are its residents what they claim to be.

Now there is enough evidence to contextualize the teachings of Perennial Wisdom in a modern setting that give them another kind of validation that we did not have before. We know where we are, and we know the unavoidable path that lies ahead of us. The only questions that we still have to ask ourselves is how much attention and intention we are willing to invest in this trip, to speed it up, and how we can use this new information to better understand the historical teachings of the Masters and put them into practice.

The purpose of human experience is to evolve and develop our consciousness, so as to be filled with wisdom and love. All human beings, without exception, have come into the world to work on our spiritual development, sharing and participating in experiences with other human beings. Life is part of the Universe's formidable educational process; Planet Earth is a "spiritual school" and each experience we live through is like one academic year.

When we note that suffering is disappearing, that inner peace becomes invulnerable and that our own ability to create, love and serve is expressed without any conditions or restrictions, it means we have attained wisdom.

In order to lay the foundations of a new civilization capable of producing a higher level of satisfaction in everyone, first we need to harmonize ourselves. This unavoidably entails studying the Universal Laws and applying the principles that lead to wisdom. The fact to remember is that only through constant practice and by discarding theories and concepts that prove to be wrong will we ever achieve wisdom, which in turn will enable us to develop peace and harmony directly on the ground, with the teaching of daily life, as this is the best school, just as nature is the best teacher.

To achieve efficiency, you just have to stop fighting the perfect order of the Universe; mental inefficiency is needed to discover, through saturation, that the Laws of the Universe do exist. When we have suffered enough, we are ready to understand the Laws. Before the external struggle stops, first the internal struggle has to stop, and this entails having accepted that everything that exists and everything that happens is perfect and necessary, because it has a purpose of Love.

Bibliography

Aurobindo, Sri: *Life Divine*.
Bucke, Richard M.: *Cosmic consciousness*.
Combs, Allan: *Consciousness Explained Better*.
Davies, Paul: Evidence of purpose: *Scientists Discover the Creator*.
Goswami, Amit: *Physics of the Soul*.
Goswami, Amit: *Quantum Activism*.
Goswami, Amit: *The Self-aware Universe*.
Goswami, Amit: *God is not Dead*.
Goswami, Amit: *Creative Evolution*.
Greene, Brian: *The fabric of the Cosmos*.
Greene, Brian: *Hidden Reality*.
Hawkins, David R.: *I, Reality and Subjectivity*.
Hawkins, David R.: *Power vs. Force*.
Hawkins, David R.: *Spirituality and Modern Man*.
Hawkins, David R.: *The I of the eye*.
Hawkins, David R.: *Transcending the levels of consciousness*.
Hawkins, David R.: *Truth vs. Falsehood*.
Hofstadter, Douglas: *I am a Strange Loop*.
James, William: *The Varieties of Religious Experience*.
Krishna, Gopi: *Higher Consciousness and Kundalini*.
Lanza, Robert: *Biocentrism*.
Laszlo, Ervin: *Science and the Akashic Fields*.
Laszlo, Ervin: *The In-formed Universe*.
Lipton, Bruce: *The Biology of Belief*.
Maharaj, Nisargadatta: *I am That*.
Marion, Jim: *Putting on the mind of Christ*.
Marquier, Annie: *Free your true self. The power of free will*.
Marquier, Annie: *The Master of the heart*.
McTaggart, Lynne: *The Field*.
McTaggart, Lynne: *The Intention Experiment*.
Moody, Raymond: Life After Life.
Peat, David: Synchronicity: *The Bridge Between Matter and Mind*.

Polkinghorne, John: *Quantum Physics and Theology: An Unexpected Kinship.*
Pribram, Karl H.: *The Holographic Brain.*
Purna, Svami: *The truth will set you Free.*
Rodriguez Dos Santos, José: *The Key of Solomon.*
Sannella, Lee: *Kundalini Experience.*
Schmedling, Gerardo: *Complete work: Escuela del Amor.*
Sheldrake, Rupert: *Morphic Resonance.*
Smith, Huston: *Forgotten Truth.*
Stapp, Henry: *Mindful Universe.*
Talbot, Michael: *The Holographic Universe.*
Wilber, Ken: *Brief history of everything.*
Wilber, Ken: *Eye to eye.*
Wilber, Ken: *Integral Psychology.*
Wilber, Ken: *Sex, ecology and spirituality.*
Wilber, Ken: *Up from Eden.*
Yogananda, Paramahansa: *Autobiography of a Yogi.*
Yogananda, Paramahansa: *The Second Coming of Christ.*
Yogananda, Paramahansa: *The Yoga of Jesus.*

In the event you would like to receive
more information about the issues tackled
here
you may enter the webpage
www.desarrolloconsciencia.org